The Hitler Assassination Attempts

The Hitler Assassination Attempts

The Plots, Places and People that Almost Changed History

John Grehan

Frontline Books

First published in Great Britain in 2022 by
Frontline Books
An imprint of
Pen & Sword Books Ltd
Yorkshire – Philadelphia

ISBN 978 1 39901 890 6

A CIP catalogue record for this book is available from the British Library.

Typeset by Mac Style
Printed and bound in the UK by CPI Group (UK) Ltd,
Croydon, CR0 4YY.

FSC www.fsc.org MIX Paper from responsible sources FSC® C013604

Pen & Sword Books Limited incorporates the imprints of Atlas, Archaeology, Aviation, Discovery, Family History, Fiction, History, Maritime, Military, Military Classics, Politics, Select, Transport, True Crime, Air World, Frontline Publishing, Leo Cooper, Remember When, Seaforth Publishing, The Praetorian Press, Wharncliffe Local History, Wharncliffe Transport, Wharncliffe True Crime and White Owl.

For a complete list of Pen & Sword titles please contact

PEN & SWORD BOOKS LIMITED
47 Church Street, Barnsley, South Yorkshire, S70 2AS, England
E-mail: enquiries@pen-and-sword.co.uk
Website: www.pen-and-sword.co.uk

Or

PEN AND SWORD BOOKS
1950 Lawrence Rd, Havertown, PA 19083, USA
E-mail: Uspen-and-sword@casematepublishers.com
Website: www.penandswordbooks.com

Contents

Introduction

The twenty-four officers and stenographers were gathered on all sides of the rectangular oak table for the meeting in the *Wolfsschanze*, Hitler's 'Wolf's Lair', in the heart of Gierłoż Forest in East Prussia. The date was 20 July 1944. It was a hot day, and all the windows were open in the *lagebaracke* which was the scene of the daily situation conferences held to discuss the war situation.

As the conference unfolded, Hitler stretched out across the table to indicate a point on the large-scale map in front of him when, at exactly 1242 hours, there was a blinding flash followed instantaneously by a deafening roar. Bluish-yellow flame shot out of the windows, hurling with it glass and splinters and a cloud of choking black smoke. 'In a flash the map room became a scene of stampede and destruction,' recalled General Walter Warlimont, Deputy Chief of the Operations Staff. 'At one moment … a set of men … a focal point of world events; at the next there was nothing but wounded men groaning, the acrid smell of burning; and charred fragments of maps and papers fluttering in the wind. I staggered up and jumped through the open window.' As the officers who were unwounded came to their senses, their first thought was for Hitler. 'Where is the Führer?' Field Marshal Wilhelm Keitel was the first to put into words the thoughts that were running through the minds of the stunned survivors. A figure pulled himself up, covered in dust, his trousers cut to ribbons, his hair on fire – Keitel answered his own question, 'My Führer! You're alive!'[1]

It was true. Hitler was injured and badly shaken, but he was still alive. Nevertheless, this was the closest anyone had come to killing the Führer even though there had been dozens of plots and numerous actual attempts on his life. These efforts had, in the main, been conducted by fellow Germans, despite the near impossibility of organizing any form of resistance or opposition movement in the heavily policed Nazi state.

There were other reasons for the lack of organized opposition to Hitler in Germany apart from the brutal efficiency of the Secret State Police, the *Geheime Staatspolizei* – the Gestapo – as was explained, in some measure, by Dr Eugene Gerstenmaier, one of the very few opposition figures to survive the *Valkyrie* plot which culminated in that failed 20 July assassination attempt in the *lagebaracke*:

> I think that no one is inwardly obliged to remain loyal to Hitler and his system for Germany's sake. Whatever may be said against the conditions in which we are at present compelled to live, we must fairly recognise that they are the consequences of Hitler's policy. Dazzled by the idea of National Socialism, disgusted by the quarrels of the parties and incomprehensibly blind to what stood behind the man – all in all, foolishly but fairly, the German people gave Hitler a chance. And, perhaps with misgivings, but without resistance, the majority surrendered to him. That is our fault, our great fault. Thereafter, it was beyond the power of an individual, indeed beyond the power of a group of men determined to do everything possible to break the bonds into which Hitler's total system of terror had been able to cast us.[2]

The German historian Friedrich Lenz saw the opposition to Hitler quite differently. In 1952, he wrote:

> In defence of their meek attitudes towards the methods employed by Hitler after his seizure of power, the opponents now plead the terrorist measures that awaited them, had they done otherwise, but they keep silent about the real reason, which is that in light of the clear wish of the people to give Hitler a chance and to help him, they could not have dared offer any practical resistance if they did not want to risk making fools of themselves or being swept away by their own followers.[3]

There were, nevertheless, groups in Germany opposed to Hitler that were active not only throughout the Second World War but even before his propulsion to power in 1933, though when he was no more than the leader of a small extremist political party he was despised rather than feared. Even when Hitler became Chancellor, in what was a surprising move undertaken by an embattled Reich President Hindenburg, the

Nazi leader was not immediately seen as a threat to the security of the country or its people. Many thought that Hitler would not last long at the Chancellery before being ousted by more sophisticated politicians. But as soon as he assumed power Hitler set about eliminating any real or perceived opponents. The merest suspicion of an individual's or a group's disinclination not to wholeheartedly support the Nazis was quickly seized upon and investigated, usually on the basis of guilty until proven innocent. A sizeable part of the Nazi machinery was devoted to neutralizing, either by death or imprisonment, a considerable portion of the German public. Between 1933 and 1939 the ordinary civilian courts convicted 225,000 people of political crimes, their sentences amounting to a total of 600,000 years' imprisonment, many spending their sentences in the fifty-plus concentration camps spread around the Reich, with some never being seen again. According to some estimates, in the years 1943–45, for example, the Gestapo alone 'neutralized' more than 40,000 men. The total number of political prisoners throughout Hitler's reign may have been as high as 3,000,000, and dissident execution possibly exceeded 12,000 men and women, with the number of capital offences increasing from three to forty-three during the first ten years of Hitler's reign.[4]

An example of this is the case of Sophie Scholl. In May 1942 she began to study biology and philosophy at Munich University. She had the temerity to join the resistance group known as the 'White Rose', which was composed of students, artists and scientists who called for a clear rejection of Hitler and his regime in order, as one of their leaflets put it, 'to strive for the renewal of the mortally wounded German spirit'.[5] That was more than enough for the authorities to arrest her, which they did on 18 February 1943, along with her brother Hans. They were seized at the university while throwing hundreds of leaflets from the gallery of the atrium of the university. They were tried in the so-called People's Court. Both were sentenced to death and duly executed the very same day.[6]

Another woman with less means at her disposal found another method of displaying her repugnance of the regime and urging others to resist. Elise Hampel began her campaign of subversion following the death of her soldier brother during the invasion of France and the Low Countries in the summer of 1940. She expressed her feelings on postcards, writing such provocative statements as 'Wake up German people, we must free ourselves from Hitler. There is no freedom under this devilish government.'

With the help of her husband, Otto, she dropped her postcards in mailboxes, left them in tenement stairwells, shop windowsills or anywhere that others might see them.[7] Most of these cards were picked up and handed to the Gestapo, often by people fearing that the cards had been left by the Gestapo to test their loyalty to the regime, but over the course of two years the Hampels wrote and displayed more than 200 postcards across Berlin, often near the district of Wedding, where they lived.

The Gestapo tried to track down the perpetrators by catching them in the act of depositing their inflammatory messages and by seeking to identify individuals purchasing large quantities of blank postcards. But, in the end, Elise and Otto were betrayed by their fellow Berliners and they were arrested by the Gestapo in the autumn of 1942. On 22 January 1943 they were sentenced to death by the 2nd Senate of the People's Court for 'demoralizing the troops' and of 'preparing for high treason'. They were guillotined on 8 April 1943 in Berlin's Plötzensee Prison.

Women also played key roles in a loose confederation of opposition groups called by the Gestapo the 'Red Orchestra'. This group sought to undermine the Third Reich in a variety of ways, most notably by passing on information about the German armed forces to the Allies, especially the Soviet Union. This was unquestionably treasonable conduct by any standards and the German security forces were so concerned about the Red Orchestra that, unusually, the Reich Security Service (the *Sicherheitsdienst*, or SD), the Gestapo, and the German military intelligence counter-espionage service, the *Abwehr*, combined resources to eliminate the group.

The Red Orchestra (so called because of its Soviet links and with its radio operators being referred to as pianists, and group leaders being the 'conductors') was made up of three different units: the Leopold Trepper unit, the 'Red Three' and the Harro Schulze-Boysen/Arvid Harnack group. The Trepper unit was based in Germany and occupied France and Belgium, the 'Red Three' was based in neutral Switzerland while the Schulze-Boysen/Harnack group was based in Berlin. Their internal activities included the printing and distribution of leaflets inciting the people to rise up against the Nazi administration.

It was the interception by the Abwehr of the radio transmissions which led to the various groups being tracked down in 1942. It is believed that as many as 400 men and women were involved in Red Orchestra activities. Arrests, torture and executions followed, with a set of gallows constructed in Plötzensee Prison where eight people at a time could be hanged.

Amongst others who met a similar fate was Helmuth Günther Hübener who was just seventeen years old when, in October 1942, he faced the People's Court. His 'crime' was read out during his sentencing, after being found guilty:

> Since the summer of 1941, Hübener has spread the contents of British news bulletins in leaflets and handbills.... All in all twenty different propaganda leaflets of this kind, either drafts or mimeographed copies, have been confiscated. In addition to the British bulletins on the war situation, the handbills contained insults and insinuations against the Führer and his lieutenants and inflammatory attacks on the measures and institutions of the National Socialist government.

Because Hübener was still a youth, the death sentence would not normally apply but, because he was of above-average intelligence, his leaflets were well written and 'no one could imagine that their author was only sixteen or seventeen, even if he knew that they were composed with the help of notes'. This meant, in the perverse wisdom of the People's Court, that because the leaflets appeared to have been written by an adult, Hübener had to be punished as an adult. The death sentence was carried out on 27 October 1942.[8]

Even earlier than this, shortly after the start of Operation BARBAROSSA the invasion of the Soviet Union, one of the civilian leaders of the opposition wrote of the atrocities being carried out in Germany:

> We have 19 guillotines working at considerable speed without most people even knowing this fact, and practically nobody knows how many are beheaded each day. In my estimation there are about 50 per day, not counting those who die in concentration camps – nobody knows the exact number of concentration camps or of their inhabitants.... We only know for certain, that scores, probably many hundreds of Germans are killed daily by the various methods, and that these people die not a glorious death as those in the occupied

> countries do, knowing that their people consider them heroes, but an ignominious death knowing that they are classed among robbers and murderers.[9]

The families of those who dared to challenge the regime and had been slaughtered for their opposition kept very quiet about what had happened to their loved ones for fear of a similar fate. This meant that the resisters died not as martyrs, celebrated for their courage, but as common criminals. This made their deaths pointless and it acted as a very effective deterrent.

As Herbert Ernst Carl Frahm who, being a member of the far-left Socialist Workers Party, fled from Germany to avoid persecution, admitted:

> we referred to ourselves as the 'opposition'. Of course, we knew about the diversity of those opposing the Nazis, and we were aware of their inadequacy … there was very little resistance deserving of the name that was not soon discovered, with the means available to the totalitarian regime at the time, or even destroyed before it got started.

Herbert Fraham changed his name to avoid being arrested. In his new guise, he returned to Germany after the war becoming Chancellor of West Germany from 1969 to 1974. Frahm is known to the world as Willy Brandt.[10] The German historian Joachim Fest agrees, calling the opposition to the Nazis as 'The Resistance that never was',[11] and his fellow historian Mommsen believes that the conditions under which Stauffenberg and the Valkyrie conspirators were forced to operate meant that 'their chances of bringing down the regime from within were virtually non-existent'.[12] This is demonstrated by the fact that no meeting of all the people destined to form the new government after Hitler had been killed had occurred before 20 July and the man earmarked as Chancellor, Karl Goerdeler, whose name will feature many times throughout this narrative, had not even been told of the impending assassination.[13]

Though the Gestapo's deadly tentacles appear to have stretched far and wide, there were fewer Gestapo agents than is customarily assumed, but their influence was all-pervasive.[14] People were encouraged to report any dissident behaviour, no matter how trivial it might seem. No one could be sure if the person they were talking to was a Gestapo plant, an agent provocateur, or merely someone seeking to curry favour with the authorities by denouncing others to demonstrate their support for the Party. An off-hand comment, or a joke about Hitler, could be a death sentence.

An example of this occurred on 10 October 1943 at a small party in the Berlin flat of the fifty-five-year-old widow Elisabeth von Thadden. Among the gathering of friends and guests was a new member of the group – a doctor at a hospital in Birkenwerder, Brandenburg, called Paul Reckzeh. Three months earlier he had been offered an assignment in Switzerland to ascertain what kind of contacts German emigrants had with the Allies, which led him to Elisabeth Thadden's flat that autumn evening.

The leading light of Elisabeth's group was Johanna Solf who had been instrumental in hiding Jewish friends from the Gestapo and providing them with documents and money to help them escape the Third Reich. The Gestapo suspected the subversive motives of the 'Solf Circle' as it became known but lacked evidence of its activities.

As the evening progressed Reckzeh made increasingly disparaging comments on Hitler's handling of the war. This encouraged others to also voice their less-than-favourable opinions of the Führer. Having gained their confidence, some of the group asked the affable young doctor if he would convey letters to their friends in Switzerland. What they didn't know was that Reckzeh was a Gestapo agent codenamed 'Robby' and he was only too happy to accept the letters he was given.

Those letters and his report were soon in the hands of the Gestapo, as were Elisabeth Thadden and members of the Solf Circle. Reckzeh received the promotion he sought to the rank of staff surgeon with the Organisation Todt, and Elisabeth von Thadden and most of the Solf Circle members were arrested and executed.

Professor Dr Walter Arndt was reported to have said in the winter of 1943–4, that 'This is the end of the German Reich. We are to blame for the war, and all that remains is to [decide] how far the guilty are brought to account and punished.' He was arrested and sentenced to death by the People's Court on 11 May 1944. A post office guard in Danzig, Georg Jurkowski was alleged to have spoken in a public street in 1943 declaring that the Führer would soon suffer the same fate as Mussolini and would be dead by January. His 'subversive' comments were reported to the authorities and the inevitable death sentence was announced in the People's Court on 14 October 1943.[15]

Despite such systematic oppression, and because of it, there were more than forty known planned attempts on the life of Hitler, as well as other schemes that were considered but not carried through and a number of impromptu, opportunistic efforts. Through inadequate planning or poor execution, but often merely through sheer bad luck, all the attempts failed. Few of those who arranged such internally devised efforts approached the Allies for direct assistance. Had they done so their chances of success would have been immeasurably improved. But the plotters were patriots, good Germans. They did not want the British or the Americans – and especially the despised French – to take the credit for toppling Hitler. It was nothing to do with the Allies. Hitler and the Nazis were their problem, and they would deal with them themselves.

There were, of course, Allied plots to kill Hitler. The most elaborate of those was the SOE's 1944 Operation FOXLEY but this was not carried through because it was considered that Hitler had, by that stage of the war, become a liability to the German war effort and that no advantage would be gained by assassinating him.

The German resistance (*Der Widerstand*) did openly approach London, Paris and Washington a number of times before the outbreak of war and clandestinely afterwards. In a bid to alert the Allies to Hitler's designs upon Czechoslovakia, Karl Goerdeler, a former mayor of Leipzig who had at one time been considered for the post of Chancellor before Franz von Papen in 1932, and led a small highly-conservative opposition group, travelled to Paris in early March 1938 and again the following month. Goerdeler met with Alexis Léger, Secretary General of the Ministry of Foreign Affairs and, though he was warmly received, it was with deep mistrust. No one in Paris could quite understand what Goerdeler's real motives were, as it was distinctly unusual for an influential German to be talking in derogatory tones about his own government to the French. Sir Gilbert Vansittart, the chief diplomatic advisor to the British Foreign Office, bluntly told Goerdeler, when he was approached by the latter in June 1937, that his actions were nothing short of treason, and Britain would have no truck with any subversive activities in Germany. The truth seems to have been that Léger and Vansittart believed Goerdeler was working for Hitler and not against him.

Goerdeler sought only to strengthen Germany's position in the world, not to weaken it, and the doubt over the motives for his visits to the UK and even the US, which he visited in October 1937, probably arose because his aims were scarcely less expansionist than Hitler's. He believed in the concept of a Greater Germany incorporating all the predominantly German-speaking territories and the return of Germany's overseas colonies. Goerdeler even demanded the elimination of the Polish Corridor, a subject which Hitler, at that time, had not yet dared to voice. His fear, which drove him to talk to the Allies, was that Hitler would push too hard and too fast and bring on a war which would benefit no one, especially the Germans: 'On no occasion did the ... Goerdeler group cease to feel that Germany's real place, by reason of her economic, political and military strength and potential was among the major powers and that she must,' wrote one German historian, 'at least on the Continent, win back her old position.'[16]

Even as late as May 1941, after Britain had withstood every effort of the German air force to beat the UK into submission throughout the Battle of Britain and the Blitz had failed, Goerdeler was still trying to persuade the British government to accept unrealistic peace terms. These still included the restoration of Germany's 1914 frontiers, confirmation of the Anschluss and the annexation of the Sudetenland, the return of all Germany's colonies taken from her in the First World War, as mentioned above, and that there should be no claim by any of the Allied or occupied countries for reparations.[17]

It must also be understood that even the perpetrator of the 20 July 1944 assassination attempt, Claus von Stauffenberg, believed that Germany should be the dominant power in Europe. He helped draft a statement of the ideals behind the group of which he had become the most resolute member. In this, he declared: 'We know that the German has powers that designate him to lead the community of the occidental nations' and 'the amalgamation of Hellenic and Christian origins in the Germanic character created western man.'[18] Stauffenberg was claiming that Germany had created the western world which should be under its control – hardly the morally-heroic character he has since been portrayed as.

There were divisions among the various Resistance groupings on the form of government that should follow the collapse of the Third Reich. While there was unanimity of intent amongst the opposition, i.e. to get rid of Hitler, there was no commonality on the outcome. Each opposition group formed its own version of the new Germany that would emerge once the Nazis were no more.

Nevertheless, one theme is identifiable as a constant, which was set down in a lengthy 'essay' produced by Generaloberst Ludwig Beck, Chief of the German General Staff, and Goerdeler, entitled 'The Goal'. This visualised a federation of European nations under German leadership 'within ten or twenty years'.[19]

Indeed, the moral gloss with which the Valkyrie conspiracy has been painted is a relatively recent phenomenon, its shine reflecting a Germany which is kinder to the modern eye. Such authors as Manvell and Fraenkel have helped to create this dazzling effect by calling the conspiracy 'a Christian crusade against the forces of evil,'[20] and many others have followed suit. Yet, as another German historian, Hans Mommsen, has made clear, 'a number of key figures in the resistance … were involved either in the planning of the war of extermination in the East, or, as many others did, participated in its execution'.[21] Many of these were ardent supporters of Hitler and his nationalistic ideals until it became obvious that Germany was losing the war. It was the prospect of defeat that motivated Stauffenberg to act against Hitler, as revealed in a paper dropped from his pocket as he was being dragged into the courtyard of the Bendlerblock to be shot after his assassination had failed: 'If the present course continues, defeat and destruction of the country's manpower and material strength is inevitable. Imminent disaster can only be averted by removing the present leadership… . Therefore, quick action is necessary.'[22]

There were, though, some military figures who opposed Hitler from the outset. These included Generalmajor Hans Oster, the deputy head of the Abwehr who was, as we will read, an early and persistent opponent of Hitler. He led a group that included Edwald von Kleist-Schmenzin who contacted a number of his English friends to enlist British support to halt the Nazis in the days before Hitler had reached the Chancellery in 1933, but his warnings were not taken seriously. Von Kleist-Schmenzin tried again in 1938, this time travelling to the UK as the emissary of Beck's and Goerdeler's group.

Being the representative of such a high ranking official, Kleist-Schmenzin was received not only by Gilbert Vansittart but also the Conservative politician Lord Lloyd and the troublesome, then backbencher, Winston Churchill. Prime Minister Neville Chamberlain, however, would have nothing to do with someone he regarded as nothing more than a revolutionary, a modern-day 'Jacobite', to use his exact words.

Oster was not deterred by this rebuff and tried again, this time through the industrialist Hans Böhm-Tettelbach who enlisted the support of a key figure in the German Foreign Ministry in London, Erich Kordt, who prepared a statement for consumption by his British counterparts which warned of Hitler's dangerous warlike ambitions. Because of the treacherous nature of the statement, it could not be carried in hard copy and was instead committed to memory. Böhm-Tettelbach actually got as far as No.10 Downing Street (albeit through the back door) and met with Lord Halifax, the British Foreign Secretary. British backing for what was, in effect, a coup d'état, was however, out of the question. Hitler, by all appearances, had enormous and widespread support throughout Germany and it was seen that Böhm-Tettelbach represented the views of a few elitist Prussians who felt marginalised by Hitler's populist policies.[23]

Others in Germany were also convinced that Hitler was leading his *volke* into war and sought help from the Allies to prevent the cataclysm they saw would inevitably unfold. The secretary of state in the German Foreign Office, Ernst von Weizsäcker, tried to warn the British as did Hjalmar Schacht the President of the Reichsbank, who met the Governor of the Bank of England, Montagu Norman, a number of times. Fabian von Schlabrendorff, an aristocratic lawyer, Helmuth Graf von Moltke, great-grandnephew of Field Marshal Helmuth von Moltke the Elder who had been the Chief of Staff of the Prussian Army, and Count Erich Schwerin von Schwanenfeld, a wealthy landowner, all tried in vain to enlist British support to oust Hitler.

It may seem incomprehensible that the pleadings of such high-ranking individuals should have been ignored. But Britain was set firmly on the path of appeasement and, however distasteful Hitler may have been, he had brought a degree of stability to a country that had witnessed mass unemployment, hyper-inflation and political turmoil in the years following the end of the First World War. The last thing that the British government wanted was another war with Germany – the last one had all but wiped out a generation of young men and virtually bankrupted the country.

The immense popularity of the Nazis in all of this is not to be discounted. The Weimar Republic which followed the First World War was regarded by many throughout Germany as nothing more than the unfortunate consequence of, as it was perceived, the treacherous surrender of 1918 and few believed it to be the kind of government that could lead Germany back to its place at the forefront of nations. From the outset it was hampered by the punitive terms of the Treaty of Versailles, its problems being compounded at the start of the 1930s by the worldwide Depression which hit Germany particularly badly. By 1932 around a third of the population had slid into poverty – and poverty bred anarchy. The Nazi Party had, meanwhile, become the largest in the Reichstag and, whilst unable to win a majority, in the March 1933 election the Nazis amassed 288 seats out of the available 647, amounting to 43.9 per cent of the vote. The nearest rivals, the Social Democrats, managed only 18.3 per cent.

When Hitler was thrust into power he may have ruthlessly eliminated all opposition groups, but this brought political stability. It may have been a bitter pill for ordinary, decent, aspirational Germans to swallow, but the medicine soon began to work. An increasingly stronger Germany began to emerge under a forceful leader. The suppression of the rights of some minority groups, homosexuals, gypsies, Jews, was a small price to pay, and was far from unpopular. Toppling Hitler would have inevitably meant a return to the chaos of the past. Such a situation was unimaginable. Only those like Kleist-Schmenzin and Goerdeler could visualise an alternative future for a post-Hitlerite Germany. But they had no public voice.

One group that did have a platform, or more accurately a pulpit, from which it could express its distain for the Nazi regime was the Catholic Church. But even that august body hesitated to vocalise its opposition following the 1933 Concordat with the Vatican in which priests were prohibited from participating in politics. Some, though at a local level, refused to remain silent, only for many of them to find themselves in the Priest Barracks at Dachau concentration camp.

There were attempts by the Catholic Church to enlist help from the United Kingdom to oust Hitler during the war through the Vatican. Talks were undertaken with British officials but they eventually proved fruitless.

Another religious organisation which attempted to take a stand against Hitler was a group of Protestant pastors which formed the 'Confessing

Church' in 1933. In 1937 one of its leaders, Dietrich Bonhoeffer, publicly opposed the Catholic stance, declaring that it was the church's moral duty to challenge the government's policies.[24] Predictably, he was soon forbidden to speak in public and was banned from entering Berlin. This served not to deter him, but instead drove him into the arms of those seeking to overthrow the Nazi regime. He joined the Abwehr which, as we will see, became the centre of the armed forces' opposition to Hitler. Bonhoeffer used his position to contact other religious bodies across Europe on behalf of the opposition. In May 1942 he met Anglican Bishop George Bell of Chichester, a member of the House of Lords and an ally of the Confessing Church, and tried, through him, to make contact with Britain's new Foreign Secretary, Anthony Eden, but his appeals were rebuffed. He was arrested on 5 April 1943 and held, without trial, at Tegel military prison before being secretly moved to Flossenbürg concentration camp, via Buchenwald. He was accused of being part of the 20 July 1944 plot and was executed at Flossenbürg on 9 April 1945.

The most powerful body that had remained aloof from the political turmoil was the Army. Its role was that of independent guardians of the state, its political neutrality being enshrined in the oath which every German soldier had to take:

> I swear by God this holy oath that I will at all times, truly and sincerely, serve my people and Fatherland and that, as a brave soldier, I will be ready at all times to give my life for this oath.

Just hours after the death of President Hindenburg on 2 August 1934, and following the removal or resignation of many senior officers, Hitler imposed a new oath, the Law of the Oath of the Wehrmacht, which again all soldiers had to commit to:

> I swear by God this holy oath, that I will give unconditional obedience to the Führer of the German Reich and people, Adolf Hitler, the Supreme Commander of the Wehrmacht and that, as a brave soldier, I will be ready at all times to give my life for this oath.

Symbolically and literally Hitler became one with the military. His decisions carried the power of orders. There was no other competing authority to which the military owed allegiance. It was hard for a good, God-fearing German to break such an oath, though, as will be seen, the Army, the *Heer*, became the most persistent and best-organised of all Hitler's domestic opponents and, ultimately, thousands of Army officers would refuse to follow the genocidal orders of their leaders and be executed as a result. Civilian officials had to swear a similar oath with the aim of bringing the military and civil society into alignment so that there was no distinction between loyalty to the state and loyalty to Hitler.

Consequently, the concept of assassinating Hitler, the legitimate head of state, had consequences which went far beyond the mere act of killing one individual. Failure would be certain to result in capture, probably torture, followed, unquestionably, by the death penalty. Even success would have the same fatal consequences for the conspirators if the Nazi Party remained in government. The only way conspirators could avoid reprisal was by mounting a fullscale coup d'état to remove not just Hitler but all the leading Nazis. This would require an enormous amount of planning and a large number of individuals to support the cause. Meanwhile, these people still had to go about their jobs in support of the state, performing them to the best of their ability for their country, as well as living within its society. It was, as one historian has put it, a 'Jekyll-and-Hyde' existence.[25]

Finding people to join such a conspiracy was, in itself, highly dangerous. The slightest indication of anti-Nazi sentiment revealed to the wrong person might lead to immediate denouncement and arrest. This was particularly the case between the differing branches of the armed forces. Inter-service rivalry, which was actively encouraged by Hitler, was intense and created an atmosphere of mutual distrust. Any attempt at regime change would need wide support across the Wehrmacht especially if post-coup conflict, with all its imponderables, was to be avoided. As Hitler had promoted literally hundreds of officers in the Heer to general rank their allegiance to the Führer was likely to be unbreakable. The *Luftwaffe*, established in 1935, was a Nazi creation, and saw itself as an elite force and its officers the beneficiaries of considerable government funding programmes to develop the most modern combat aircraft. The German navy, which had been compelled to hand over almost all its warships and submarines after the First World War, had been reborn as the *Kriegsmarine*, also in 1935, and its officers had heard Hitler promise the building of great battleships to rival, once again, the Royal Navy. Its admirals were hardly going to turn against a man who offered them so much. The ships, and therefore the personnel, of the Kriegsmarine were also dispersed around the globe making the assembly of large numbers of men to assist in overthrowing the government virtually impossible. Where then was support for an assassination of the Führer to be found?

It was a similar story with the business community. Many industrialists had no liking for Hitler, but they hated and feared the Communist far more. Hitler's rearmament programme was also of benefit to lots of industrialists – war, or the threat of war, and big business are, after all, hardly incompatible as the USA has so often demonstrated.

The Nazis' opposition to Communism must not be undervalued. Communism was perceived as an even greater threat to the Western democracies than Fascism in the 1920s and '30s. Hitler saw himself, and his ultimately inappropriately named National Socialists, as the main bulwark against Communism in central Europe, and many in the West were conscious of this. The Communists were, unsurprisingly, responsible for a number of the early attempts on Hitler's life before the movement was suppressed throughout the Reich.

Likewise, the unions, large organized left-wing bodies, were soon outlawed by Hitler. They were replaced by the German Labour Front, which was controlled by the Nazi Party. This ensured that the workforce of the country worked for the benefit of the state rather than that of its members.

Little wonder then, that politicians in the UK offered no encouragement to German opposition groups, for they were unquestionably in the minority in their own country. None could demonstrate the kind of backing across the armed forces or the business community which would ensure success. Not that there was a single resistance movement for the Chamberlain administration to support, merely a number of unconnected little groups, each with a different message to impart. If Britain was, by some means, to depose Hitler, what or who would replace him? Better possibly the devil you know?

When war was declared in 1939 the Allies knew exactly what devil they had to deal with. They also knew they had lost their chance to topple Hitler for, whilst they were aware that there were many influential individuals who wished to bring down the Führer, they could no longer be contacted through normal means of communication. Following its formation in 1940, the SOE's Section X, which was responsible for co-ordinating operations in Germany, saw little prospect of enlisting serious practical support from within the Third Reich. The anti-Nazi elements in Germany were, 'in the vast majority of cases neither willing nor able to undertake any subversive activities against the German regime', judging that most of the people were 'solidly behind the Nazi leadership'.

The German opposition was therefore left to its own devices and whereas, before 1939, Britain and France were fellow European neighbours, now they were Germany's mortal enemies. As patriotic Germans they could not bring themselves to aid the enemy in time of war.

There was, though, always the possibility that it would not be an organised group which would kill Hitler, as he conceded after one assassination attempt, that by Maurice Bavaud in 1938, came close to achieving its end:

> not a soul can cope with an assassin who, for idealistic reasons, is prepared quite ruthlessly to hazard his own life in the execution of his own object. I quite understand why ninety per cent of the historic assassinations have been successful… . In the midst of crowds it is easy for some fanatic armed with a telescopic sighted firearm to take a shot at me from some corner or other.

Hitler doubted the capability of the police or his security teams to detect or stop such lone assassins, citing the time when he entered Vienna during the Anschluss when the Gestapo dressed in plain clothes were so obvious that 'any moron could recognise them for what they were at a glance'. The only preventative measure one can take, he concluded, 'is to live irregularly – to walk, to drive and to travel at irregular times and unexpectedly'.[26]

Such a policy served Hitler well over the succeeding years, to the immense frustration of those who sought to remove him from power. Nevertheless, the likes of Beck, Oster, Schwerin von Schwanenfeld and others continued to conspire against Hitler, but they did so with little internal support and no outside help. They would have to deal with Hitler themselves or, as would be the case with most of them, they would die trying.

Chapter 1

Hofbräuhaus, Munich, Socialist and Communist Activists, 4 November 1921

As early as 1920 Communists in Germany had made numerous attempts to kill one of their fiercest rivals, the leader of the *Nationalsozialistische Deutsche Arbeiterpartei*, known as the NSDP or Nazi Party, Adolf Hitler. One of these is known to have taken place in 1921 in Munich.

The beer halls of the Bavarian capital were the battleground of political ideas, and of rival political movements, in the turbulent years after the First World War in southern Germany. It was in these rough and dangerous back-street buildings that Adolf Hitler fought to be heard and fought his enemies. On 4 November 1921 Hitler addressed a large crowd in the Hofbräuhaus am Platzl. It was at this beer hall that, in February 1920, Hitler and the National Socialists had held their first meeting in the Festsaal, the Festival Room, on the third floor.

As it happens, we have an eyewitness to the events of that evening, Adolf Hitler himself. What he later wrote in his quasi-autobiographical book, *Mein Kampf*, about the incidents that took place must be taken with a large measure of salt, but his account is the most detailed available. Hitler aimed to deliver a vitriolic denunciation of the assassination the previous month of Majority Socialist Reichstag Deputy Erhard Auer, with the inflammatory title 'Who Are the Murderers?' Assassination as a means of political change, or to eliminate political opponents, was disturbingly commonplace in Germany, even before the turbulent 1920s. Otto von Bismarck, the 'Iron Chancellor' who had engineered the unification of Germany and was seen as a great national hero, had survived two assassination attempts. But it was after Germany's defeat in the First World War, as the country sought to re-discover its identity, that politics became a particularly dangerous occupation, and by 1923 there had been more than 370 political murders.

Hitler was well aware of the dangers he faced and, at some time between 1800 and 1900 hours on the evening of his pre-arranged speech, he was informed that members of the Independent Socialist Party and the Communist Party, among other left-wing groups, intended to turn up in large numbers to break up the meeting. The Nazi Party had moved headquarters earlier that day and the telephones in the new premises had not been connected. Several earlier attempts had been made to warn Hitler by phone of the plan to disrupt his speech, but the callers had been unable to get through. Consequently, Hitler did not have time to increase the number of members of the paramilitary wing of the Nazi Party, the recently-formed SA – the *Sturmabteilung* (or Storm Detachment) – to help control the crowd. There would be around 300 people in the Hofbräuhaus and only forty-six men of the SA to protect Hitler. Another reason why there were so few of the SA on duty that night was because it was thought that the Hofbräuhaus was too small for a major confrontation. Had it been a larger venue, we are told, a full squad of 100 men would have been present.

Hitler, though, was not the kind of man to be deterred by the threats of his enemies, and he arrived at the Hofbräuhaus at 19.40 hours, determined to deliver his speech: 'The hall was filled, and for that reason the police had barred the entrances,' wrote Hitler.[1]

> Our adversaries, who had arrived very early, were in the hall, and our followers were for the most part outside. The small bodyguard awaited me at the entrance. I had the doors leading to the principal hall closed and then asked the bodyguard of forty-five or forty-six men to come forward. I made it clear to the boys that perhaps on that evening for the first time they would have to show their unbending and unbreakable loyalty to the movement and that not one of us should leave the hall unless carried out dead. I added that I would remain in the hall and that I did not believe that one of them would abandon me, and that if I saw any one of them act the coward I myself would personally tear off his armlet and his badge. I demanded of them that they should come forward if the slightest attempt to sabotage the meeting were made and that they must remember that the best defence is always attack.
>
> I was greeted with a triple 'Heil' which sounded more hoarse and violent than usual.

> Then I advanced through the hall and could take in the situation with my own eyes. Our opponents sat closely huddled together and tried to pierce me through with their looks. Innumerable faces glowing with hatred and rage were fixed on me, while others with sneering grimaces shouted at me together. Now they would 'Finish with us. We must look out for our entrails. To-day they would smash in our faces once and for all.' And there were other expressions of an equally elegant character. They knew that they were there in superior numbers and they acted accordingly.
>
> Yet we were able to open the meeting; and I began to speak. In the Hall of the Hofbräuhaus I stood always at the side, away from the entry and on top of a beer table. Therefore, I was always right in the midst of the audience …
>
> Before me, and especially towards my left, there were only opponents, seated or standing. They now began to order litre mugs of beer, one after the other, and to throw the empty mugs under the table. In this way whole batteries were collected. I should have been surprised had this meeting ended peacefully.

Despite numerous interruptions, Hitler was able to speak for about an hour and a half before a man jumped on a seat and shouted 'Freedom'.[2] It was the signal Hitler's opponents had been waiting for.

'In a few moments the hall was filled with a yelling and shrieking mob,' continued Hitler.

> Numerous beer-mugs flew like howitzers above their heads. Amid this uproar one heard the crash of chair legs, the crashing of mugs, groans and yells and screams.
>
> It was a mad spectacle. I stood where I was and could observe my boys doing their duty, every one of them.
>
> There I had the chance of seeing what a bourgeois meeting could be.
>
> The dance had hardly begun when my Storm Troops, as they were called from that day onwards, launched their attack. Like wolves they threw themselves on the enemy again and again in parties of eight or ten and began steadily to thrash them out of the hall. After five minutes I could see hardly one of them that was not streaming with

> blood. Then I realized what kind of men many of them were, above all my brave Maurice Hess, who is my private secretary today, and many others who, even though seriously wounded, attacked again and again as long as they could stand on their feet. Twenty minutes long the pandemonium continued. Then the opponents, who had numbered seven or eight hundred, had been driven from the hall or hurled out headlong by my men, who had not numbered fifty. Only in the left corner a big crowd still stood out against our men and put up a bitter fight. Then two pistol shots rang out from the entrance to the hall in the direction of the platform and now a wild din of shooting broke out from all sides. One's heart almost rejoiced at this spectacle which recalled memories of the War.
>
> At that moment it was not possible to identify the person who had fired the shots. But at any rate I could see that my boys renewed the attack with increased fury until finally the last disturbers were overcome and flung out of the hall.
>
> About twenty-five minutes had passed since it all began. The hall looked as if a bomb had exploded there. Many of my comrades had to be bandaged and others taken away. But we remained masters of the situation.

Hitler continued his speech and only declared the meeting over when he decided he had said enough and made his point.[3]

Eventually, the police arrived and closed down the meeting. It is said that the police found 150 smashed steins as well as chairs and tables, and the hall was strewn with lengths of brass pipe, brass knuckles and other weapons. There is little doubt that the target of the beer mugs was Hitler and, had his opponents' aim been more accurate, they could have caused him serious harm. It is said that the man who fired the gun had taken the loaded weapon into the Hofbräuhaus with the express intention of killing Hitler.[4] He might have been the first man who sought to shoot Hitler but he would not be the last.

Chapter 2

Thuringia, 1923, Persons Unknown; Tübingen, 1923, Persons Unknown; Feldherrnhalle, Munich, 9 November 1923, Bavarian Police

As the Nazi Party continued to grow in both numbers and notoriety, its leader was the subject of three known attempts on his life in 1923.

In April of that year Hitler and his friend, the German-American businessman Ernst Hanfstaengl, were driving in Hitler's green Selve with Nazi Party devotee Emil Maurice at the wheel. At a town on the outskirts of Leipzig, an area largely controlled by Communists, they were stopped at a roadblock manned by 'Red' militia. Hanfstaengl showed the Communists his Swiss passport and in a broad German-American accent told them he was a paper manufacturer from abroad who had come to visit the Leipzig fair. The other two men with him were his chauffeur and his valet. The ruse worked and they were allowed to pass through. As they drove away, a relieved Hitler commented that, 'They would have had my head.'[1]

Of the three actual assassination attempts made that year, one occurred in Thuringia where shots were fired at Hitler from a crowd. Shots were again fired at Hitler in Leipzig, this time at Hitler's car, as was the case in the third attempt which took place in Tübingen. In none of these instances were the perpetrators known, and these would seem to be opportunistic, rather than planned assassination efforts.

Despite such opposition, the time seemed ripe for Hitler to make his bid for power. The German economy was collapsing under the burden of the massive First World War reparations that had to be paid to the Allied nations, and inflation within the Weimar Republic was spiralling out of control. With prices of even the most basic of items reaching astronomical sums – even a postage stamp cost five billion marks – the German currency had lost all credibility, and individuals found that their life savings were worth nothing. There were food riots in the streets with workers being paid in what had become a virtually worthless currency. A change was needed, and Hitler believed the moment had come for the Nazi Party to lead that change.

He had read of Mussolini's National Fascist Party's march on Rome in October 1922. Thousands of Blackshirts had entered the Italian capital, forcing the incumbent government of Luigi Facta to cede power to the populist movement. It was Hitler's inspiration. He saw himself leading the National Socialists to Berlin where he would be propelled into the Chancellery on an overwhelming tide of popular support.

First, though, he had to seize power in Bavaria, which Hitler declared could become an autonomous region of Germany. In speech after speech, attended by ever-increasing numbers, Hitler roused the disaffected Bavarians to calls for revolution and separation from Berlin. His powerful right-wing policies appealed to the traditionally conservative police and army, and the Bavarian government had difficulty in ordering its forces to curb Hitler's dangerously subversive language and, often brutal, tactics when challenged.

In fact, it was the actions of the Weimar government which gave Hitler the opportunity he sought. Concerned at Hitler's growing popularity, General Otto von Lossow, the head of the Reichswehr in Bavaria, was instructed to clamp down on Hitler's activities and shut down his party's newspaper the *Völkischer Beobachter*. Lossow refused and was dismissed by the authorities in Berlin. This interference in local affairs angered the Bavarians still further. It also prompted Lossow to suggest that the Bavarians should march on Berlin and throw out the Republican politicians.

This led to the declaration of a state of emergency by Lossow in which he, State Commissar Gustav von Kahr and Colonel Hans Ritter von Seisser, the chief of the Bavarian state police, took over control of the Bavarian regional government.

In reality, Hitler had no wish to see Bavaria separated from the rest of the country, but the turmoil that was being created, which he had largely helped to manufacture, was the ideal setting for the Nazis to make their move to take over the regional government as the first step in seizing power in Berlin.

Hitler began to plot. He would use the words of the separatists against them. Their actions could certainly be considered treasonous and so the Nazis would step in to restore order and legitimacy, taking over power in the process. By this time the Nazi Party was the strongest and best organised of the anarchical groups with a following of some 55,000 angry Bavarians. It also had the backing of General Erich Ludendorff, who had led the German Army in the First World War before resigning shortly before the Armistice. After the war Ludendorff had taken up a political career on the far right and saw Hitler as an ally. Hitler and his followers were now a force to be reckoned with but just how they were to seize power remained unresolved. Then fate leant a hand.

It was announced that Commissar von Kahr was to hold a public meeting (which he called a 'patriotic demonstration') in which he would spell out the objectives of the new regime. On the podium with von Kahr would be Lossow, Seisser and Minister President Eugen von Knilling. The meeting offered Hitler the chance to take all these men at gunpoint and persuade them to accept his leadership. If they refused, they would be bundled away and imprisoned.

Hitler knew that he could not achieve power in Bavaria without the support of these powerful and, now that they had defied Berlin, popular, men and if they did not co-operate with him he knew his chances of a successful coup were slim. But his party members were growing increasingly vocal in their demands for action. If he did not act soon Hitler might find his influence waning. The date of the patriotic demonstration was 9 November. It would always be remembered in German history as the date of the Beer Hall Putsch.

By the time that Hitler arrived at the 3,000-capacity Bürgerbräukeller every seat had been taken. As with every gathering those days in Munich there was a possibility that there would be trouble and 125 municipal policemen were there to control the crowd. On their way by truck were 603 SA, with their field-grey windjammers and swastika armbands. Hitler advised the police on guard at the door that they would be wise not to try and impede his stormtroopers when they entered the building. At 20.30 hours the trucks emptied and the well-armed Nazis surrounded the building and waited for the signal. That signal was the arrival of the Führer's personal 100-strong, steel-helmeted bodyguard.

Led by Captain Hermann Göring, the bodyguard, armed with machine pistols, entered the hall. The police in the hall made a token attempt to block the Nazis but, on being ordered out of the way, they meekly stood back. With his Browning pistol in his hand, Hitler, accompanied by a small group of supporters, which included Rudolf Hess, pushed his way through the throng towards the speaker's platform.

There was uproar, tables were overturned as people began either to try to stop Hitler or to leave the hall. Brownshirts, however, had blocked both the front and rear exits. Hitler could not push his way through the melee, so he fired a shot into the ceiling and called out, 'Quiet!'

The crowd was stunned into silence: 'The National Revolution has begun!' Hitler shouted. 'No one may leave the hall. Unless there is immediate quiet I shall have a machine-gun posted in the gallery. The Bavarian and Reich governments have been removed and a provisional national government formed. The barracks of the Reichswehr and police are occupied. The Army and the police are marching on the city under the swastika banner!'

At gunpoint Kahr, Lossow and Seisser were ushered into the side room. With a mixture of threats and promises, Hitler tried to convince the three men to support his cause, without success. Meanwhile the audience was becoming restless, despite another shot being fired into the ceiling, this time by Göring.

Not quite sure what to do next, Hitler left the three men in the side room watched by Ulrich Graf, Hitler's personal bodyguard, who was armed with a machine pistol, and re-entered the hall. Hitler was in a difficult situation with the coup in the balance, but he rose to the occasion, delivering one of his mesmerizing speeches to the audience. His passion communicated itself to the crowd which soon was shouting its approval. Hitler, though, was still nothing more than an anarchist in the eyes of many Bavarians. What he needed was a figure of national standing to add legitimacy to his cause – and at that moment General Ludendorff marched into the Bürgerbräukeller. It had been agreed that Ludendorff would once again take control of the German Army after Hitler had seized power.

Though he was angry that Hitler had started the putsch without him, Ludendorff went into the side room with Hitler and managed to persuade Kahr, Lossow and Seisser if not to support Hitler then at least not to stand in Hitler's way. The five men returned to the main hall, with Hitler telling the now wildly enthusiastic crowd that he would not rest 'until on the ruins of the wretched Germany of today there should have arisen once more a Germany of power and greatness, of freedom and splendour'.[2]

Of course, Hitler could not hope to take control of the Bavarian government with a few hundred men, however committed they might be. He needed strength in numbers to back his strength of character. Across the River Iser, 2,000 men of the paramilitary group the Bund Reichskriegsflagge and the remainder of the SA were packed into another beer hall, the Löwenbräukeller, waiting for word that the coup had succeeded. At 20.40 hours the telephone rang with a message from the Bürgerbräukeller. It was the signal. Captain Ernst Röhm walked up to the podium and announced that the Kahr regime was at an end and Adolf Hitler had declared a national revolution. Amid cheers, wild exclamations and the waving of hats, Röhm led the noisy crowd out of the Löwenbräukeller and through the Maxvorstadt district accompanied by a local brass band.

The procession was stopped by a motorcyclist with fresh instructions from Hitler. The men were to be divided into three columns, with one going to the monastery in the St Annaplatz square to pick up a cache of 3,000 rifles stored in its basement; the second group was to march to the Schöfeldstrasse to take over General von Lossow's headquarters, with only the third group continuing to join Hitler at the Bürgerbräukeller.

Röhm bluffed his way into the Army headquarters, persuading those guards on duty to lay down their arms or face a battle whilst, at the Bürgerbräukeller, Hess was taking prisoner every senior political figure at the gathering. Other Nazis set off to secure key establishments across the city, including a bank and the police headquarters. At this stage it appeared that the putsch was going to plan, especially as it received the support of 1,000 young and impressionable cadets from the local infantry school. Then Hitler made a terrible mistake. He received word that his men were having trouble gaining entry to the Army's engineer barracks and Hitler decided to go there and resolve the matter in person, leaving Ludendorff to look after the situation in the Bürgerbräukeller.

While he was away, Lessow told Ludendorff that he needed to go to his headquarters to issue orders to his men regarding the new government to be set up under Hitler. Ludendorff believed him and allowed Lessow to leave, along with Kahr and Seisser. As far as Ludendorff was concerned, an agreement had been reached with the three men; under Hitler's new regime Kahr would become Regent of Bavaria, Seisser would be police minister and Lessow would be army minister. He saw no reason why they should still be detained. He was duped.

As soon as he was free, Lessow made for the 19th Infantry barracks from where he telephoned the headquarters of the battalions stationed in the surrounding localities, ordering them to Munich by train as quickly as possible to put down the putsch. Similarly, Commissar Kahr had rushed to his headquarters where he received a message from Bavaria's Crown Prince, Rupprecht, to quash the coup 'at any cost'.

Kahr's headquarters had been surrounded by the cadets from the infantry school, where they were confronted by armed police. Though the cadets far outnumbered the police they were reluctant to open fire on fellow Bavarians in uniform. After a stand off lasting deep into the night, the cadets withdrew after lengthy negotiations with the commissar. The putsch was stalling.

Unaware that things were not going to plan, across Munich the Nazis were conducting themselves in a manner to which they became infamous, dragging known opponents and prominent socialists from their beds and holding them hostage. This, of course, included Jews, and even people with Jewish-sounding names selected from the Munich telephone directory.

Lossow, meanwhile, had issued a message to all German wireless stations at 02.55 hours:

> State Commissar General v. Kahr, Col. v. Seisser and General v. Lossow repudiate the Hitler Putsch. Expressions of support extracted by gunpoint invalid. Caution is urged against misuse of the above names.
>
> v. Lossow.

Kahr followed this up by outlawing the NSDAP and declaring that the leaders of the putsch would 'ruthlessly be made to suffer the punishment they deserve'. Hitler learned of this at 05.00 hours, and he responded in the only way he knew how – violently. As the Brownshirts and other Nazis re-assembled in the beer hall, they were told of the treachery of

Kahr and the others. It was now that the senior Nazi figures showed their mettle, in particular Julius Stricher, who restored the putschists' ardour with a rousing speech.

Still determined to continue with the coup, Hitler and his closest comrades discussed their next course of action. The conversation dragged on indecisively through the early morning with the armed and angry men in the Bürgerbräukeller itching for action. To keep the increasingly frustrated troops quiet, Hitler sent some of his SA men to seize bundles of 50-billion mark notes directly from the printing presses to distribute to his unsettled supporters.[3]

At 10.00 hours word was received that truckloads of Bavarian state troopers had arrived and set up two heavy machine guns at one of the bridges, the Ludwig Bridge, across the River Isar which cuts Munich in two. Everything now depended on the putschists' next move. After a proposal to withdraw to the Austrian border to try and rally support had been rejected, the decision was taken to march through Munich, believing that the people would flock to join the march. The march of the *Münchners* would become unstoppable and von Kahr and his traitors would be forced to flee. 'We would go to the city,' Hitler later testified, 'to win the people to our side … and then we would see how Kahr, Lossow and Seisser would react to public opinion.'

Ludendorff believed that he was held in such high esteem that the soldiers would never shoot him, and Hitler was equally confident that support for the Nazis was so strong that the Army would not dare to stop the marchers.

The Nazis assembled outside the beer hall, organised into line by Freikorps fighter Hermann Kriebel. At the head of the procession were a number of selected marksmen in the centre of which were eight men carrying the swastika and the black-white-red Nazi flags which would become so well known. Behind these came Hitler and the other leaders, followed by three heavily-armed columns, which included Hitler's 100-strong bodyguard. Many in the main group behind these three columns were also armed with rifles, bayonets and pistols. In total, there were around 2,000 extremely committed individuals, from the street bruisers of the SA, and the smartly-paraded cadets of the infantry school, to ordinary businessmen and office workers.

It was almost midday before the march began. The first obstacle that lay in the path of the marchers was the contingent of armed police at the Ludwig Bridge. The police commander ordered the marchers to halt but he and his men were quickly overwhelmed without a shot being fired. Gaining in confidence in the cold Bavarian air, the Nazis saw increasing numbers of people joining them, singing patriotic songs as they marched into the Marienplatz and onto the Feldhernhalle eight abreast. Ahead of them was a line of state police. Seeking to seize the initiative, Senior Lieutenant Baron Michael Freiherr von Godin ordered his men forward. The police jogged up towards the head of the column but the putschists kept moving forward. There was a clash of bayonets, and then a shot rang out. It hit a sergeant who fell to the ground. 'For a fraction of a second my company stood frozen,' recalled Godin. 'Then, before I could give an order, my people opened fire, with the effect of a salvo.'[14]

Hitler's men returned fire as most of the marchers near the front and the watching crowd fled for cover. Ulrich Graph, Hitler's bodyguard threw himself in front of the Führer, stopping the fusillade of bullets aimed at the Nazi leader. As he fell to the street, he grabbed at Hitler so violently that he dislocated the Führer's left arm. All the leading Nazis were either cut down by the gunfire or dropped to the ground to avoid the police bullets.

It is said that Ludendorff was the only one that stayed on his feet (though this is disputed) and marched on to be taken prisoner. Behind him eighteen men lay dead or dying. Hitler staggered to his feet, nursing his left arm, believing that he had been shot on his left side.

Unaware of what was happening ahead, those in the rear of the column pushed on, adding to the rapidly escalating confusion. In the midst of the chaos Hitler made his getaway with the help of chief surgeon of the SA, Dr Walter Schultze, and reached his car. Hitler told the driver to go back to the Bürgerbräukeller, but he was now a wanted man and at the Marienplatz the car came under machine-gun fire, being forced to swerve to avoid the spray of bullets. When they reached the Isar they found the Ludwig Bridge again blocked by troopers. Unable to get back to the beer hall, there was nothing for it but to leave Munich and head for the Austrian border.

Hitler left his ardent followers to their fate. The Nazis scattered around Munich, seeking refuge wherever they could. The triumphal march had turned into an ignominious scramble for safety. Though abandoned by their Führer, whom they believed had been wounded, the surviving Nazis did not lose heart entirely and they considered Kahr, whom they thought wanted to keep power for himself, to be the man who had betrayed them. The failure of the putsch was seen by the angry men who sought to overthrow the establishment not as a botched affair in which they were let down badly by their leaders, but as further proof of the corruption and treachery of the ruling elite.

Hitler was taken to the country house of his friend the German-American businessman Ernst Hanfstaengl at Uffing. Hitler was completely crushed by the result of the putsch and, when he was informed that the police were on their way to Uffing, he picked up his revolver intent, it appeared, to shoot himself, claiming there was no point in carrying on. Frau Hanfstaengl demanded to know what he was doing: 'How can you give up at the first reverse?' she asked. 'How can you leave all the people you have got interested in your idea of saving your country – and then take your own life?'

Those words saved Hitler and the Nazi Party.

Hitler was arrested and, along with others such as Röhm, Hermann Kriebel and Rudolph Hess, was tried in a special People's Court for treason. Found guilty, on 1 April 1924 Hitler was sentenced to five years' imprisonment at Landsberg Prison. Adolf Hitler's political career was, to all appearances, at an end. Appearances, however, can be deceptive.

Chapter 3

Hotel Kaiserhof, Berlin, January 1932, Persons Unknown

Hitler's trial for high treason gave him his day in court and the opportunity to expound his views, which were widely reported in the local press. Though found guilty, his views had resonated with many across Germany, and his attempted putsch indicated that he had the strength of will to bring about the changes that were so desperately needed if Germany was to rise again to the position it held before the First World War. Hitler had gained many supporters in positions of influence and he served only nine months of his five-year sentence and was granted the most lenient form of imprisonment.

It was during his time in prison that he wrote *Mein Kampf*, which gave him the chance to assemble his ideas into a somewhat more cogent form. He was not ready to form a government in 1923 and the failed coup made Hitler realize that he could not seize power by force, but that, as his philosophies continued to gather popular support, he might do so through the strength of his words and his conviction.

It would be many years, though, before his words could be heard across all of Germany as he was banned from public speaking in much of the country until 1927 and in Prussia, the largest state, until 1928. Nevertheless, over that time Hitler gradually became seen not just a leader of a right-wing group, but the leader of the right wing, with the Nazis being the most important of such organizations. This, though, still meant that Hitler and his party were political minorities, as conditions in Germany began to improve and opposition to the Weimar Republic softened.

The recovery in Germany began with the replacement of the existing mark, which, because it had no gold to back it was a paper currency with no real value, with the *Rentenmark*.[1] The brilliant idea behind this move was to base the new currency on the land used for agriculture and business as security. This gave the currency a tangible value. The Rentenmark was introduced, on 15 October 1923, at a rate of one Rentenmark to one million old marks.

Sebastian Haffner described the experience of spending Rentenmarks after their introduction:

> When you offered them in payment for the first time, you waited in suspense to see what would happen. Nothing did. They were actually accepted, and you were handed your goods – goods worth a billion marks. The same thing happened the next day and the day after. Incredible… . On Thursday, you could still buy something for the money received on the previous Friday.[2]

The Rentenmark was changed to the *Reichsmark* in 1924, at the same rate. Following the stabilization of the German currency, a new plan, the Dawes Plan, also of 1924, was agreed upon which saw the end of the Allied occupation of the Ruhr and a staggered and more realistic payment plan for Germany's payment of its war reparations.

Living standards improved rapidly, there was an increase in house building, the shops were full of modern goods, industrial output exceeded pre-war levels and people could afford to indulge in luxury goods and leisure pursuits. Germany's borders were confirmed by the Locarno Treaty of 1925, and Germany was allowed entry into the League of Nations in 1926 with a permanent seat on the Council in recognition of her status as a great power. Germany was back in the fold and few were interested in extreme right-wing parties.

With regards to the political front, whilst there had been four changes of administration between 1923 and 1926, there had been much continuity because these changes were from one coalition to another formed from all the principal mainstream parties. Support for the right across the country dwindled and when the Nazi Party stood in the Reichstag elections under its own name for the first time in 1928, it received just 2.6 per cent of the vote. This gave the Nazis twelve seats out of the 491 in the Reichstag.

The significance of this, however, was considerable. It demonstrated that Hitler, who only five years earlier had tried to bring the Weimar Republic down by armed revolution, had joined, and had been accepted by, the existing political system. Or so it would seem.

Despite its poor showings in the Reichstag election, growing unrest amongst the farming community caused by a revision of the Dawes Plan by Owen D. Young (known unsurprisingly as the Young Plan) saw the Nazis perform well in regional elections in 1929. Party membership rose dramatically to some 100,000 – twice as many as at the time of the Beer Hall Putsch.

Nevertheless, the Nazis' seemingly weak performance in the 1928 elections demonstrated that the party was of little relevance to most people and the government lifted its public speaking ban on Hitler. He quickly took advantage of this and his impassioned speeches drew large crowds. Hitler's magnetism gripped audiences and he soon had a strong cult following. Hitler was becoming bigger than the party.

Despite Hitler's growing appeal, there was no possibility of him ever becoming anything other than the leader of a collection of protest groups on the fringe of the German political system. Something almost cataclysmic would have to happen before most decent, hardworking Germans would listen to Hitler's rhetoric – and it did.

On Tuesday 24 October 1929 the New York stock market collapsed and the world was thrown into chaos. The effects were felt particularly severely in Germany with its post-war economy having been built on foreign capital, mostly loans from America, and was heavily dependent on exports to generate income to service those debts. World trade shrank dramatically and, when those loans were called in by the desperate financiers in the US, the Germans were in terrible trouble. As export orders declined, so workers were laid off and unemployment soared. Worse still was the failure of many banks, with people seeing their life's savings lost overnight.

The latest of the coalition governments, known as the 'Grand Coalition' did not survive the disaster and was replaced in March 1930 with an administration headed by Heinrich Brüning which was imposed upon the Reichstag by President Hindenburg. The coalition of moderate parties was seen as being too weak to deal with Germany's mounting problems, and Brüning and Hindenburg sought to reduce the influence of the Reichstag and concentrate power in the hands of the Chancellor and the President. They, unwittingly, were preparing the ground for a Hitler dictatorship – and the Nazi leader was on the rise.

In the Reichstag elections of September 1930 the Nazi Party's share of the vote rose to more than eighteen per cent, with 6,371,000 people casting their votes in its favour. The twelve seats won two years earlier had shot up to 107.[3] No one had expected such success, not even Hitler. But the other main parties had been in the various coalitions and had been seen to fail. Not so the Nazis, who remained untainted by the disasters that had brought the country to its knees.

Hitler had run an energetic election campaign, offering the Germans something new, with Goebbels organizing hundreds of meetings in halls, huge marquees and in the open air. As a 'little corporal' who had fought and been wounded and decorated, he was, in modern parlance 'a man of the people'. Yet it was this year, Hitler's breakthrough year, when he was subject to what might have been the first consciously-planned assassination attempt at the Hotel Kaiserhof on Berlin's Wilhelmstrasse.

Hitler, we are told, loved the luxurious hotel which was situated near the Reichstag in the capital's government district. Until he later moved his party permanently to Berlin, the Kaiserhof became Hitler's headquarters in the capital where he maintained a suite and where he would dine with key members of the Nazi Party to discuss tactics. On one such occasion in January 1932, all those who dined with him fell ill from food poisoning, less than an hour after the dinner. The symptoms suffered by Hitler's dinner guests included stomach cramps, vomiting and general weakness. Doctors were summoned and one of the diners, Hitler's adjutant Wilhelm Brückner, was so badly affected that it was feared he might not recover.[4] Hitler was least affected by the poisoning. This has been attributed to his strict vegetarian diet. Hitler suspected that members of the kitchen staff had attempted to kill him. As it transpired no one died but, from that moment on, Hitler was wary of food served in outside establishments and that explains why he only drank water at the Hofbräuhaus. Though the precise date of this incident is not known, one of Hitler's close friends at that time, the German-American businessman and intimate friend, Ernst Hanfstaengl, recalled that on his birthday that year, 20 April, Hitler received numerous cakes from his female well-wishers which he refused to touch. After the names and addresses of the senders were recorded, the birthday cakes were disposed of.[5]

It is not known who the perpetrator or perpetrators were or whether it was merely a case of poor kitchen hygiene, but many people throughout

Germany were alarmed at the rapid growth of the Nazi Party and, as there is no record of any other guests being ill at the Kaiserhof, this must be regarded as an attempt to get rid of the entire leadership. No such chance would present itself again. Certainly, Goebbels' wife, Magda, believed that it had been no accident and, from that time onwards until Hitler became Chancellor, she supervised all the meals prepared for Hitler at the Kaiserhof.

Once he was installed in the Chancellery in 1933 Hitler was able to impose very tight controls over all the food that was served. He even brought his old cook from the Party's headquarters in Munich, the Brown House, to take charge of the Chancellery kitchen.

Chapter 4

Munich to Weimar Train, 15 March 1932, Persons Unknown; Kurt Lutter, 4 March 1933, Königsberg; Czech Nationalists, 20 March 1933, Tiergartenstraße, Munich

The legitimacy bestowed upon Hitler in the Nazis' electoral success in the Reichstag elections of September 1930 enabled him to widen his appeal, for he was no longer seen as an extremist outside the political norm. People of all classes could now quite openly admit to being supportive of Hitler's policies and the Führer unashamedly promised everything to everyone. Workers, businessmen and wealthy landowners alike were seduced by Hitler's belief that Germany could become, once again, the foremost nation in Europe. At his speeches and rallies he ranted against materialism and social injustice, the Jews and the communists, but in talks with the industrialists he offered tax reductions and import duties on foreign goods. His ideas were also spread through the written word with *Mein Kampf* becoming a best seller – selling 54,086 copies in the year following the 1930 electoral triumph.

The German economy continued to slide as the Depression deepened. The Reichsmark could not be exchanged for any currency and foreign investment flowed out of the country. By 1932 six million Germans were out of work, which meant that around a third of the workforce was unemployed. Between 1929 and 1932 there was a huge increase in crime, mostly due to a rise in theft, as people became increasingly desperate. 'Hate exploded suddenly without warning, out of nowhere; at street corners, in restaurants, cinemas, dance halls, swimming baths; at midnight, after breakfast, in the middle of the afternoon,' wrote the Anglo-American novelist Christopher Isherwood who had moved to Berlin in 1929. 'Knives were whipped out, blows were dealt with spiked rings, beer-mugs, chair-legs or leaded clubs.'[1]

In the midst of this mounting chaos two further attempts were made on Hitler's life in 1932, not long after the Hotel Kaiserhof incident. The first occasion was on 15 March when Hitler was travelling by train from Munich to Weimar. Bullets were fired at the carriage carrying Hitler, Josef Goebbels and William Frick. No one was hurt. The second incident occurred in June of that year near the town of Straslund and, once again, it was as Hitler was on the move, this time in his car. It is said that a group of men were waiting to ambush Hitler as the car slowed down to navigate a very tight bend. Hitler, and the car, got away unscathed.

More violence was shown to Hitler in July 1932 and, though the incident cannot be considered an assassination attempt, this time he was hurt. On the 29th he delivered a speech at a rally in Freiburg. Either just before, or just after his speech, stones were thrown at his car, one of which struck Hitler's head.[2]

By this time, few continued to believe in the Weimar Republic, including President Hindenburg who dismissed Brüning, replacing him with Franz von Papen on 30 May 1932. This move, it has been said, marked the end of democracy in Germany until the post-war era. Most of the men selected by von Papen had no connection with any political party and did not have a seat in the Reichstag. An unelected body now ran Germany.

Papen hoped to rule in a manner that transcended politics, but his appointment without a mandate from the people only served to drive more of them to the polls in the July 1932 election. If 1928 had been the breakthrough year for the Nazi Party, 1932 was when it consolidated its position as the most important political organization in Germany since the end of the Great War. The Nazis won a staggering 230 seats in the Reichstag – almost 100 more than their nearest rivals, the Social Democrats. The Communist Party also saw a moderate increase in its share of the vote, indicating how in times of adversity political opinion becomes polarized. Papen, though he did try, failed to dissolve the Reichstag with the aim of ruling by presidential decree, and was forced to resign.

He was replaced as Chancellor on 3 December 1932 by General der Infanterie Kurt von Schleicher, who also sought to establish an autocratic regime without reference to the Reichstag to prevent the left-wing parties from having any say in how Germany was governed. But, predictably, he was obstructed by the elected representatives and, most notably, by the Nazis. Hitler now had his sights set on the Chancellery and Schleicher stood in his way.

Seeing no prospect of controlling the Reichstag, Schleicher stood down from the Chancellorship suggesting to Hindenburg that the President should simply dispense with the Reichstag and rule as a de facto dictator. This was not something Hindenburg was willing to consider.

Yet, with the largest party – the Nazis – being opposed at every turn by the Communists and the Social Democrats who together had more seats than the Nazis, the country was becoming ungovernable. Somehow, Hindenburg had to find a man amongst the political parties that had a mandate from the electorate and was also strongwilled and ruthless. It was a perfect description of the leader of the Nazi Party.

The prospect of Adolf Hitler becoming Chancellor was something that deeply troubled Generaloberst Kurt Gebhard Adolf Philipp Freiherr von Hammerstein-Equord. Hammerstein had a profound dislike of the Nazis and, in 1932, had vowed that the Army (the Reichswehr) would never allow Hitler into power.

Hammerstein had served alongside Kurt von Schleicher during the First World War in the 3rd Foot Guards with the two men becoming friends, and he was therefore angry with the way Hitler had opposed Schleicher during his brief reign as chancellor. As the Commander-in-Chief of the Reichswehr, Hammerstein was uniquely placed to get rid of Hitler by force. Indeed, so powerful had become the armed wing of the Nazi Party, the SA, the Army was the only body with the military muscle to take on Hitler.

In early 1933 Hammerstein discussed with Schleicher the practicality of using the Army to mount a coup in which Hindenburg would be deposed, a military dictatorship established, and Hitler eliminated once and for all. Hammerstein's conscience, however, held him back. He felt great loyalty to Hindenburg who had also assured him that he would never allow Hitler into a position of power. This troubling question of loyalty, which bound officers to their oaths of duty, would become a familiar obstacle over the following years, and the Army's failure to unshackle itself from this would see repeated opportunities to avert disaster lost at crucial times. So, with little alternative, on 30 January 1933, at Hindenburg's invitation, Adolf Hitler became Chancellor of Germany.

Hindenburg and Schleicher believed that they could control Hitler, who would be forced to include members of other political parties in his cabinet, but the entire political landscape changed abruptly when, in the early hours of 27 February, the Reichstag building was burnt to the ground. The arsonist, a Dutch immigrant and Communist Party member called Marinus van der Lubbe, was apprehended at the scene of the crime, declaring that he had started the fire as 'a cry to rally the German workers against fascist rule'.

Nothing could have suited Hitler better. The fire, he declared, was evidence that the communists were aiming to bring down the government, providing, it was claimed, information that a revolution was about to be launched. With this 'proof' Hitler persuaded Hindenburg to sign an emergency decree allowing the Nazis to apprehend the ringleaders. The SA was ordered to round up all the communists it could find and around 4,000 were arrested, with Goebbels gleefully reporting: 'Arrests upon arrests. Now the Red pest is being thoroughly rooted out.'

This was the start of Hitler's complete dominance of the German political scene. He called it '*Gleichaltung*' which roughly translates as 'bringing into line'. Across the country Nazis began infiltrating and taking over local communities and organizations, and this included social as well as political gatherings. Germany was to be Nazified.

This naturally alarmed many people and it prompted a spate of assassination attempts against Hitler. The most considered of these efforts was undertaken by a ship's carpenter called Kurt Lutter. He was part of a small group of communists who wanted to end Hitler's reign as Chancellor before his grip on the country became absolute.

On 4 March 1933 Hitler was due to address a political rally in Königsberg in support of his candidates in the Federal elections, prompted by the Reichstag fire, which were to take place the following day. The Lutter group planned to blow up the speaker's platform as Hitler gave his address. The group met twice in February to discuss their plans, but one of their number was a police informer who notified the authorities. The group was rounded up on 3 March. Under interrogation, none of the group admitted to planning a political assassination and no explosives were ever found. Eventually, they were all released.

The 5 March Federal elections gave the Nazis 288 seats, another increase, but still not enough to command a majority in the Reichstag which this time numbered 647 seats. Hitler knew that public opinion, which had swung so dramatically in his direction, could just as easily swing away. What Germany needed was stability and Hitler managed to convince Hindenburg of this, the latter issuing the Decree of the Reich President for the Protection of People and State. This act allowed a temporary suspension of most civil liberties, including the right to free expression, the freedom of the press and privacy of postal and telephonic communications.

This was a major triumph for Hitler who could now do almost anything he wanted. To celebrate this success, a ceremony was organized for 23 March at the Garrison Church (*Garnisonskirche*) in Potsdam. The *Garnisonskirche* was the parish church of the Prussian royal family and where the kings of Prussia, including Frederick the Great, were buried.

By this time the police were receiving reports of assassination plots against the new Chancellor almost every week. One such was reported in *The Times* of 21 March 1933, the information coming from Heinrich Himmler, the recently installed chief of the Munich police. According to his statement, the previous day, three 'Checkists' drove up in a motor car with Berlin number plates to the Richard Wagner monument by the Tiergartenstraße in Munich, which Hitler was to pass by later that day. There, they planted three bombs. They were spotted by the police but they swiftly made their escape and were not caught. The bombs were secured and made safe. Announcing the incident to the press, Himmler said: 'The authorities saw in every attempt of this kind the gravest danger to public order and security' and that 'From his own knowledge of the public mood and from the reports of subordinate officials, he was convinced that the firing of the very first shot – whether it hit its mark or not – might lead to unequalled chaos throughout Germany and to a great programme which no power of the state or the police would be able to prevent.'

With such scant detail, the veracity of this announcement is certainly questionable, and it appears to set the ground for the security services to impose even harsher measures against political dissidents. To further reinforce the apparent need to seek out those who sought to oppose the now legitimate German head of state, numerous debatable reports were received by police forces around the country of plans to kill Hitler. These ranged from spraying Hitler with prussic acid concealed in a bunch of flowers to sending him the gift of an exploding pen and presenting him with a rabid dog with sharp claws.[3] There were reports of assassination threats from Jews planning Hitler's demise in Basle, and schemes were supposedly afoot in Barcelona, Holland, Morocco and Spain.[4]

It is difficult from this distance in time to know how serious these threats were and whether, like the Reichstag fire, they were a convenient excuse to clamp down on any perceived dissident activity.

According to the German historian Will Berthold, the reason why we know so little about the numerous plots to assassinate Hitler at this early period in his chancellorship is because Hitler came to power as the beloved Führer of the German people and it could not be seen that some wished to see him dead. Such plots were, therefore, concealed from the general public and the only incidents which were revealed were those that could not be covered up.[5] This is echoed by another German historian, Hans Rothfels who, writing in the late 1940s about Georg Elser's Bürgerbräukeller bomb of November 1939, stated: 'This is the only bomb incident to be made public from the pre-war period, but it can be assumed that other attempts were made which were not so generally known.'[6] It is equally likely that some of these alleged plots were concocted by Himmler to increase the perceived importance of his police force to Hitler's safety.

Security was, consequently, tightened for Hitler's Potsdam visit, especially when a clairvoyant claimed that a tunnel had been dug under the church where dynamite had been placed which was to blow up Hitler and his entourage, which included Hindenburg. The police investigated and they did indeed discover that a tunnel had been dug under the church – to allow the installation of cables as the event was to be broadcast on German radio.[7] The presumption that the tunnel was for some sinister purpose indicates just how nervous Hitler's security team had become.

The church, which was badly damaged by the RAF in 1945, was finally destroyed under the post-war communist regime. Plans to rebuild the church in 2014 met with fierce opposition as it is considered to be the place where the Third Reich was born.

As for Kurt von Hammerstein, he continued to urge Hindenburg to rein in Hitler. But the ageing president told the general that he should stop meddling in politics and concentrate on running the Army. Due to his continued opposition to Hitler, Hammerstein's relationship with Hindenburg became increasingly strained and, on 31 January 1943, Hammerstein was forced to resign his post.

Chapter 5

Chicago, Illinois, 19 December 1933, M. X. Kimball; Washington, 23 March 1933, Daniel Stern; Palaiseau, France, 18 February 1933, Ludwig Assner

The declassified files of the CIA have revealed a previously undeclared assassination plot against Hitler in 1933. A report made by Special Agent H.H. Reinecke disclosed the following details:

> Shortly before October 13, 1933, a man called on German Consul Yaeger, now in Germany, at Chicago, and refusing to give his name and address, said for an immediate $1,000 cash consideration, [he would] divulge details of a plot being hatched among educated Jews of Chicago to send an emissary to Germany to kill Chancellor Hitler, with an additional $4,000 if the plot were frustrated as a result of his information.
>
> On October 20th, this same individual, giving the name of M.X. Kimball, called at [the] German Embassy, Washington, D.C., with the same story and demands; later calling the Embassy by phone and demanding $50,000, saying he was going to New York to see [the] German Consul, where he later called by phone, but never put in his appearance. No description, address, or connections of Kimball [are] available in Chicago.[1]

As a result of all this, the FBI felt obliged to investigate further and an agent went to speak to the German Consul General, Dr Nuhring, at 520 North Michigan Avenue, Illinois. Dr Nuhring said that he believed it was his assistant, Dr Tannanberg, who dealt with the person in question. When spoken to, Dr Tannanberg explained that it was indeed Dr Nuhring's predecessor, Consul Yaeger, to whom the individual had spoken. However, he was able to provide a few more details. This individual stated that he knew the name of the person who had agreed to go to Germany to carry out the deed as well as the individuals involved in the plot. He said that the man was of Jewish extraction, although he did not look like a Jew, and that he was to go to Germany by way of London at which place he was to receive further instructions 'by which he would be able to get into the presence of Chancellor Hitler in his office where the murder was to be committed'. The would-be assassin said that he was willing to sacrifice himself for the purpose of solving the Jewish problem in Germany, provided that his mother and brothers were taken care of after he had been arrested or killed. The report concluded that Consul Yaeger was somewhat sceptical of the man's ability to deliver the information he promised.

The Bureau decided not to take any action until more specific information was provided by Kimball. As there are no further references to this in the files, it would seem that Mr Kimball did not return.

Another tale of a plot being hatched in America earlier in 1933 has also come to light. This began with yet another letter to the German Ambassador in Washington:

> Dear Sir, I have asked President Roosevelt to publicly remonstrate with your government [about] the outrages committed upon the Jews in Germany, and to demand an immediate and complete end of this persecution.
>
> In the event that he does not make such a statement, I notify you that I shall go to Germany and assassinate Hitler. Yours sincerely, Daniel Stern

The letter, dated 23 March 1933, was passed on to US Attorney General Homer Cummings. There had been street protests and rallies in many cities across the United States against Hitler's anti-Semitic policies since he had become Chancellor. German consulates, businesses, and stores selling German products had also been picketed. The threat from Stern had to be taken seriously.

Cummings forwarded the letter to J. Edgar Hoover, director of the Justice Department's Division of Investigation, asking Hoover to find Stern and arrest him. Hoover's agents mounted a nationwide search to find Stern but to no avail. Then, in April, the Justice Department received a letter addressed to the German embassy and postmarked Highbridge Station, New York. It read:

> Having overheard a conversation between several Jews in New York, I learned that there is a movement on foot to assassinate Chancellor Adolf Hitler and that a young American Jew has already been selected to commit this murder. The Jews present were joyfully enthused over this plan. I communicate this to you in order that, if possible, any such act be prevented. Very respectfully, C. Portugall.

Other similarly tantalizing but unspecific bits of information came to the attention of Hoover's agents throughout the course of the summer until the case file was closed on 2 September.[2]

Amongst the assassination alerts that came the way of the German authorities throughout 1933 and 1934, fourteen were considered serious enough to be investigated by the criminal police. These included a report from the Bavarian Legation in Berlin, concerning a Ludwig Assner (Aßner in German). While it is usually said that Assner was a former Nazi turned communist, this is actually the wrong way round. He was, at an early stage, the chauffeur-cum-bodyguard of the Jewish Social Democratic Party leader Kurt Eisner before the latter was assassinated in 1919, and had long held left-wing views.

There is much doubt about his affiliation with the Nazis. It is said that he joined the Party but only, allegedly, to act as a 'stalker' on behalf of the communists, though there is little proof of this. He certainly stood in the 1924 Bavarian elections as a candidate for the right-wing, anti-Jewish Völkisch-Social Block. He was elected but was unable to take his seat on a technicality, having been sentenced to four months in prison just weeks before the election.

By 1933 Assner had left Germany and was living in France and had developed a deep hatred of Hitler. This might have stemmed from the fact that, from his cell in Landsberg prison, Hitler had registered his objection to Assner being allowed to take his seat in the Bavarian elections.

Assner threatened to kill Hitler, before he 'plunged Germany into misery'. Writing from Palaiseau in France on 18 February 1933, he declared that he would not rest until either he had shot Hitler or Hindenburg had removed him from power. An unknown source close to Assner alerted Nazi Party officials that Assner intended to send a personal letter to Hitler which would be impregnated with a deadly poison.[3] However, Assner's threat was discounted when he said he would not carry out his plan if he was given a large sum of money.

Unlike Assner, any threats made by Anton von Padua Alfred Emil Hubert Georg Graf von Arco auf Valley had to be taken very seriously indeed. The descendant of a long line of Catholic noblemen, Arco-Valley had been enraged by events in Bavaria at the end of the First World War. Like Hitler, Arco-Valley was an Austrian who became a German national and, just as with Hitler, he had fought in a Bavarian regiment during the war and was a fervent nationalist. He was also a proclaimed anti-Semite despite the fact that his mother, Emily Freiin von Oppenheim, was from a wealthy Jewish banking family. But, unlike Hitler, who sought a vast pan-German empire embracing all ethnic German territories, Anton-Valley wanted a return of the Bavarian monarchy and a federal Germany.

That monarchy took the form of the House of Wittelsbach which had ruled Bavaria for 700 years until 7 November 1918 when the incumbent, Ludwig III, fled Munich under growing dissatisfaction with his perceived subservience to Prussia which had led to widespread civil unrest. The man who led the opposition to the Wittelsbach dynasty was the declared republican, the Jewish-born Kurt Eisner. As a member of the Independent Social Democratic Party of Germany (Unabhängige Sozialdemokratische Partei Deutschlands), Eisner organized the overthrow of Ludwig, declaring Bavaria to be a free republican state. On 8 November 1918 Eisner became the first Minister-President of the People's State of Bavaria.

In the chaos of the months following the end of the war, Eisner's administration was unable to quell the riots and the fighting between the various political groupings and, in the January 1919 election, his party was soundly beaten, only registering 3 per cent of the vote. Eisner had also made himself unpopular with large sections of the community by blaming the outbreak of the war on a 'small horde of mad Prussian military'. He epitomized everything that was exactly the kind of person that the aristocratic Arco-Valley hated: 'Eisner is a Bolshevist, a Jew,' Arco-Valley declared, 'he isn't German, he doesn't feel German, he subverts all patriotic thoughts and feelings. He is a traitor to this land.'

Consumed with such feeling on 21 February 1919, as Eisner was on his way to the Bavarian Parliament in Munich to tender his resignation, Arco-Valley sneaked up behind Eisner walking along the bustling Prannerstrasse and fired two bullets into the back of his head. Eisner crumpled to the sidewalk, dying instantly, and his bodyguards returned fire, severely wounding Arco-Valley, who was dragged away from the scene, presumed to be dead.

After Eisner's assassination, riots and looting broke out all over the city and, within days, radical anarchists and communists staged a series of revolts in an attempt to install a Soviet-style government in Bavaria. Aristocrats were arrested and wealthy businessmen were taken hostage, ten of whom were massacred at a local Munich high school. But right-wing paramilitary groups, the Freikorps, fought back and, after more than 600 people were killed in brutal street fights, wrested control of the city from the Bolsheviks.

Though wounded in the head, chest and spine, Arco-Valley survived and was tried for murder in January 1920 and sentenced to death. But Arco-Valley was seen as a hero by a large percentage of Bavarians and a sympathetic judge commuted the sentence to five years in prison. That prison was Landsberg, Cell number 7. On the morning of 11 November 1923 Arco-Valley was moved to make way for another new inmate – Adolf Hitler.

One month later Arco-Valley was released. Despite his right-wing leanings, Arco-Valley's monarchist sympathies, and his aristocratic background, saw him at odds with Hitler and he was heard to say that he would gladly commit another political assassination if he perceived it to be necessary. He continued to make such comments after Hitler had become Chancellor in 1933. Predictably, he was arrested, but was released after giving his word as an aristocrat that he would not harm the new German Führer. Arco-Valley kept his word.

What appears to have been an even more credible threat in 1933 came from someone who, unlike Assner and Arco-Valley, kept very quiet about his plans. In the autumn of 1932 the sales of *Mein Kampf* had enabled Hitler to purchase the Haus Wachenfeld on the slopes of Obersaltzberg mountain above the town of Berchtesgaden in the Bavarian Alps. This became Hitler's mountain retreat and, when he was propelled into the Chancellery, it developed into one of the key Nazi locations. Over time the house was renovated and the land around what became known as the Berghof (mountain farm) was ceded by the Bavarian government or taken by compulsory purchase to create a considerable estate, with houses for senior Nazi Party members and barracks for the troops that guarded both the people and the property.

Hitler used to enjoy walking around the Obersaltzberg with his companions and, of course, his bodyguards. This was open countryside, popular with hikers and criss-crossed with public paths. It was not unusual for Hitler to meet others out walking, and even for the Führer to offer his greetings to passers by. What did strike Hitler's bodyguards as unusual, however, was the repeated appearance of a man they did not recognize in an SA uniform. The man seemed to be watching Hitler's group intently and his actions aroused the suspicions of Hitler's security team. He was stopped and searched. On him was found a loaded handgun. This was a serious offence, and the man was duly arrested.[4]

Such incidents served to demonstrate how increasingly difficult it was becoming for Hitler's security staff to ensure his safety. Part of the problem was that Hitler had little confidence in his security detail being able to protect him. 'One day,' he said to the head of the Gestapo, SS-Oberführer Rudolf Diels, 'a completely harmless man will establish himself in an attic flat along the Wilhelmstrasse. He will be taken for a retired school-master. A solid citizen, with horn-rimmed spectacles, poorly shaven, bearded. He will not allow anyone into his modest room. He will install a gun, quietly and without haste, and with uncanny patience he will aim it at the Reich Chancellery balcony hour after hour, day after day. And then, one day, he will fire.'[5]

He was to repeat this theme on more than one occasion: 'There will never be anyone in the future with as much authority as I have … I can, however, be removed at any time by some criminal or idiot.' 'No one is safe against some idealist of an assassin,' Hitler only too clearly understood, 'who ruthlessly stakes his life for his purpose.'[6]

Hitler believed more in 'providence' or 'destiny' and his own unique instinct for survival than the endeavours of his security team. As will be seen over the following years, Hitler would often change his travel plans at almost the last moment, distressing those who had to plan ahead to secure his safe passage but equally dumbfounding those who sought to intercept him.

Despite Hitler's reservations about the effectiveness of any security measures being able to stop a lone, anonymous assassin, an enormous amount of time and resources were put into safeguarding the new Chancellor.

On 15 March 1933, the Führer Protection Commando, the nine-strong *Führerschutzkommando* (FSK) was formed which had to guarantee Hitler's unconditional safety wherever he was.[7] It was headed by SS-Standartenführer, later SS-Gruppenführer, Johann Rattenhuber and was composed of criminal-police detectives (*Kriminalkommando*) of the Bavarian state police, and was under the control of Heinrich Himmler, the ambitious Chief of the Bavarian Political Police. Being composed of Bavarian policemen, this unit's jurisdiction ended at the Bavarian border. Beyond Bavaria Hitler's protection was already in the hands of an eight-member bodyguard known as the SS-*Begleitkommando des Führers*, which was founded on 29 February 1932.

Himmler was keen to secure control of all the policing duties across Germany and continued to push for an extension of his powers. This he achieved in the spring of 1934, with the FSK replacing the SS-Begleitkommando for Hitler's overall protection throughout the country, though the SS-Begleitkommando, which was expanded to become the *Führerbegleitkommando* (FBK), retained responsibility for the close personal protection of the Führer.

In 1935 the FSK squad for Hitler's protection was made up of seventeen men, with a further seventy-six assigned to the protection of other senior Party members, such as Hermann Göring, Rudolf Hess, Joseph Goebbels and, of course, Himmler himself. The next development came in March 1935 with the formation of the RSD of which Himmler became its chief that October.

In terms of the division of responsibilities, when Hitler was on the move, it was the duty of the RSD to check the route, the buildings along the route and the places which Hitler was to visit. It would work in conjunction with the respective local Gestapo which was expected to pass on any information which had come its way regarding possible assassination plans. The FBK maintained its role as Hitler's trusted personal bodyguards and its members were the only armed personnel Hitler allowed to be near him.

Confusingly, a further layer of protection was introduced in the form of the SS-*Stabswache* Berlin to guard the Führer in the Chancellery. Drawn from the *Leibstandarte* SS Adolf Hitler, under the command of SS-Gruppenführer Josef 'Sepp' Dietrich, it was responsible for guarding the Führer's person, offices and residences. This body replaced the Army soldiers who had previously guarded the Chancellery. This unit's name was changed twice, firstly being the SS-*Sonderkommando* Berlin then, temporarily in November 1933, the Leibstandarte Adolf Hitler before, on 13 April 1934, becoming the Leibstandarte-SS Adolf Hitler (LSSAH).[8]

Rochus Misch, an *oberscharführer* (sergeant) with the LSSAH who served as Hitler's bodyguard for five years, wrote of the arrangements for guarding Hitler at the Chancellery, which were surprisingly lax:

> There were about twenty of us and we worked three shifts around the clock: from six to two; two to ten; and ten to six (the night shift). Each shift had one senior and three men on detached duty, a messenger and two men on watch duty. In order to raise alertness, the watch, telephone, courier and messenger duties were alternated.
>
> One of us would sit on sentry duty at a small table downstairs, at the kitchen entrance to the Old Chancellery. From there, a stairway led directly up to Hitler's suite, twenty-two steps in all. It was guarded by just one man. In my first days, the sparse security precautions struck me. Before going on duty, I had a long walk through the New and Old Chancelleries … I cannot recall having met a security man once on the whole walk.[9]

Hitler did not expect to be attacked by any large group, only by some lone individual as described to Rudolf Diels and the few utterly dedicated men on duty at the Chancellery were perfectly sufficient to deal with such threats. But should any organized body seek to assassinate or arrest Hitler there is no doubt they could succeed, and this was not lost on many who wished to see an end to the Nazi regime.

Chapter 6

Reich Chancellery, Spring 1933, Josef Römer; München-Bad Wiessee, 30 June 1934, Members of the SA

Like so many disillusioned ex-soldiers after the supposed 'stab in the back' that saw Germany surrender in 1918, former Captain Josef 'Beppo' Römer joined one of the paramilitary Freikorps which sprang up across the country to combat communism and to try and protect the disputed eastern border with Poland. Römer was with the Freikorps Oberland, one of the largest of these groups, but he soon turned to the Communist Party of Germany (KPD), even secretly channelling some of the Oberland's funds into the KPD. When this was discovered he was expelled from the group.

Römer studied law, obtaining his degree in 1922, but remained active in the political scene writing for the KPD periodical *Aufbruch* (New Start) and, after officially joining the KPD in 1932, he became *Aufbruch*'s editor in chief.

Römer proved to be one of Hitler's most determined opponents and he appears to have drawn a surprisingly large number of people to his side. This included a group led by Dr Paul Joseph Stuermer. The group was quite widely supported and included several Wehrmacht officers, some university professors, businessmen and even government employees. Along with another lawyer, Nicholas Christoph von Halem, Römer sought the means to kill the man he believed was leading Germany into the abyss. Halem, who called Hitler 'the messenger of chaos'[1] offered Römer the funds to find and hire an assassin who could eliminate Hitler by shooting him or using a grenade. Instead Römer took it upon himself and, in the spring of 1933, attempted to gain entry to the Reich Chancellery only to be arrested. He was imprisoned at Dachau concentration camp, being released in 1939. His incarceration did not diminish his determination to oppose Hitler's regime; it would, though, lead to his demise.

He joined a communist opposition group in the north of Berlin (the *Revolutionary Workers and Soldiers*) and again planned to assassinate Hitler – 'cutting off the snake's head' as he put it. The group formed anti-fascist cells among German workers as well as producing inflammatory pamphlets on the premises of a sailing club on Lake Tegel. Copied in large numbers, the pamphlets, inconspicuously packaged, were sent from various post offices in Germany to hundreds of addresses around the country and abroad, in particular the Soviet Union. These were then dropped as leaflets by the Soviet Air Force on the German soldiers fighting in Russia. One of the members of this group, Stenbock-Fermor, wrote in his memoirs:

> Our most important illegal pamphlet was the 'Information Service' published by Römer, our military expert. He carried out detailed analyzes of the military situation on all fronts, of the political situation, and called for active resistance to National Socialism and war… . We carefully covered our tracks after each session. Only Beppo Römer, reckless, stuffed sheets of paper that were often written on carelessly into the wastebasket. We found them later when cleaning up and burned them in the kitchen.[2]

It may have been this recklessness which led to the group being discovered by the Gestapo in February 1942. Römer and two others were arrested and sentenced to death. This was carried out on 25 September 1944 at Brandenburg-Görden Prison. During his incarceration, Römer was tortured, revealing the earlier assassination plot involving Halem who was then also arrested. Halem was beheaded, also at the Brandenburg-Görden Prison, on 9 October 1944. Altogether, 150 people were implicated in Römer's opposition activities, more than 100 of whom were executed.[3]

A more serious threat to Hitler came in the form of yet another former Freikorps leader, Ernst Julius Günther Röhm. In 1933 Hitler passed the so-called Enabling Act (*Gesetz zur Behebung der Not von Volk und Reich*) which gave his administration the power to enact laws without the involvement of the Reichstag. Over the course of the months following the passing of the act, Hitler strove to eliminate all opposition, including that within his own party, and one person in particular, Ernst Röhm.

Röhm had been a leading figure in the Nazi Party from its earliest days. A decorated war veteran, he was the co-founder of the SA, leading his Brown Shirts, it may be recalled, in the Beer Hall Putsch. When Hitler began rebuilding the Nazi Party, he asked Röhm to become the SA Chief of Staff.

As the Nazi Party grew, so did the SA, battling the communists on the streets, and silencing any persons who dared raise their voices or their fists against the Nazi revolution. Without Röhm and the SA it is likely that Hitler's message would never have been heard beyond the Munich beer cellars. The SA was composed to a great degree of violent thugs but Röhm, who as well as winning the Iron Cross on the battlefield had also served as a staff officer, organized them into a tough fighting force. When Hitler was endeavouring to establish his position at the top of the political tree, he needed the SA, but, after his elevation to the Chancellery, and particularly after the introduction of the Enabling Act, Hitler could call on all the services of the state to enforce his decrees. There was no longer a role for Röhm and his brownshirted bullies.

Understandably, Röhm had a different take on the situation the Nazis now found themselves in. Firstly, it seemed to Röhm and many of his followers that Hitler had aligned himself with German leaders and with the aristocracy-lined officer ranks of the Army. The members of the SA, predominantly simple working-class men, expected radical social reform when Hitler came to power but instead it seemed the Führer had turned his back on them after he had moved into the Chancellery. Such was their growing disenchantment with Hitler, it was reported that a man in an SA leader's uniform was noticed acting strangely at the Berghof in 1933 and, when arrested, was found to be carrying a gun with the aim of assassinating Hitler.[4]

Röhm wanted what he termed a 'second revolution' for the *volk* to take over the land and much of the means of production as well merging the SA with the old Reichswehr to form a new 'people's army' with, obviously, Röhm at its head. Whilst Hitler now had almost unlimited power over the civilian population, the one body that could still depose him and, which he had no control over, was the Army. Hitler knew that the generals would utterly oppose Röhm's plans, and Hitler dared not risk alienating the Army. Röhm had to be stopped, but he was a tough and powerful figure backed by the full weight of the SA. Hitler would need a good reason for deposing such a loyal Nazi as Röhm, and so one had to be concocted.

Senior SS and SD officers were ordered to Berlin on, or around, 25 June 1934, where Reichsführer-SS Himmler and Sturmbannführer Heydrich warned them to take measures to resist a possible attempt to overthrow the Nazi leadership by Röhm and the SA.

As belief in a revolt by the SA swiftly gained ground, a pre-emptive strike against Röhm was planned, with the Reichswehr only too willing to help, offering to provide the SS with weapons and transportation. Everything was ready within a few days and, on 29 June, Röhm's adjutant was ordered by telephone to summon all SA leaders to attend a meeting with Hitler at Bad Wiessee, a lovely little Bavarian spa town on the western shore of Lake Tegernsee, on the morning of 30 June.

Hitler's scheme was working well, as members of the SA had heard the rumours of action being taken against the SA and in some towns groups of the SA had already taken to the streets, confirming, it would seem, that the SA was on the verge of revolt against the government. When Hitler arrived in Munich from Berlin in the early hours of 30 June, he was met with abuse from some 3,000 armed, angry and no doubt confused SA troopers who had rampaged through the city.

Hitler and his entourage drove to Bad Wiessee, stopping outside the Hotel Hanselbaur at 06.30 hours, where Röhm and SA leaders were still sleeping off the effects of a heavy night's drinking. Hitler, pistol in hand, and his group, which included an SS security contingent, rushed up to Röhm's room, where the Führer denounced the bewildered leader of the SA as a traitor and ordered his immediate arrest.

Röhm and other SA leaders were taken down to the hotel's cellar until the arrival of a coach which had been hurriedly hired from the Bad Wiessee bus company, whereupon the prisoners were transported to Stadelheim prison in Munich.[5]

Hitler also aimed to return to Munich but, just as he was preparing to leave, a truck carrying heavily-armed SA bodyguards, or Stabwache, drew up. On hearing that their chief had been arrested, the men took up what has been described as a 'combative' stance.[6] This was clearly a tense, and very dangerous, moment for Hitler. One wrong move and the leader of the Nazi Party would be gunned down. Yet somehow, Hitler persuaded the Stabwache to retire, and they drove off down the road to Munich. But, after just a few minutes, the men realized that they had just lost an opportunity to kill Hitler, which would enable them to rescue Röhm and the other SA leaders. So they stopped.

They knew that Hitler would be bound to return along the road to Munich which gave them a chance to intercept him. They quickly concealed the truck well off the road and set up an ambush, with their machine-guns placed on either side of the highway – and waited.

Hitler knew that he had been fortunate to avoid a bloodbath outside the hotel and, just in case the Stabwache had a change of heart, he decided to drive in the opposite direction and take an alternative, albeit longer, route back to Munich. There can be no doubt that decision saved his life.

Chapter 7

Berghof, Obersalzberg 1935, Heinrich Grunow; Berghof, Obersalzberg, 1935, Gruppenführer Kraus; Frankfurt, 1935, Helmuth Mylius

Following his arrest on 30 June 1934, Ernst Röhm was shot the next day. The supposed SA revolt was put down mercilessly. There were waves of arrests and executions across Germany, not just of the SA leadership but of anyone who it was imagined might be a threat to the new regime. All this was done quite openly and extrajudicially – Hitler wanted everyone to know what would happen to those who dared oppose him. The killings went on throughout the last day of June and the first day of July and will forever be remembered in Germany as the 'Night of the Long Knives'.

Röhm had been murdered and the SA neutered to appease the officers of the Reichswehr, the irony of which is that it would be those very Army officers who would ultimately prove to be Hitler's most inveterate enemies. The Reichswehr had been complicit in the suppression of the SA revolt, but the brutal actions of those horrific twenty-four hours alarmed many of its officers, particularly as two of its own were arrested, and the seeds of the Army's resistance movement were sown that night.[1]

The nature of the opposition to Hitler now took on a different form. People of standing, both civilian and military, feared for Germany's future under the Nazis and saw only one solution – the assassination of the Chancellor. These were not the kind of individuals who, under normal circumstances, would ever have contemplated such an extreme measure, but normality had been swept aside with the passing of the Enabling Act and buried during the Night of the Long Knives.

One such group of individuals was led by the most unlikely of assassins, a doctor – a man whose Hippocratic Oath bound him to 'Do no Harm'.

What industrialist Dr Helmuth Mylius wanted to do was 'less' harm to the German people by removing Hitler. A powerful and prominent figure, Mylius was head of the Party of the Radical Middle Class (Radikale Mittelstandspartei) and editor of the Frankfurt-based right-wing political and economics weekly publication, *Die Parole der radicalen Staats-und Wirtschaftreform.*

The first major obstacle that Mylius and other likeminded people faced was that he could no longer express his views openly for fear of immediate arrest. From 1 July 1934 all dissenting voices had to be uttered in a whisper. Nevertheless, Mylius, along with a retired Navy captain, Hermann Ehrhardt, developed a plan to infiltrate Hitler's SS bodyguard units with their own supporters. So successful were they that 160 men penetrated SS security and began accumulating data on Hitler's movements. But Mylius' plans came to nothing as the group was in turn infiltrated by the Gestapo in 1935 and most of the members arrested. Mylius avoided arrest by joining the Army, thanks to the influence of his friend, General Erich von Manstein.

Mylius' group was probably too large to remain secret. With so many members it was almost inevitable that some would prove to be indiscreet. The more durable opposition groupings would prove to be small, closely-knit and very circumspect in their dealings with those other than people they knew and could trust.

As might be expected, many members of the SA sought to bring down Hitler after the purge of its leadership. These men had been ardent followers of Hitler and sworn party members. They felt betrayed by the man they had previously revered and sought bloody revenge. One of those was a man named Heinrich Grunow who approached a known opponent of Hitler, Otto Strasser. Otto's brother Gregor was amongst the earliest members of the Nazi Party and became the regional head of the SA in Lower Bavaria and participated in the Beer Hall Putsch. From September 1926 until the end of December 1927, he was responsible for the party's propaganda and he played a key role in the rise of the Nazis in the Reichstag elections. Otto also joined the Nazi Party, but over time Gregor's and Otto's views began to diverge from those of Hitler and they started publishing a new daily newspaper in Berlin, the *Nationaler Sozialist*, which enabled them to convey their own version of Nazism. This led to a breach with Hitler and the brothers were expelled from the Nazi Party in the summer of 1930.

Following his expulsion, Otto set up his own party, the Black Front, composed of radical former Nazis, in an attempt to split the party. But when Hitler became Chancellor, Otto went into exile, first in Austria and later Prague, Switzerland and France. Gregor, who had been invited by Franz von Papen to take the position of Vice-Chancellor before Hitler was offered the Chancellorship, was killed in the Night of the Long Knives. So, when Heinrich Grunow wanted to assassinate Hitler, he knew Otto Strasser would be certain to help him.

Whilst in exile in 1943, Otto Strasser wrote his memoirs, *Flight from Terror*, in which he described his first meeting with Grunow:

> One day a stranger was admitted who brought me a strange proposition. 'I sent in my name as Reinhardt,' he said easily, after we had greeted each other and he had been seated. 'That isn't my name. I am really Heinich Grunow. I was afraid either you or your guards would recognize the name, since I am a member of Hitler's secret bodyguard at his Berchtesgaden retreat.'
>
> 'And your purpose in coming to me?' I prompted.
>
> 'I intend to kill Adolf Hitler,' Grunow said straightforwardly.[2]

Naturally, Strasser pointed out that Grunow, as one of Hitler's bodyguards, was in a perfect position to kill the Führer himself and did not need Strasser's help. Grunow replied by pulling out a photograph which showed him and Ernst Röhm arm-in-arm. 'Röhm was my best friend,' Grunow explained. He then told Strasser his aims:

> I want his [Hitler's] death to be more than a mere act of violence – an isolated assassination, a sudden crime of passion. I want his death to mean something to the German people; through the spectacular event I want them to examine further.
>
> In other words, I want the death identified with some movement, so that the principles of that movement will be emphasized as a result. Then his death will mean something; it will serve a purpose.

The ideals of the Black Front were well known, so, by associating himself with it, everyone would understand why Hitler had been killed. Grunow then told Strasser of his plan:

> I know Hitler's routine. I know, for instance, that they're building a new road to Berchtesgaden – have completed it, in fact – and I know,

> too, that in its present condition it doesn't allow for fast driving. Now, there's a bad curve along the way, at which point Hitler's car slows down to fifteen miles an hour. A man concealed beside the road with a rifle wouldn't have to be an expert marksman to pick off a moving target at that point. And that's my strategy. It's wild country and escape afterward wouldn't be difficult, especially if a fast car were parked nearby, but on some other highway, to avoid being spotted beforehand. Hitler's chauffeur, should he escape, could never summon help before I was miles away. With no possible way of identifying me, how could I then be searched for and apprehended?

Strasser approved Grunow's plan and offered to provide him with all the money and equipment he needed from Black Front funds as well as the help of a man called Eitel Sturm. Grunow said that he was setting off the following morning as Hitler was due to make his weekend visit to the Berghof in two days' time. 'It will be a journey Hitler will never complete,' were Grunow's parting words.

Strasser waiting anxiously for two days before receiving the news. Then Sturm returned to Black Front headquarters, but on his own. Sturm told Strasser that Grunow was dead – but so was Hitler!

'Grunow knew his business,' Sturm reported:

> Just as he'd said, we found that twist in the Berchtesgaden road. We left our own car, hired in a false name, parked about a mile away, arriving just about dusk and taking no chances that we'd miss Hitler when he passed, for we had no way of knowing when he'd leave Berlin. For weary hours we remained there, crouched in the bushes, armed with high-powered rifles. I can't tell you of the suspense, the silent, motionless waiting. Every car that swished past on the highway below might have been the one we were waiting for; each one that passed brought with it a separate climax. Grunow's personal hate seemed to make him a man of steel, without nerves. He never once even shifted position, as I was forced to do, but simply crouched there, silent, unmoving.
>
> At last we saw the car, far below, its headlights sending their beams from side to side as the car lurched and twisted up the hill. We could hear the low groan of climbing gears. They would have to pass at a snail's pace on the curve directly at our feet. At this moment

> Grunow made the one sound of that entire period: his breath came out in a long shuddering sigh.
>
> Grunow got the first shot – the first two shots, in fact. His muscles seemed to react more quickly than mine, cramped as I was. When Hitler's car was directly below us – occupied only by two men, the Fuehrer and his chauffeur – Heinrich Grunow bounced to his feet, snapped the rifle to his shoulder, and let go twice. The ear-splitting roars of those shots were like the twin cracks of doom – and I guess they were that, actually, for Hitler.
>
> He was only a shadow in the seat beside the chauffeur – though we could make out his features, his mustache, easily enough – and simultaneously with the shots he came to his feet in the moving car, screaming and clawing at the air. The chauffeur slowed without thinking – and that's when I let him have it with my own gun. You know I'm a perfect shot, Herr Strasser. At that range I couldn't miss. Outlined against a moonlit sky, standing, I drew a bead on his head the way I would on a clay pigeon – and shot with as little compunction.
>
> The screaming stopped abruptly then. The standing figure flopped over into the back of the car, and the chauffeur, panicky, jammed the gas pedal down and the car lurched and skidded out of sight.[3]

According to Sturm, Grunow then told him that his mission was complete and pulled a revolver from his jacket pocket, rammed the muzzle against the roof of his mouth and pulled the trigger. He was dead when his body hit the ground. Sturm left Grunow where he had fallen and made his escape back to Prague.

Unfortunately for Grunow he died in vain, as Hitler was not dead. Hitler had decided to drive himself that day, something he did quite often. His chauffeur, Schreck, was quite similar to Hitler in appearance – the chauffeur even affecting a small mustache like his master; he had at times in the past even doubled for Hitler. Since both he and the chauffeur wore leather jackets and peaked caps, and even resembled each other, it would have been easy to confuse them even in broad daylight. Consequently, Eitel Sturm and Heinrich Grunow had assassinated the wrong man.

The official report which was presented to the press two days after the incident was that Schreck had died from an infected tooth! In reality, so

Strasser wrote, he had secretly received a copy of the autopsy carried out on Schreck which showed that he had been shot once through the shoulder, the bullet deflecting into the chest; another bullet had penetrated his jaw, and a third had pierced his right temple. If Hitler had been in the passenger seat of the car as usual, he would have died that day.[4]

This is a great sounding story; sadly, none of it, or at least most of it, is true. Heinrich Grunow did work for Strasser, acting as his courier on trips to France, Switzerland, Holland, Denmark and Spain. But he did not shoot himself in 1936. Grunow did indeed talk of assassinating Hitler in 1939 in Paris and was arrested by the French police for this in January 1940. He died in March 1945 as a prisoner in Sachsenhausen concentration camp. It is true that Julius Schreck died on 16 May 1936, not of an infection, but of meningitis. Why Strasser wrote what he clearly knew were lies is unclear; possibly he sought to portray the activities of his organization in a more positive light. The story, though, does not quite end there. According to the Humanitas International historical timeline Schreck died 'in a traffic accident', and a paper in the archives of the D.H. Ramsay Library of the University of North Carolina notes that Schreck 'was involved in an accident and was killed'.[5] The *Chicago Times* adds further to the mystery by declaring Schreck and Hitler were travelling in a car to the town of Bernau and, as with Strasser's version, Hitler was at the wheel: 'They reached a railway crossing and slowed up. As they did so, shots fired with unerring accuracy burst from the roadside. The man in the passenger seat slumped. The wrong man had been assassinated.'[6] Did Hitler come closer to death than the regime was willing to admit and was the consequence of the differing versions of Schreck's fatal illness due to a confused cover up?

Another doubtful story of an attempt on Hitler's life is one which took place whilst he was at the Berghof in 1935, told in the memoirs of Bridget Hitler, Adolf's Irish sister-in-law. Bridget Dowling had met Adolf's half-brother Alois in Dublin. The two eloped to England where they married, living in London and then Liverpool. They had a son, Patrick, but later the couple divorced. Bridget and Patrick visited Adolf in Berlin and at the Berghof. This is the story she relates:

> An S.A. group leader named Kraus, who was granted permission to present a petition personally to the Führer, was the would-be assassin

> who came nearest to succeeding. But sitting among others, waiting to be relieved, he fired at the Führer, as the latter came down the stairs to pass through the hall to the study, and he missed. If he had waited until he was faced with the Führer, the history of the Third Reich might have been quite different.[7]

According to Bridget, Gruppenführer Kraus was gunned down by Hitler's bodyguards in less than thirty seconds, five of them firing simultaneously. Elements of her *Memoirs* have been considered 'fanciful' by some historians and, despite the degree of detail in her tale, this story is difficult to authenticate. It also seems unlikely that someone with a sidearm would have been allowed inside the Berghof, particularly a member of the SA after the Night of the Long Knives purge.

Chapter 8

Mannheim Railroad Bridge, March 1936, Franz Steinberg and Wolfgang Eberle; Nuremberg, 21 December 1936, Helmut Hirsch; Berlin Sportplast, 1937, Unidentified person

The Black Front allegedly sponsored further assassination attempts on Hitler. Amongst these was an effort to destroy a railway bridge at the moment Hitler's train, the *Führersonderzug*, was passing over. Once again this is another story related by Otto Strasser in his 1943 autobiographical book *Flight from Terror* and is equally hard to substantiate.

According to Strasser it was towards the close of February 1936 that he was approached in Prague by a man called Franz Steinberg. Strasser described him as a shy, little middle-aged man, whose sparse brown hair was flecked with grey. The Nazis had killed his brother, sent his parents to a concentration camp and seized his business in Essen. He said that he had been a construction engineer and that he had a friend, Wolfgang Eberle, who also hated the Nazis who had formerly been a railroad despatcher. Steinberg offered his help to the Black Front, in whatever form that may take. As it happened an opportunity would soon present itself for the two men to prove their commitment to the Black Front cause.

On 7 March of that year, the German Army marched into the Rhineland which, by the terms of the Treaty of Versailles, was to be a demilitarized zone. This move was unopposed by the Allied powers who did not want to be dragged into another conflict with Germany so soon after the First World War. This was a major triumph for Hitler whose popularity throughout Germany soared.

To celebrate this major event, celebrations were held across the country, with Hitler attending an event at Speyer Cathedral, the resting place of eight German kings and emperors. He was scheduled to leave Berlin at 10.00 hours and the route the train would follow included crossing the Mannheim railroad bridge.

When Strasser mentioned this to Franz Steinberg, he declared: 'The bridge! I know the bridge! I know enough of explosives and bridges to bring it down without fail – and Wolfgang Eberle knows his railroad organization. That's our mission.'

Eberle claimed that he knew all about Hitler's routine for railroad travel. Just ahead of the train that carried the Führer ran a guide car to test the track the official train had to run upon. Any tampering with the rails, any explosives or other impediments would first be struck by the guide car. This meant that the would-be assassins would need to have a clear sight of the track at that point so that they could blow the bridge after the guide car had passed. In addition to the guide car, there was, of course, a constant and vigilant force of men observing and inspecting the right of way when it was known that Hitler was to travel over a certain route. Despite all of this, Eberle felt certain he knew enough of railroading and railroad men to carry the plan through safely. Steinberg said that all he needed was a ten minute warning to enable him to lay a rack of dynamite sticks and wire them to a detonator. The explosives and materials were readily provided by the Black Front and the two saboteurs set off for Germany.

Once again, Strasser waited hopefully for the news of Hitler's demise. Two days went by, with no word from either of the assassins, or any wireless announcements. Concerned with the fate of Steinberg and Eberle, Strasser sent another of his Black Front men to find out what had happened. What the man discovered was that the two men had reached the bridge undetected and had succeeded in accomplishing the technical part of their scheme. That was clear from the fact that all the centre section of the bridge had been blown away, its girders dragging in a stream below; that much the man could see. The rest of the story had to be pieced together bit by bit. Steinberg and Eberle had waited for the guide car and had let it pass safely, as planned; then, on the approach of the second train, had sent a section of the bridge rocketing into the air when it was too late for that train to stop. The train had hit the gap;

the locomotive, tender and two cars went over the brink and crashed to the rocks below. But, unfortunately for the assassins, it wasn't Hitler's official train.

In what Strasser called 'one chance out of a hundred', an important troop train bound for the Rhineland had been allowed to cut in ahead of the official train. Of course, when it was wrecked, there was still plenty of time to safely flag down Hitler's train following behind. Steinberg and Eberle were caught at the scene. Their bodies were found in the nearby woods, each with his hands tied behind him, bearing the signs of a frightful beating, and each riddled with bullets.[1]

Exactly which bridge was destroyed is difficult to ascertain. It was certainly not the main Mannheim-Ludwigshafen railway bridge across the Rhine which in fact was named after Leo Schlageter, a former highly regarded member of the Nazi Party, in the same year Strasser claimed it had been destroyed – 1936. In reality this bridge remained intact until destroyed by German forces on 20 March 1945. Furthermore, the two saboteurs escaped into, and were shot in, nearby woods, which again excludes the Mannheim-Ludwigshafen bridge as there were, and still are, no woods in the vicinity of the bridge. Once more, this whole episode appears to have existed only in the fanciful mind of Otto Strasser.

Be all that as it may, Strasser's Black Front really did support an actual assassination plot devised by Helmut Hirsch, a young, handsome Jewish boy of twenty, who came from Stuttgart. His action was prompted by the introduction of the Nuremberg Laws in September 1935 which were expanded in November. These were anti-Semitic regulations which imposed severe restrictions on top of the laws already imposed by Hitler in 1933. Hirsch sought to destabilize the Nazi regime by blowing up the Nuremberg building of *Der Sturmer*, a weekly Nazi tabloid newspaper.

Hirsch arrived in Stuttgart on 20 December, from where he would travel to Nuremberg to receive the bomb from another of Strasser's disciples. That person, however, had been stopped whilst crossing the German-Polish border with the bomb. Under questioning, he revealed both the plot and the would-be perpetrator. As Hirsch had booked into a hotel near the Stuttgart railway station under his own name, it was an easy matter for the Gestapo to find and arrest him.

There are, however, other versions of this story. The first is that Hirsch intended to plant a bomb under the speaker's platform at one of the famous Nazi rallies.[2] Unfortunately, the timing is all wrong for this to be true, as the rallies always took place in September, just as they did that year. The other is that Hirsch would take the bomb, concealed in a suitcase, to the Nazi Party headquarters in Nuremberg and in a 'heroic act' detonate the bomb.[3]

On 8 March 1937 Helmut Hirsch was tried, with full details of the plot being revealed which has led to the belief that he was betrayed by someone within the Black Front organization. Though his target was not specifically Hitler, at his trial he admitted that if the opportunity presented itself he would kill the Führer. He was convicted and sentenced to death by beheading. Despite international appeals for clemency, the execution was carried out on 4 June at Plötzensee Prison.

The Nuremberg Laws also drove Croatian Jew David Frankfurter to attempt and, in his case, succeed in assassinating a leading Nazi. Frankfurter was a medical student who was studying in Germany when Hitler came to power. Amongst the new laws was a ban on Jews studying in German universities, so Frankfurter moved to Berne, Switzerland. As some 60 per cent of Swiss were German-speakers, the Nazi movement, and the new German nationalism, gained many supporters. Worried that Switzerland would go the same way as Germany, Frankfurter decided to take matters into his own hands.

There was no possibility of Frankfurter being able to kill Hitler, though the Führer was his preferred target, but there was a chance of him being able to attack the leading Nazi in Switzerland, Hitler's deputy, *Landesgruppenleiter* Wilhelm Gustloff. Frankfurter bought a Browning revolver in Berne (supposedly for only ten francs) and went to Gustloff's home in Davos, the address of which he found in the telephone directory.[4]

On Tuesday 4 February, with snow crunching under his feet, Frankfurter walked up to the front door of the Gustloff residence. Gustloff's wife, Hedwig, answered the door. As her husband received many visitors, she invited Frankfurter into the house and showed him to Gustloff's study and asked him to wait as he was on the telephone. Frankfurter waited patiently, sitting opposite a signed picture of Hitler.

A few minutes later Gustloff walked into his study. Frankfurter introduced himself as a Jew and promptly shot the Nazi five times in the head, neck and chest.

Frankfurter calmly left the house, went next door, and telephoned the police. He then went to the local police station and handed himself in. Frankfurter wanted the world to know that a Jew had killed Gustloff.

At his subsequent trial, Frankfurter was sentenced to eighteen years in jail. On 1 June 1945 he was granted a pardon.

It is said that a year later it was learned that Gustloff's murder was part of a failed assassination plan against Hitler by a Paris-based group known as the Alliance Israélite.[5]

Throughout 1937 and 1938 various German émigré groups in Britain, Czechoslovakia and Switzerland plotted to kill Hitler, but none came to fruition. There was also an incident on 26 November 1937 in Berlin. A mental patient by the name of Joseph Thomas from Ebersfeld was arrested trying to enter the Reich Chancellery in a supposed bid to shoot both the Führer and Reichsmarschall Hermann Göring. Thomas was carted away by the Gestapo and never heard of again.[6]

Another failed plot took place in 1937. Dr Johannes von Dohnanyi (who became Hans von Dohnanyi) of the Abwehr, personal advisor to Reich Minister of Justice Franz Gurtner, had disapproved of Hitler and his Nazi Party almost from the beginning when, through his post in the attorney general's office in Hamburg, he was exposed firsthand to Nazi brutality, and was particularly shocked with the atrocities committed during the Night of the Long Knives. He eventually became an important member of the Oster group, of which more will be revealed in due course, but, as early as 1937, Dohnanyi tried to recruit Hitler's adjutant, Fritz Wiedemann, in a plot to shoot the Führer. This, though, came to nothing.[7] Wiedemann, who had been Hitler's commanding officer during the First World War, nevertheless, through his close personal contact with Hitler, became to realize that Hitler was a danger to world peace and nothing would deter him from trying to achieve his ambition of a Greater Germany.

In 1938 Wiedemann met Lord Halifax and warned him that Hitler was set on solving the Sudetenland problem by force and, after being sent to the United States as German Consul General to San Francisco in January 1940, he met secretly met with a senior British intelligence representative, Sir William Wiseman, in a San Francisco Hotel. There Wiedemann offered to denounce Hitler publicly to the Americans (the USA, it will be recalled, was not at war with Germany at that date) and that, following defeat in the Battle of Britain, Hitler was 'reeling' and that 'was the time to strike back at Germany hard'. Wiedemann also stated that a number of his associates in Germany were prepared to 'act' against Hitler if they could be assured of British support, including Hjalmar Schacht, the president of the German Central Bank and Hitler's economics minister. Again, nothing came of this and Wiedemann remained in the service of the Third Reich, though kept at arm's length. When war broke out between Germany and the United States, he was posted to China 'as far out of Hitler's way as possible'.[8] Dohnanyi continued to plot against Hitler and his name will appear again later in these pages.

There is another alleged assassination attempt that went wrong which is frequently, and always briefly, mentioned. This is that an unidentified man in SS uniform sought to blow up Hitler when he delivered a speech at the Berlin Sportplast in 1937, but the man in question became stuck in a toilet and was unable to carry out his deadly deed.[9] Unfortunately, though Hitler gave a number of speeches in the Sportplast, none of those was in 1937. The speech given by Hitler nearest to that date at that venue was 26 September 1938.[10] This, it would seem, was just another false, if amusing, story which is perpetuated despite having no foundation in fact.

Chapter 9

Munich, Maurice Bavaud, November 1938; Zurich, Switzerland, Wilhelm Abegg, 1938

It was while Swiss-born Maurice Bavaud was studying to become a Catholic missionary at the French seminary of École Saint-Ilan Langueux in Brittany that he helped form a current affairs discussion group, the *Compagnie du Mystère*. The meetings of this group, led by fellow student Marcel Gerbohay, enabled Bavaud to vocalize his growing concerns over the Nazi Party's persecution of the Catholic Church and led him to the conclusion that the persecution, and Hitler, had to be stopped.

His plan was to move to Germany and pretend to be an ardent National Socialist, thus allowing him access to Hitler. In the summer of 1938 he abandoned his studies and returned to his family home in Neuchâtel, in west Switzerland. Here he began reading a French translation of *Mein Kampf* and started to learn German. On 9 October 1938 Bavaud left on his mission to kill Hitler. He travelled to Baden-Baden to stay with relatives, but he was unable to find work and, after only ten days, he moved on. He sent his luggage on to Berlin while he travelled down to Basle. There he purchased a 6.35mm Schmeisser semi-automatic pocket pistol and ammunition before catching the train to Berlin, which he reached on 21 October. Bavaud found lodgings and began to reconnoitre the military district and consider how he could carry out his mission. What he did discover was that Hitler was not in Berlin. He was at the Berghof.

Bavaud had the bit between his teeth and, not willing to wait indefinitely for Hitler to return (probably because his funds were limited – he had left Switzerland with 600 Swiss francs he had stolen from his mother[1]) he took the train once again to travel the 350 miles to Berchtesgaden. He checked in to the Stiftskeller hotel and, somewhat surprisingly, was able to purchase more ammunition. With this he went into the woods which surround the Obersalzberg and practised his marksmanship on the trees. He came to the conclusion that if he could get to within twenty-five feet of Hitler he would be able to shoot him.[2]

Luck was not on young Maurice's side for, soon after he arrived at Berchtesgaden, the Führer went to Munich, news of which he received when he reached the Berghof's outer perimeter before being turned away. But luck, albeit fleetingly, took a sudden turn in his favour. One afternoon, while at lunch, he fell into conversation with two Frenchmen. He declared his admiration for Hitler, saying how he would love to meet the Führer. Sitting at a nearby table was Captain Karl Derkert, who could not help overhearing the conversation. Believing Bavaud's words, Derkert told him that he was connected to Hitler's personal security and that it would not be possible to have an audience with Hitler without a letter of introduction from a highranking official. On the other hand, if he wanted to see Hitler close up, his best chance would be at the anniversary of the Beer Hall Putsch in Munich. On 9 November each year Hitler led a procession through the city along the route from the Bürgerbräukeller taken by the Nazis in 1923.

So Bavaud was back on a train up to Munich. He must have been running very low on funds at this point and becoming increasingly desperate. He knew that this would be his one and only chance to kill Hitler before he would have to return to Switzerland. Knowing that he was likely to only have a few seconds to shot Hitler as he came into range, Bavaud had to be certain that he would not miss. He therefore found a spot outside Munich where he could safely practise his skills with the Schmeisser once more.

At last the day came. It was a cold, clear day and Bavaud wore a heavy coat with the semi-automatic in one of its deep pockets. By posing as a Swiss journalist, Bavaud managed to obtain a complimentary ticket for a seat in one of the temporary grandstands which overlooked the route of the procession. He chose a seat near the Heilig-Geist-Kirche (Holy Ghost Church) at a point where the procession had to slow down to pass through an archway before it turned towards the Feldherrnhalle.

At last the procession made its way towards him along the route lined with men of the SA which partially obscured the road, limiting his field of fire. Nevertheless, Bavaud gripped the pistol in his pocket as the noise of the crowd increased. Then the moment arrived. The head of the column reached Bavaud's position but then a 'forest' of right hands shot up to deliver the Nazi salute, briefly blocking any chance of a clear shot at the moving target. It also seems that Hitler, flanked by Himmler and

Göring, was walking over the far side of the road and well beyond the range of twenty-five metres Bavaud had expected. Nor could he leave the grandstand and run across the road to shoot Hitler at point-blank range as he would never be able to push his way past the double row of SA guards.[3] Within moments the procession had passed and with it Bavaud's only opportunity.[4]

Bavaud was not going to be thwarted by this setback, but his subsequent actions betrayed his increasing desperation. He returned to his hotel and reconsidered his original idea of addressing Hitler in person. Taking on board what Captain Derkert had said, Bavaud purchased some expensive stationery and forged a letter of introduction to Hitler from French Foreign Minister Pierre Flandin. The letter stated that Bavaud carried a second letter that was for the Führer's eyes only. That he should have thought that such a ruse would have worked demonstrates how irrational his thinking had become.

Bavaud travelled once more down to Berchtesgaden and walked up to the Berghof. Not only was he stopped at the outermost perimeter and told that he could only be granted access if he carried an invitation, but again, he had failed to establish Hitler's whereabouts as the Führer was not in residence. Bavaud took the train back to Munich.

Still hoping to gain access to Hitler, he forged yet another letter. This time he had hired a typewriter to give the letter a more official appearance. Armed with this letter, on the morning of 12 November, the increasingly frustrated Bavaud went to the *Braunes Haus* (the Brown House, so called because of the original brown uniforms worn by the Nazis) the Nazi Party Headquarters in Munich and asked for a personal interview with the Führer. This, of course, was denied, the party official inviting Bavaud to leave the letter with him so that it could be passed on to Hitler or, if he preferred, he could post it.

Bavaud had criss-crossed Germany in his bid to kill Hitler with no detailed knowledge of the Führer's movements. This resulted in him taking the train back down to Bischofswesen, a station near Berchtesgaden, that very afternoon. By the time he had walked the six or seven miles to the Berghof it was dark, and even the deluded young Swiss realized that he would not be permitted to see Hitler that night.

He walked all the way back to the station, having, at last, recognized that he was never going to be able to get close enough to Hitler to kill him.

He was also broke. All Bavaud could hope for was that he would be able to escape back to France. What little money he had he spent on a train ticket, but he did not have enough even to reach Munich. Nevertheless, he got as far as Augsburg before he was caught by a ticket inspector, who called the railway police, who, in turn, passed Bavaud on to the Gestapo. Though at first just charged with possession of a pistol and travelling without a ticket, when his baggage was retrieved from Berlin it was found to include maps of Munich and Berchtesgaden, as well as additional ammunition. He eventually confessed his true intentions and was sent for trial in the People's Court in Berlin. He admitted his guilt, telling the court at his trial that he had acted 'for the benefit of humanity and all Christendom'. He was duly sentenced to death.

Maurice Bavaud was executed at dawn on 14 May 1941. Whilst Bavaud's ill-conceived assassination attempts may have been fruitless, they did have a lasting consequence as 1938 was the final time the Beer Hall Putsch was celebrated with a march through the streets of Munich.

The postscript to this story is that when Germany invaded France in May/June 1940, Brittany was occupied. The Gestapo had not forgotten Bavaud's assassination plot and Marcel Gerbohay was arrested and, like his former friend, was beheaded.

Though the Swiss government made no effort to intervene on Bavaud's behalf during his trial, in 2008 the Swiss government honoured the life and effort of Maurice Bavaud and, in 2011, a small monument was erected in Hauterive near Neuchâtel.

Bauvard was not the only person seeking to kill Hitler in 1938. Wilhelm Abegg was born into an influential family Berlin in 1876. He studied law, achieving a doctorate in 1903, and took a post as an administrative lawyer in the Prussian civil service. In 1923 he became Assistant Secretary of State and Permanent Representative of the Prussian interior minister. He was particularly concerned with the lawlessness which prevailed in Germany after the First World War and Abegg is regarded as the man who established a modern police force in the country to combat the violent activities of groups such as the fledgling Nazi Party. As Germany drifted further to the right with the installing of Franz von Papen as Chancellor, Abegg went into politics in opposition to the national government.

In a bid to stop the escalating violence between the Communists and the increasingly confident Nazi Party, a ban had been placed on gatherings of the SA and SS. On 28 June 1932 Papen lifted the ban which led to open street fighting between the rival political factions and, within a month, there were ninety-nine deaths and 1,125 injuries in Germany, mainly involving National Socialists and communists. In particular, a march on 17 July by the SS and the SA through the workers' quarter in a town called Altona, which was at that time a part of Schleswig-Holstein, triggered a major confrontation between 7,000 National Socialists and Altona's communist residents, leading to massive police intervention. Eighteen people, including two SA members, were killed, most of them by police bullets.

Papen used this as an excuse to impose emergency measures by which he could act without reference to the Reichstag, effectively granting Papen dictatorial powers. Abegg tried to oppose this and was summarily dismissed from the civil service.

Abegg, fearing for the future, emigrated to Switzerland (from where his family originated). Settling in Zurich, he became an international lawyer helping refugees from Germany. He also plotted to kill Hitler and other high-ranking Nazis – or at least that is what some historians have led us to believe.

It is said that he formed a team of ten assassins, all of whom were former Prussian police officers who had served time in Nazi concentration camps from where Abegg had rescued them by paying off the authorities. Abegg's scheme was for the assassins to dress in stolen uniforms of Italian Army courier officers, with each one given a different leading Nazi to assassinate. They were to approach their respective targets under the guise of delivering an important message from Italy, pull out their side arm and shoot the intended victim. The only exception to this was regarding the man who would kill Hitler. Aware that the security round the Führer would be tighter than other Nazi officials, the man destined to kill Hitler would be a suicide bomber who would blow himself up in the presence of the Führer. For this last part of the plan to work, Abegg needed to find an explosive of sufficient power to kill Hitler but which was small enough to be concealed about the person of the assassin without it being easily detected.

Whilst trying to solve the problem of the manufacture of a suitable bomb, Abegg learned of a resistance movement in the upper echelons of the German Army – men far more adept at killing than he – and his unlikely scheme was shelved.[5]

There is some doubt over the truth in the Abegg assassination story. Swiss historian Klaus Urner has examined the 'Abegg Archive' and concluded that the documents that relate to the assassination plot are post-war forgeries, with financial gain being the motive.[6]

Chapter 10

Reich Chancellery, Berlin, Friedrich Heinz/ Hans Oster, September 1938

A significant change in the opposition to Hitler took place in 1938. Hitler had regained control of the Saar region on 1 March 1935 and had marched German troops into the Rhineland in repudiation of the terms of the Treaty of Versailles almost exactly a year later, receiving overwhelming support from the German people and its armed forces.

But already disquiet over Hitler's actions was growing in the Army and a small group of officers had shared their concerns over the direction in which their country was heading. The man at the centre of this group was Oberstleutnant Hans Paul Oster, who was deputy head of the Abwehr, the German military intelligence organization. Like so many officers in the Reichswehr, Oster had initially welcomed Hitler's firm hand on the tiller of state, but this appreciation of the Nazis soon turned to anger after the Night of the Long Knives, and then hatred following the shocking excesses committed during the destruction of Jewish property and the killing of Jews during the infamous *Kristallnacht*. Yet it was not just these appalling events that prompted Oster into drawing fellow officers into his plans to assassinate the German head of state – it was also the fear that Hitler would thrust his country into a war against Britain and France; a war it could not win.

Until early in 1938 the Army had managed to retain its independence from government, at least to some degree. It remained the one major cohesive body that Hitler had limited control over. That all changed in February 1938. The Commander-in-Chief of the Armed Forces and Minister of War, Generalfeldmarschall Werner von Blomberg, was compelled to resign his post following revelations concerning his recently-married wife's long criminal record for prostitution. The man who replaced him, Generaloberst Werner von Fritsch, was also forced to resign due to concocted accusations of homosexuality made by Himmler. Both these generals had voiced their concerns over Hitler's expansionist ambitions and had paid the price.

These 'scandals' enabled Hitler to re-organize the command structure of the German armed forces, placing the Army, Navy and Air Force under a new body the Oberkommando der Wehrmacht (OKW) or Supreme Command of the Armed Forces, under Generalfeldmarschall Wilhelm Keitel, while command of the Army was put in the hands of a man that Hitler knew would do his bidding, whether he liked it or not, Generalfeldmarschall Walther von Brauchitsch. At the same time, Hitler ordered the summary retirement of fourteen senior generals. He then replaced Konstantin von Neurath, the Minister of Foreign Affairs, who had also expressed his disapproval of Hitler's policies, with the 'dull but obedient' Joachim von Ribbentrop. The consequence of all these machinations was that if Hitler decided to go to war there was now no one in Germany who could stop him.

With all the power he needed in his own hands, Hitler was ready to take the next step in his plans to create a Greater Germany encompassing all the German-speaking peoples of central Europe. According to Hitler's personal adjutant, Captain Fritz Wiedemann, Hitler's ultimate goal was even more ambitious: that of a German Empire which would include Poland, the Ukraine, the Baltic States, Scandinavia, Flemish Belgium, Luxembourg, Burgundy, Alsace-Lorraine and Switzerland.[1]

His first target was Austria. Towards the end of 1918 and into 1919 negotiations had taken place to try and unite the two great Germanic nations Germany and Austria, but this had been blocked by the Allies and, under the terms of the Treaty of Versailles, had been expressly forbidden. As he had broken the terms of the Treaty by re-militarizing the Ruhr, creating an air force and expanding the army, with little opposition from Britain and France, Hitler was confident he could absorb Austria into the Third Reich without fear of repercussions.

Consequently, on 12 March 1938, German troops crossed the border, being greeted by cheering crowds and Nazi salutes. The *Anschluss* (joining) was legitimized by the Austrian government and confirmed in a plebiscite four weeks later, in which 99.7 per cent of voters agreed to the union with Germany.

The world held its collective breath to see what the response of Britain and France would be to the *Anschluss*. The answer was soon forthcoming, with Prime Minister Neville Chamberlain conceding that 'nothing could have arrested what has actually happened [in Austria] unless this country and other countries had been prepared to use force',[2] and no one was prepared to use force. Hitler had gambled yet again on allied acquiescence as he had when he had re-occupied the Rhineland and the Ruhr, and once more had won.

Senior officers throughout the Army had feared the worst when German troops marched into Austria and the roots of the Army's resistance to Hitler, which had become firmly established in the wake of the Blomberg-Fritsch affair, began to spread. It was, in fact, the day after Fritsch had been forced to resign, when Generaloberst Ludwig Beck, Chief of the General Staff, met with Admiral Wilhelm Canaris, head of the Abwehr, and his deputy, Hans Oster. These men, and others in the Army, believed that Himmler had deceived Hitler over the entirely false charges of Fritsch's homosexuality and that it was Himmler who should be driven from office and not Fritsch. Himmler wanted to considerably expand the size and fighting capacity of his SS and to bring the Army fully under Nazi control – something Fritsch had fought to resist. Fritsch was seen as an obstacle in the path of Himmler's ambitions and had paid the price.

Along with fellow members of the Abwehr and other supporters, Oster planned to occupy Gestapo headquarters in Berlin, arrest Himmler and his deputy, Reinhard Heydrich, and present to Hitler all the evidence showing that the accusations against Fritsch were false. So that the public would know what was going on, they intended to publish the material at the same time they handed it over to the Führer. As it transpired, the evidence against Fritsch was demonstrated to be false and the case against him collapsed. On 31 March 1938 Fritsch received a letter from Hitler confirming that he had been acquitted of all charges, though no apology was offered, and he was not reinstated at the head of the Army.

The upper echelons of the Army knew that its independence was threatened, and it was after Oster was arrested in 1943 on suspicion of helping Abwehr officers caught helping Jews escape Germany that he admitted that the dismissal of Fritsch was the tipping point: 'I made the Fritsch business my own. Our intentions were initially to remove

Himmler and the Gestapo because we believed that their influence was against the common good.'

Oster became the driving force of the opposition and was the vital link between Beck and Canaris, with the latter's headquarters the communications hub of the Army's resistance. Canaris, who spoke six languages, had risen to prominence during the First World War when he escaped from Chile where he and other members of the crew of the scuttled cruiser SMS *Dresden* had been interned. He was then employed by the Kriegsmarine in intelligence-gathering duties in Spain, later becoming a U-boat commander in the Mediterranean.

Canaris was fiercely opposed to the Treaty of Versailles and after the war was sent to Japan to supervise a secret U-boat construction programme in direct violation of the terms of the treaty. He was a vocal supporter of Hitler and the Nazi Party and, on 1 January 1935, Canaris happily accepted the position of chief of the Abwehr. Unlike Oster, Canaris was unmoved by the Blomberg-Fritsch affair, but he was concerned with Hitler's expansionist aims, fearing, like others, that Hitler would drag Germany into a war it was ill-prepared for.

That certainly appeared to be a distinct possibility as, with Fritsch out of the way, Hitler planned to undertake the second part of his dream of creating a Greater Germany which would embrace all the Germanic people. This next step was to dismantle Czechoslovakia, the artificially constructed state to the east of Germany, which had been carved from the former Austro-Hungarian Empire after the First World War. Within its borders were two important features. One was the Sudetenland, where more than 3,000,000 ethnic Germans lived; the other was the Skoda works which had previously been the principal arms manufacturer for the Austro-Hungarian Army. Hitler intended to seize both.

Relieved that Britain and France had accepted the *Anschluss* with little fuss, the Army leaders could not believe that these two nations would sit on their hands if Hitler invaded an independent sovereign country. Hitler would have to be removed from power before he could move against Czechoslovakia and bring about a war that would destroy Germany; Oster and his co-conspirators began to plot the Führer's downfall.

But these men alone could not topple the Nazi Party, so Oster sent 'missionaries' to the headquarters of the twelve military districts into which Germany was divided to garner support. No coup could succeed in toppling the government if it was opposed by the commanders of the military districts. Equally important was that another civil administration was ready to step into the vacuum created by the removal of the Nazi leadership. So, drawn into what would become known as the Oster Conspiracy, were Hans-Bernd Gisevius, former member of the Gestapo and employee of the Ministry of the Interior; Karl Goerdeler; and Hjalmar Schacht, a former minister of economics and the then president of the Reichsbank, amongst others.

As we have discussed earlier, Goredeler repeatedly tried to convince politicians in Britain and France to stand up to Hitler and support his efforts at regime change, only to be rebuffed. But at least the leaders in London and Paris had been informed that Hitler had designs on Czechoslovakia and that if they stood firm and frustrated his territorial aims there was a chance that opposition groups in Germany could oust the Führer. In support of this, Theodor Kordt, brother of Erich mentioned earlier and fellow conspirator, was the Chargé d'Affaires at the German Embassy in London and he appealed to Halifax to have the BBC 'broadcast a warning to the German people' that they should get 'their Army leaders' to 'intervene against Hitler's policies by force of arms'.[3] The appeal was rejected, but it kept up the pressure on the British Government to act – and everything depended on how the politicians in London and Paris would act over the course of the next few months, as Hitler increased his rhetoric over the alleged 'plight' of the Sudeten Germans.

Since the *Anschluss* the Sudeten Germans, claiming to be a persecuted minority, had been agitating noisily for their own union with the Third Reich. The leader of the Sudeten German Party, the Sudentendeutsche Partei, Konrad Henlein, demanded autonomy for the region which the Czech government could not accept.

As the manufactured crisis escalated, Hitler told his generals to prepare to attack Czechoslovakia no later than 2 October. This prompted Generaloberst Beck to submit a memorandum to von Brauchitsch predicting that a move against Czechoslovakia would lead to a protracted and costly war, warning that 'Germany is not fit for a long war'. Brauchitsch dared not be seen as condoning Beck's negative view and the memo was not passed on to Hitler.

On 19 May 1938 German forces were observed massing on the Czech border. Two days later the Czechs mobilized. Britain and France issued stern communiques, threatening that a move against Czechoslovakia might result in a 'European conflagration'. Much to the surprise of the Western leaders, Hitler did not call their bluff, and von Ribbentrop was able, for once, to tell the truth (but not the whole truth) when he assured them that Germany was not on the verge of invading Czechoslovakia. He did not say what might happen in the future.

But the threats that had emanated from Paris and London further reinforced the conviction of the Oster group that when, for it was no longer *if*, Hitler invaded Czechoslovakia, Britain, France and, probably, the Soviet Union would declare war on Germany.

Beck tried again to point out the risks he believed that Hitler was running in planning to occupy Czechoslovakia, but his advice was dismissed out of hand by the Führer who was becoming increasingly annoyed with the Chief of Staff's pessimism. For his part, Beck saw that his efforts to deter Hitler with reasoned analysis had failed and that the only way of preventing another European war was by removing Hitler.

Throughout June and July diplomatic efforts by Lord Halifax and Prime Minister Chamberlain appeared to be bearing fruit as tensions eased after the May crisis. Indeed, towards the end of July, Chamberlain had managed to persuade the Czech government and the Sudetens to agree to a British mediator, the shipping magnate Lord Runciman, to find a solution to the problem. The situation, Chamberlain now believed, was under control. Germany, meanwhile, prepared for war.

Aware that the date of Hitler's proposed invasion was drawing closer, Beck took steps that could, quite reasonably, be considered treasonable. On 4 August, for the first and only time in the history of the Third Reich, the Army's senior generals met without having been summoned by the Führer. The Chief of Staff had called them together to present them with his apocalyptic view of what would happen if Germany invaded Czechoslovakia. He hoped that he could convince them to refuse to carry out Hitler's instructions. There was a degree of unanimity amongst the generals, with much consideration given to Beck's call for them to resign en masse. Mutiny was in the air, with Beck warning the officers that as well as preparing for war they should be ready for 'an internal showdown at home'.[4] Only two generals rebuked the others for their treacherous words, and one of them, General Walther von Reichenau, went off to tell Hitler all that had transpired.

The Führer responded by convening his own meeting with the military hierarchy on 15 August. Hitler was nothing if he was not persuasive, and he convinced many of the generals that neither Britain nor France would lift a finger to help the Czechs. Beck was unmoved by Hitler's words, but he now saw that nothing he could say would stop the invasion. If words were not enough, then possibly deeds might. So, the Chief of Staff of the Army resigned.

Beck hoped that others would follow but the naturally conservative officers baulked at taking such an extreme measure. Even Beck's replacement, General Franz Halder, who had previously called Hitler a 'madman' and a 'criminal', now vacillated. The cautious generals decided to wait and see what would happen.

Beck, and the group that had gathered round himself and Oster, now knew that they were on their own. They also knew that without the support of the other generals they could no longer openly conspire against Hitler.

Time was running out for the resisters to draw the men necessary for a successful coup into the conspiracy. One man they were able to recruit, and possibly the most important, was General Erwin von Witzleben, commander of III Military District, within whose jurisdiction was the Berlin Defence District. Witzleben became an enthusiastic member of the conspiracy, drawing General der Infanterie Walter von Brockdorff-Ahlefeldt into the plot and allocating him the task of formulating the plan of action for the coup. He also provided Gisevius with a room in his Military District Headquarters at 144 Hohenzollerndamm which could only be entered through Witzleben's office where he could safely document and map out the details of the coup.[5]

Brockdorff-Ahlefeldt had to work out how all the important locations around Berlin could be quickly taken with the troops at Witzleben's disposal. The Army headquarters at the Bendlerblock, the main radio transmitter, the Gestapo headquarters and the Chancellery had to be secured. All these places had to be carefully scrutinized to ensure they were swiftly seized and, so as not to arouse suspicion by wandering around these buildings, they were driven across Berlin by a woman, Elisabeth

Strüenck, whose husband Theodor had been enlisted into the Abwehr, and the plot, by Oster.

As other generals around the country were drawn into the conspiratorial web, the plan began to take shape. Brockdorff-Ahlefeldt's 23rd Division was to move into Berlin from its quarters in Potsdam to seize the key installations and arrest a long list of Nazi officials, aided by Generalmajor Paul von Hase's Berlin-based 50th Infantry Regiment. Meanwhile, the tanks of Generalmajor Erich Hoepner's 1st Light Division were to block the road from Munich to Berlin to prevent the 1st SS Panzer Division Leibstandarte Adolf Hitler from interfering with the coup.

Of paramount importance was a defiant stand by the British. If Chamberlain made it abundantly clear that the invasion of Czechoslovakia would result in a declaration of war against Germany, Hitler would have to stand down his army and the myth of the Führer's brilliant political manoeuvring would be dispelled and his standing across Germany diminished. The task of explaining this to the British Government was handed to the influential monarchist Edward von Kleist-Schmenzin. 'Bring me certain proof that England will fight if Czechoslovakia is attacked,' he was told by Oster before he left Berlin, 'and I will make an end of this regime.'[6]

Exactly how Hitler was to be disposed of when the time for action arrived was the subject of much discussion. An outright assassination was repugnant to many of the officers, most preferring to see Hitler arrested and tried for the many crimes his regime had committed against the German people, or even declared insane by a panel of doctors and committed to an asylum.[7]

The plan eventually agreed upon was that Witzleben would march to the Chancellery with a squad of young officers and Abwehr agents under a certain Major Friedrich Wilhelm Heinz. If Hitler's SS guards attempted to stop Heinz's men from entering the Chancellery, they would be shot. Witzleben would demand Hitler's resignation. If he refused, Hitler would be arrested and taken to a secret location where he would be held until the coup had been completed before being forced to resign. What many of the conspirators did not know was that Heinz, along with Oster, believed that 'Hitler alive has more weight than all the troops at our disposal', and had decided that he would provoke a situation of some kind which would result in a gun battle in which the Führer would be killed. It must be said that, as was the case with many who opposed Hitler, Heinz was no saint. He had previously worked as a journalist for the Nazi Party until, incredible as it may seem, he was dismissed for being *too* violent.[8]

In preparation for the assault upon the Chancellery, Admiral Canaris took guns and explosives (to blow in the doors of the Chancellery if necessary) from the Abwehr arsenal and secreted them in 'safe houses' around Berlin for Heinz's assault squad. That squad was to consist of 'courageous, unscrupulous motivated but politically unambitious men' who would be willing to stand aside after Hitler had been killed and allow the leading conspirators to take over the reins of power.[9] These included twenty or thirty active Wehrmacht officers, a few student and labour leaders, and some of Heinz's old friends from his time with a right-wing Great War veterans group, the *Stahlhelm*. In total Heinz's group numbered fifty-sixty hardline anti-Nazis. A motley crew it was indeed but the disparate composition of the group was intentional, the aim being to reflect how widely spread the opposition to Hitler had become.[10]

Having gathered together his team, exactly how the attack upon Hitler could be carried out had then to considered. In the Chancellery there were between twelve and fifteen men of the Leibstandarte SS Adolf Hitler on duty at any one time around the clock. One of these stood guard at the main entrance and another at the entrance to Hitler's quarters. Another soldier patrolled the yard with a dog at night. The other guards were posted at other points around the Chancellery.

The conspirators now waited on the response to their mission to London. Kleist met Lord Lloyd, an outspoken critic of Hitler, and Sir Robert Vansittart, permanent under-secretary at the Foreign Office, advising them that the invasion of Czechoslovakia was a certainty, unless Britain took decisive action. 'The mobilization plans are complete, zero day is fixed, and the Army group commanders have their orders. All will run according to plan at the end of September, and no one can stop it unless Britain speaks an open warning to Herr Hitler.'[11]

Vansittart took this information to Lord Halifax who, in turn, passed it on to Chamberlain. None of these politicians saw anything other than Kleist being the representative of a group that merely sought power in Germany for its own ends. To Chamberlain they were merely a 'gang of traitors'.

Hans Oster, meanwhile, had been rapidly extending his network and had his spies in government ministries and the police. Even Halder, who saw the date of the invasion of Czechoslovakia looming, declared he would back the coup, but only if Hitler issued the order to attack the Czechs. One man who remained outside the conspiracy was Brauchitsch. If the Army commander could be persuaded to counter Hitler's orders, there would be no invasion, war would be averted, and the Führer's authority permanently held in check. Though he was told that 'the destiny of the German army and thus the destiny of the German people' lay in his hands, Brauchitsch remained unmoved.

Also unmoved was the situation between Berlin and Prague. The Sudetens continued to demonstrate for the Sudetenland to be ceded to Germany and towards the end of August Lord Runciman had to confess that he was unable to reconcile the differences between Konrad Henlein and the Czech President, Edvard Beneš. The Germany army was also conducting manoeuvres close to the border with Czechoslovakia. It seemed that the repeated warnings that Hitler was set on seizing the Sudetenland by force were all too true.

Chamberlain called an emergency Cabinet meeting on 30 August. Only one item was on the agenda for that day – should Britain announce that it would go to war to uphold Czechoslovakia's sovereignty? The arguments for and against such a declaration were obvious to all. But no one could predict what would happen if Britain did take such a bold step. Would Hitler back down, or would Europe be flung into another, and even more terrible, war with Germany? Like Hitler's generals, Chamberlain's ministers decided to wait and see.

Oddly, this was exactly what Chamberlain wanted, for he had a scheme to write his name in the history books as the man who brought peace to the troubled Continent. It was termed 'Plan Z'. Chamberlain suspected that if Britain did not threaten to go to war with Germany, Hitler would continue his preparations against the Czechs. So, just as the Germans were on the verge of launching their attack, Chamberlain would fly, unannounced, to meet the Führer and save the day with a typically British compromise.

With Hitler's self-imposed deadline looming, Theo Kordt tried yet again to persuade the British government to stand firm against Hitler. In a secret meeting on the night of 5 September, Kordt told Halifax and

Britain's highest ranking civil servant, the head of the civil service and secretary to the treasury, Sir Horace Wilson, that, if Britain opposed Hitler, the 'political and military circles for whom I speak, will take arms against a sea of troubles and, by opposing, end them'.[12] But the British still refused to be drawn into internal Germany politics.

Meanwhile, Oster and the others continued with their own plans which included an approach to Count Wolf Hendrick von Helldorf, the President of the Berlin Police, for if the police resisted the actions of Brockdorff-Ahlefeldt's and Hase's men and gun battles broke out in the streets, the chances of swiftly seizing Berlin were remote. Such a move had to be taken with extreme care, for Helldorf's loyalties remained untested. It was Gisevius who made the approach and, to his immense relief, Helldorf was willing to stand his men down during the coup. Oster could now be certain of securing Berlin, with significant elements of the Army and now the police willing to accept his orders. While certain key buildings would have to be seized on the day of the coup, it was thought most government departments would accept the change of regime with little fuss and that, after a brief period of military rule to ensure the leading Nazis were rounded up, the country could be handed back to the civilians. The SS would resist, of course, but at that time there was only the one SS division, the Leibstandarte Adolf Hitler, and even if this eventually broke through the 1st Light Division, by the time it reached Berlin, the conspirators would have already seized power.

Everyone now waited for the signal which would see Major Heinz's assault squad storm the Reich Chancellery. That signal was the implementation of 'Plan Green', the invasion of Czechoslovakia. Halder would be given at least twenty-four hours notice to enable him to issue his instructions to his corps commanders – twenty-four hours to topple Hitler and his hated regime before Europe was plunged into war.

Halder finally conceded that action needed to be taken against Hitler to prevent what he saw as a looming disaster, which was noted by Helmuth Groscurth, one of Canaris' Abwehr officers and a committed member of the opposition: 'With tears in his eyes H[alder] says that for weeks he had been going to see Emil [i.e. Hitler] with a loaded pistol in his pocket in order eventually to gun him down.'[13]

But then it happened. On 14 September, the British prime minister sent a message to Hitler telling the Führer that he was flying to

Germany the next day to offer a solution, once and for all, to the Czech problem.

Hitler decided to meet Chamberlain at the Berghof and arrangements were rapidly made to receive him, who was taking his first ever flight in an aeroplane. The two leaders met face-to-face in a small study in the Berghof with Hitler's interpreter the only other person present. At the recent Nuremberg rally, Hitler had called for a plebiscite in the Sudetenland to determine if its people wanted to remain part of Czechoslovakia or join the Third Reich. Hitler asked Chamberlain if he supported the principle of self-determination. In response Chamberlain said that 'It was immaterial … whether the Sudeten Germans stayed in Czechoslovakia'. Hitler was going to be given what he wanted.

Chamberlain returned to advise his Cabinet, following which Lord Halifax had discussed the prime minister's proposal with the French and the Czechs. The French had agreed that if the majority of the Sudetens wanted to join Germany then they should be allowed to. President Beneš was given no choice.

It seemed to the conspirators that Hitler was going to have his way and that war would be avoided. But then Hitler made further demands: that the Polish and Hungarian minorities in Czechoslovakia should also be granted the right of self-determination and that any plebiscites would only take place *after* the German Army had marched into Czechoslovakia. This amounted to the forced dismemberment of the country – this, surely, could never be agreed to by Britain and France? Hitler was clearly bent on war.

This drove even more senior figures into the Oster conspiracy. Heinz and his men were poised for action. Chamberlain was not.

With Hitler declaring that the German Army would march into Czechoslovakia on 1 October unless his demands were met, Heinz's squad assembled at the Bendlerblock, a short distance from Abwehr headquarters on 28 September. The day had come.

But then, to the amazement – and consternation – of the conspirators, Hitler agreed to a proposal from Mussolini to hold a conference with the major powers in Munich to resolve the Czechoslovakia problem. Maybe a peaceful solution could be found after all? Heinz's men were stood down.

Chamberlain flew to Munich for his third meeting with the Führer on 29 September and in the early hours of the following day the two men, plus the French prime minister, Édouard Daladier, and Mussolini thrashed out a deal. They all signed the Munich Agreement which gave the Sudetenland to Germany, with an international commission to decide the future of other disputed areas – though this, effectively, gave Hitler control over the fate of the rest of Czechoslovakia. In return for Chamberlain's compliance over Czechoslovakia, Hitler agreed to sign a peace treaty with Britain. Both men believed they had achieved everything they had set out to accomplish.

Chamberlain returned to London, driving through crowds that cheered and waved as his car took him to Buckingham Palace to brief the King. He then returned to 10 Downing Street, where he famously declared to the exultant throng he had achieved 'peace with honour … peace for our time'.[14]

The rejoicing of the people in Britain was more than matched by that of the German *volk*. Hitler would never be more popular than at this moment. As the German tanks rolled across the Czech border into Sudetenland unopposed on 1 October, the conspirators knew that there was no longer any hope of mounting a coup against the Führer. Oster, Gisevius, and Schacht met at Witzleben's house, where they tossed 'their lovely plans and projects into the fire'.[15]

Chamberlain believed he had saved Europe. In reality, it was Hitler he had saved. But, as Goerdeler prophetically wrote a few days later: 'By shrinking from a risk, Chamberlain has made war inevitable.'[16]

Chapter 11

Wilhelmshaven, Czech Nationalists, 1 April 1939; British Embassy, Berlin, Colonel Mason-Macfarlane, 20 April 1939

His name was Noel Mason-MacFarlane. He was the British Military Attaché to Berlin and he wanted to kill Hitler. An artillery officer, he had received the DSO, MC and *Croix de Guerre* during the First World War and was a tough and shrewd old soldier, who would go on to add a Bar to his Military Cross during the Second World War. 'Mason-Mac' had pondered the subject of overturning the Nazi regime, and thus of preserving peace, for some time. But he was well aware that there were many dangers to such a course of action, warning the British ambassador in Berlin that 'any bungling of an attempt to interfere with German domestic politics from without during Hitler's lifetime would most assuredly lead to exactly what we wish to avoid'.[1] In other words, the only hope of bringing about regime change in Germany was with Hitler's death.

The date on which Mason-MacFarlane wanted to shoot Hitler, though, was in early 1939 and no such action could be sanctioned by the British authorities. Mason-MacFarlane had calculated that, during the celebratory parade for Hitler's birthday on 20 April in Berlin, the German leader would be on a raised dais within easy rifle shot of Mason-MacFarlane's drawing-room window. Mason-MacFarlane told the story of the assassination plan to Ewen Butler *The Times*' correspondent in Germany from 1937 to 1939:

> He discussed the plan with me in the summer of 1938 as I sat looking out of the window of his Berlin flat – the window from which his rifleman would, if the Colonel (as he then was) had had his way, have fired the shot which would have ended Hitler's career. Mason-Mac believed then, as I did and still do, that the Führer's

> death at that time would have brought about the collapse of the National Socialist regime. He was well aware of the forces inside the Oberkommando der Wehrmacht which would have seized the opportunity to overthrow a system they had every reason to hate and to fear. Mason-Mac told me that he had put the plan up to London but without the slightest hope that it would be accepted. If by any wild chance it were approved he said, he himself would be the rifleman if necessary.
>
> I protested that the murder of the Chancellor by the British Military Attaché would create a really formidable diplomatic incident. He agreed but added that nobody in Germany would go to war on that account, whereas while Hitler lived war was certain. A few weeks later it so happened that by a combination of luck and bluff I stood for some minutes within 20ft. of Hitler outside the Anhalter station in Berlin. In my case the Gestapo security arrangements had collapsed. I was not searched although I had no right to be where I was and might have had several Mills bombs in my pocket. In that case I could have disposed not only of the Führer but of most of his accomplices. I told Mason-Mac about this and he reproached me bitterly for having missed such an excellent opportunity.[2]

Apparently, Mason-MacFarlane declared that he could 'pick the bastard off from here as easy as winking. There'd be hell to pay, of course, and I'd be finished in every sense of the word. Still … with that lunatic out of the way we might be able to get some sense into things.' He later mused on this chance he had of killing Hitler:

> My residence in Berlin was barely 100 yards from the saluting base of all the big Führer reviews. All that was necessary was a good shot and a high-velocity rifle with telescopic sight and silencer. It could have been fired through my open bathroom window from a spot on the landing some 30 feet back from the window.[3]

The British Foreign Secretary, Lord Halifax, was nevertheless unimpressed by Mason-MacFarlane's proposal. 'We have not reached that stage … when we have to use assassination as a substitution for diplomacy.' It was a decision not just Britain, but the whole world would live to regret.

As it happened, there had been another plot to kill Hitler earlier that same month. Hitler was due to attend the launching of Germany's last great battleship, *Tirpitz*, at Wilhelmshaven on 1 April. The day before the ceremony, Gestapo agents searched the quays near *Tirpitz* and arrested two Czech nationals carrying automatic weapons who had gone there expressly to shoot Hitler. According to a report in the *Daily Mirror* of 12 April, a raid on a nearby house, owned by a Sudeten German, resulted in four more arrests. Two others managed to escape across the border into Holland.

All those arrested were found to be armed and, apparently, 'confessed calmly' to their plans. A Dutch journalist, the only witness to the arrests, was also taken into custody and 'flung' into prison. He was released the following morning and forced to sign a statement that he would not publish anything about the plot.

Chapter 12

Osteria Bavaria, Munich, Alexander Foote, August 1939

Hitler had made his detestation of Bolsheviks in general, and those in power in the Soviet Union in particular, very well known. Whilst he was in Landsberg Prison after his failed coup attempt in 1923, Hitler began work on *Mein Kampf*, in which he set out his political ideology and his future hopes for Germany. In this he wrote, with reference to the First World War:

> If new territory were to be acquired in Europe it must have been mainly at Russia's cost, and once again the new German Empire should have set out on its march along the same road as was formerly trodden by the Teutonic Knights, this time to acquire soil for the German plough by means of the German sword and thus provide the nation with its daily bread.[1]

Hitler was fixated with the acquisition of more territory for the expanding German nation – the infamous *Lebensraum*, or living space – and he made it quite clear where that living space would be found: 'We shall soon reach a point beyond which the resources of our soil can no longer be exploited,' he wrote, 'and at the same time we shall reach a point beyond which our man-power cannot develop … If we speak of soil in Europe today, we can primarily have in mind only Russia and her vassal border states.'[2]

Remarkably, he was able to find a justification for seizing Russian territory:

> One must calmly and squarely face the truth that it certainly cannot be part of the dispensation of Divine Providence to give a fifty times larger share of the soil of this world to one nation than to another. In considering this state of affairs to-day, one must not allow existing political frontiers to distract attention from what ought to exist on principles of strict justice. If this earth has sufficient room for all,

> then we ought to have that share of the soil which is absolutely necessary for our existence.[3]

There was another factor, not just the uneven distribution of land, which impelled Hitler to contemplate seizing Russian territory – the supposed racial superiority of the Germans over the Slavs of Russia, Belorussia and Poland. In adopting Darwin's theory of evolution, which in its simplest form can be defined as the consequence of the survival of the fittest, Hitler believed that the superior Germans should flourish at the expense of the inferior races. 'In order to preserve a certain culture, the type of manhood that creates such a culture must be preserved. But such a preservation goes hand-in-hand with the inexorable law that it is the strongest and the best who must triumph and that they have the right to endure.' If any should doubt how 'the best' should triumph, Hitler made it quite clear, 'He who would live must fight. He who does not wish to fight in this world, where permanent struggle is the law of life, has not the right to exist.'[4]

While such ideologies may sound outrageous to us today, at the time many, if not most, people throughout Western Europe and North America, believed that the superiority of the Aryan race above all others was a scientific fact. So strongly did many Nazis feel about this 'Social Darwinism', they took it with them, quite literally, to the grave, as expressed at the post-war Nuremberg Trials: 'Their political dictionary was replete with words like space, struggle, selection, and extinction. The syllogism of their logic was clearly stated: "The world is a jungle in which different nations struggle for space. The stronger win, the weaker die or are killed."'[5] Little wonder, then, that the Soviets sought to kill Hitler before he killed them.

Strangely, the first Soviet plan to assassinate Hitler was devised by a Briton. Alexander Foote was born in Lancashire but was raised mostly in Yorkshire by his Scottish-born father and English mother. He developed an intense hatred for fascism and joined the Republicans in the Spanish Civil War, following which he volunteered to undertake clandestine work for the Soviets in Germany. The enigmatic Foote became a radio operator for a Soviet espionage operation based in Switzerland, but was, in fact, an MI6 (SIS) double agent.

It was in his guise as a Soviet spy in Munich, that one day, when looking for somewhere 'cheap' for lunch, he bumped into Hitler at the small restaurant in Munich called 'Osteria Bavaria'. He had been told by his Soviet handlers merely to keep a general eye on Hitler's movements and he soon discovered that Hitler ate at the restaurant sometimes as often as three times a week, enjoying eggs and mayonnaise, vegetables and pasta, and compote of fruit or a raw grated apple and Fachinger Wasser, which was a mineral water recommended for those with digestion troubles.[6]

Over the course of a few weeks, this observation of the German Chancellor had morphed in the minds of those in Moscow into a full-blown assassination 'scheme' to be carried out by Foote and his co-spy Bill Philips, and the prospects of killing Hitler at the Osteria Bavaria were quite 'promising'. Despite Hitler's worries about being assassinated, security appeared to be surprisingly lax, as Foote wrote in his memoirs: 'As far as we could gather there was no special surveillance of the place, and no extra precautions were put in force when the Führer honoured it with his presence.' Apparently Hitler farted frequently throughout the meal but no one ever complained.[7]

This relaxed mood, so different to the tense atmosphere of later years, was noted by Unity Mitford, the British socialite whose aunt was Clementine Churchill. Her sister, Diana, had married Oswald Mosley, leader of the British Union of Fascists, and Unity had similar designs on Hitler. She discovered that the Führer's movements could easily be ascertained, as one narrator explained:

> It's one of the extraordinary things about Hitler's daily life that he was so available to the public. You knew which café he'd be in, you knew which restaurant he'd be in, which hotel, and he would just go and meet people over sticky buns and cakes, and it was possible to meet him like that. And he was in the habit of eating in the Osteria Bavaria in Munich and she started sitting in the Osteria Bavaria every day.[8]

Like Unity Mitford, Foote did not have any trouble coming up with a simple plan to get close to Hitler, nor of concocting a scheme to eliminate him at the restaurant. Hitler always lunched in a private room, which was only separated by a thin wooden partition from the corridor leading from the restaurant to the toilets. It was along this partition that the coats of the customers were hung: 'What could be easier, we argued, than to put a time bomb in an attaché case along with our coats, and having had an early lunch, abandon the lot in the hope that our bomb would blow Hitler and his entourage, snugly lunching behind the boarding, into eternity.'[9]

When he published his memoirs in 1949, Foote remarked that, looking back on the scheme, he considered it 'well-nigh fool-proof'. The other three sides of the corridor were solid Bavarian stone which would have deflected the blast directly at the thin partition beyond which Hitler sat. But the two men, merely private individuals in the heart of Munich, were simply unable to obtain explosives, so another scheme had to be thought up.

They had seen that Hitler walked through the restaurant on his way to his private room 'acknowledging the plaudits of the lunchers, who, not unnaturally, rose to their feet on the entrance of the head of the State'. It would have been very easy for one of the 'lunchers' to pull a concealed pistol from his or her pocket and gun Hitler down.

Just to see how practicable such an action would be, the two men mounted a trial run, as Foote described: 'One day Bill stationed himself at the table next to the gangway, and as Hitler approached put his hand rapidly and furtively into his pocket – and drew out a cigarette case.' Foote watched this from the other side of the room, to see the reaction of the members of Hitler's entourage and the rest of the guests among whom, Foote believed, must have been a fair sprinkling of 'trigger-happy' Gestapo agents. Nothing whatsoever happened.

Though Foote was encouraged to carry out the assassination, he knew only too well that he would never have left the Osteria Bavaria alive but, to pacify those urging him to act, he promised to continue planning, though he had no intention of sacrificing his own life to kill Hitler. As it transpired, the political landscape changed abruptly when Germany and the Soviet Union signed the Molotov-Ribbentrop Non-aggression Pact on 23 August 1939. With this Hitler had become Stalin's ally and Foote was ordered to stand down.

The Osteria Bavaria, now the Osteria Italiana, still stands at Schellingstrasse 62 and retains its old 1930s feel. Visitors can sit at the very table occupied by Hitler – exactly where the Führer just might have been blown to bits.

Chapter 13

The Vatican, Pope Pius XII, 1939–1940; Reich Chancellery, Erich Kordt, November 1939; Switzerland, Ulrich von Hassell, 22 February 1940

It was a remarkable coincidence that at the same time the Nazi Party was growing in strength throughout Germany, the man who would become Pope was the Apostolic Nuncio – the Vatican's ambassador – to Germany. Italian-born Eugenio Pacelli, who had served the Roman Catholic Church in Germany from 1917 to 1930, became Pope Pius XII on 2 March 1939, just six months before Hitler invaded Poland and plunged the world into war.

The new pope still had many friends in Germany and the persistent Hans Oster saw this as a chance to use the pope as an intermediary between Germany and Great Britain before the conflict between the two countries escalated to the point of no return. Even though all their previous attempts to gain backing from Britain for a coup had been rebuffed, now that their warnings about Hitler's ambitions had been shown to be frighteningly accurate, the Oster group hoped that the British Government would finally see the sense in supporting the opposition. But with the two countries at war, no direct contact could be made with the UK. So, another means of communicating with London had to be found, and no one could be considered more trustworthy, more respected and more discreet than the pope.

The man whom Oster and Canaris thought would gain a ready audience with the Pope was Dr Joseph Müller, who had been a close friend of the pontiff for many years and was a known member of the (largely toothless) Catholic resistance movement. Müller, known to his friends as 'Joey Ox' because he had worked his way through school driving an ox-cart, was a lawyer and legal advisor to numerous church officials and highly respected throughout the Roman Catholic community in Germany, was summoned to Abwehr headquarters on 27 September 1939 by Canaris. Yet it was not the admiral who attended Müller but his deputy.

Oster told Müller that he was aware of his involvement in the Catholic resistance. Müller must have feared what was to happen next but, to his surprise, Oster said that the Central Division of the Abwehr 'is also the central directorate of the German military opposition under General Beck'.[1]

Müller had been passing details of the treatment of Catholics in Germany to the Vatican for years. His law firm had become the central repository of details concerning anti-Christian decrees issued by the Third Reich, press censorship, and the manner in which priests were hindered or obstructed in their clerical duties. These details, and other acts against the Church, were collected from across Germany and taken to Müller where the reports were evaluated and then summarized for onward transmission to the Vatican. Passing on that intelligence to Rome was no easy matter. The SS kept a careful watch on all the Church's communication with the outside world, tapping the telephones of the bishops and opening their mail to stop their criticisms of the regime being known in other countries. The only way to pass on the summarized reports was by personal contact – and the main courier was Müller himself.

Müller had a small, single-seat sports aircraft and it was in this that he flew over the Alps with the documents to Merano in Italy's South Tyrol. There he would meet someone who would take the documents down to the Vatican and hand them over to Pacelli, who, at that time was the Holy See's Cardinal Secretary of State. Pacelli used Müller's bulletins to write protests to Berlin. Little wonder that Oster saw Müller as the perfect conduit for his group's appeals to Britain for support of their plans to assassinate Hitler.

Oster and Müller talked for three hours. Convinced that Oster was sincere in his desire to rid the world of Hitler, on a shake of hands and a sworn oath, Müller joined the conspiracy. Now he needed to tell his contacts in Rome.

When he flew once again over the Alps in the first week of October, it was to the Italian capital that he made his way. There he met Monsignor Ludwig Kaas. The former chairman of the banned German Catholic Centre Party, he was the pope's advisor on German affairs. It took two weeks for Kaas to make up his mind about Müller's story, no doubt contemplating the moral issues of associating the pope with the murder of a head of state and the potential risks involved not just for Pius XII, but for the Catholic Church across Europe, which Hitler had threatened to 'squash like a toad'. It took the pope less than a day to come to his decision.

The Catholic Church has always found means of justifying its actions and despite God's Fifth Commandment, popes had a long history of sanctioning religious wars and of engaging in the murder of individuals from the executions of the Knights Templar to the atrocities of the Inquisition. Pius, therefore, had no qualms with aiding the German resistance for the greater good of mankind.

Around 17 October Müller received Pius' reply. He would help to restore peace through the complete overthrow of the Nazi regime by persuading the British that it was in their interests to give its support to the conspirators and the government they would form after the removal of Hitler.

One of the first effects of the pope's participation in the plot was for him to tone down his public criticisms of the Nazis and eventually to keep silent altogether so as not to draw attention to Catholics in Germany which might imperil their subversive activities. Meanwhile, at Abwehr headquarters, Oster and Canaris began to lay out their scheme. As the best disguise is to hide in plain sight, Müller was made an Abwehr agent, with the rank of lieutenant, who, due to his contacts in Italy, could sound out opponents to Mussolini and his pact with Hitler and report his findings back to Berlin. This would all be explained beforehand to the Gestapo, so that he could meet with dissident groups in Italy – Germany's most important ally – quite legitimately with official backing.

Canaris met Müller in person and laid out the ground rules of the scheme. The conspirators would negotiate only with Britain. They could not be seen to be playing one of the Allies against another, so contact would be attempted solely with London. Then the admiral explained how Müller would pass on information from Rome. In each report he made on the activities of the pacifists in Italy, he would include a section with the title 'Current Possibilities for Peace' in which Müller would make coded references to the plan to remove Hitler.[2] Once again, this would help disguise Müller's real intentions.

Müller was back in Rome on 7 November. This time he met Father Robert Leiber, the pope's private secretary and closest advisor, at his apartment at 4 Piazza della Pilotta. Leiber explained that Pius could not meet Müller in person, but the pope was determined to handle the channel of communication with London personally. If word of the pope's involvement in talks with Britain to overthrow Hitler became known, Pius did not want the church to be implicated, so Müller was told that, when mentioning the possibility of peace talks with Britain, the conspirators must only ever refer to the pope and never the Vatican. In true covert fashion, codenames were to be used. Müller was to be 'Herr X', Father Lieber, who taught at the Universita Gregoriana, was to be 'Gregor' and Pius was to be the 'Chief'.[3]

All this scheming would be for naught unless some means could be found of carrying out the deadly deed itself – and time was pressing. It was known by the military that Hitler aimed to launch his invasion of France and the Low Countries on 12 November. Once that tipping point had been reached there would be little chance of arranging a peace deal. The conspirators needed to act swiftly and, conscious of what they believed was looming disaster, the Foreign Ministry's Erich Kordt decided he would be the one to end all the doubt and uncertainty. On 1 November he asked Oster to get him the bomb with which he would kill Hitler. As Ribbentrop's senior official, Kordt was a trusted individual and one of only a few who had easy access to the Führer without being checked for weapons. Oster was not going to miss out on this offer, and he told Kordt he would have the bomb by the 11th.

Oster contacted Generalmajor Erwin von Lahousen, fellow conspirator and the head of Abwehr Department II, and asked him to help. As Department II's responsibilities included sabotage, Lahousen could withdraw the explosive material and fuses from the stores without arousing suspicion. He could also arrange for Kordt to undergo a quick course on explosives at the Abwehr's secret training camp at Lake Quenz near Brandenburg.[4] Kordt had seen that Hitler often walked into the antechamber of his office at the Chancellery to greet visitors and to issue orders. It would be there that Kordt would strike. So that his face would become a familiar one at the Chancellery he invented reasons to visit there frequently over the days following his meeting with Oster.

In the midst of these clandestine collaborations, the blast from George Elser's bomb on 8 November (which is discussed in a later chapter) sent shock waves reverberating around the offices of the Abwehr. Hitler really did seem to have the luck of the Devil. Did Erich Kordt have any realistic chance of killing Hitler, or would it be a disaster which would lead to the exposure of the conspiracy?

News of Elser's assassination attempt had the reverse effect in London. It demonstrated that there were indeed people willing to kill Hitler and perhaps he was not as popular in Germany as had been portrayed. The British government's renewed interest in possible regime change in Germany was quickly extinguished, however, when British Secret Service agents Best and Stevens were seized in neutral Holland the following day (see Chapter 16). In Rome there was confusion. Pius wanted to have all the pieces in place before Hitler was removed to avoid mayhem in Germany and was shocked with Elser's premature rogue action. Oster's conspiracy was floundering. Yet, with the invasion of France and the Low Countries looming, Kordt was as determined as ever to stop Hitler. But von Lahousen was unable to obtain the explosives because of tighter controls having been put into place due to the war situation. Kordt was exasperated: 'Along comes a civilian, such as myself,' he complained, 'who is prepared to run the kind of risk that our gallant generals should have run long ago, and these bloody professional heroes … are not even in a position to supply an uncompromising diplomat with something as simple as a small bomb.[5]

Despite this setback, Kordt was still intent on killing Hitler and, if he could not get a bomb, he told Oster he would use a pistol instead. 'There is not a chance in a hundred,' warned Oster. 'Don't try an act of insanity. You can't get Hitler alone, and in the antechamber there are all those adjutants, orderlies and visitors. You wouldn't have an opportunity to fire.'[6]

There seemed to be no way to stop Hitler from launching his disastrous attack upon the West. Nevertheless, D'Arcy Osborne, the British ambassador to the Holy See, through whom the pope communicated with the British government, wanted to keep the plan alive. As it transpired, Hitler postponed his attack in the West, which gave the conspirators some breathing space to reconsider their options and, anyway, there were more immediate concerns for Oster and his co-conspirators – Müller's activities had been uncovered.

An old enemy of Müller, a Benedictine monk and agent of the SS Intelligence Unit II/B, Herman Keller, had been following Müller's movements and, through his contacts in Rome, had found out what Joey Ox was involved in. As the report Keller submitted to his SS handlers had foreign connections, it was passed on to the Abwehr. It was understood that Müller would be arrested within days.

Müller was told to see Canaris. The admiral had a plan.

Canaris instructed Müller to write one of his usual reports for the Abwehr, but in this one he would detail information he had received from the Vatican of a pre-war plot to remove Hitler from power. The report would be deliberately vague but was to include the names of a general who had already been killed during the invasion of Poland as well as General Walter Reichenau, an ardent Hitler supporter. Canaris knew that if the plot included Reichenau, Hitler would not believe a word of it. Canaris proved to be right, with the Führer dismissing the report as '*schmarren*' (nonsense).[7] Though disaster had been averted, Müller stayed away from Rome throughout most of December to let the dust settle.

For his part, the pope was undeterred by recent setbacks and, on 12 January 1940, Pius saw Osborne in person and committed himself to discussing the overthrow of Hitler with Britain. Osborne relayed the conversation in writing to Lord Halifax, marked 'Secret'. 'If the German generals could be assured of peace with Great Britain … they were prepared to replace the present German Government by a "*Verhandlungs-fänige Regierung*" – a government with which it was possible to negotiate – and then to reach a settlement in Eastern Europe with the British Government.' This would see the restoration of Poland and Czechoslovakia, but the Anschluss with Austria would not be affected.

Pius was, understandably, very careful with his words. He made it quite clear to Osborne that he was unable to guarantee the German generals 'could effect the change of government of which they spoke or that, even if they did so, they would be any more reliable than Hitler'.[8] Pius, though, did state that the generals in question were in no way associated with the Nazi Party. He also emphasized to Osborne the need for absolute secrecy for, if Hitler got wind of the plot against him, the lives if the unnamed generals would be 'forfeit'.

Osborne took the pope's warning onboard. He spoke to no one else about his meeting and wrote his report personally and made no copies. It was sent directly to Halifax by diplomatic bag, not trusting to any telecommunications system that could potentially be hacked.

Osborne's next meeting with the pope was very cloak and dagger. Osborne was summoned to a midnight rendezvous in the Vatican on 7 February 1940. He was told not to dress formally as he usually would for an audience of the Pope and if anyone should find out about his nighttime excursion he was to state that his meeting was with the head of the pope's private household, the Maestro di Camera.

In his papal apartment, Pius told Osborne that he had been contacted again, 'by a reliable intermediary [no doubt meaning Müller] of German military circles'. Osborne pressed Pius for the names of these generals but all that the pope would concede was that they included a well-known and high-ranking general 'of sufficient importance to be taken seriously'.

In his report on the meeting he sent to Halifax, Osborne related how the overthrow of Hitler was seen by the Abwehr conspirators:

> A part of the Army (proportion and influence unspecified) would like a change of government and to get rid of Hitler. They would not propose to start their action, if they take it, in Berlin, but elsewhere. There would be, for a time, two governments and a more or less serious civil war in Germany. The anti-Hitler authority would have to be a military dictatorship, but this would be temporary. It would be replaced by a government, described as 'democratic', 'conservative' and 'moderate'. It would be decentralised and federal in nature.

Austria and the Sudetenland would remain as part of a Greater Germany. It was made clear that the conspirators would only act against Hitler if they received the assurances they sought from Britain.[9]

Halifax discussed Osborne's letter with Chamberlain and even sent a copy to King George. Remarkably, the king had been told two weeks earlier by his cousin, Queen Marie of Yugoslavia, that she had heard of a German plot to assassinate Hitler. It really seemed that there was an opposition movement that was gathering momentum inside Germany. This, coupled with Osborne's stated belief that the pope seriously appeared to believe that the conspirators meant business, gave the British government real hope.

Halifax replied to Osborne on 17 February. Though willing to discuss a deal with the conspirators, the British could not commit to any peace arrangements without the consent of their French allies: 'If His Majesty's Government were [sic] convinced that the intermediaries who approached

His Holiness represented principals in Germany who had both the intention and the power to perform what they promised, His Majesty's Government would be willing to consider with the French Government any enquiries that those principals might make.' Here, then, we have in writing, the British government demonstrating its willingness to support the assassination of the head of state of a foreign country, though, of course, not in quite so many words.

The sticking point, unfortunately, was France. No German could forget what had happened after the First World War, when France had imposed punitive reparations upon Germany which led to a virtual collapse in the German economy and the social unrest which had led to the rise of the Nazi Party. Through Müller, the conspirators had made it clear that there would be no 'Compiègne' and no change to Germany's Rhine border with France. If Halifax and Chamberlain could have known how quickly France would be overrun in just a couple of months' time their response to the conspirators' appeals might have been quite different, and the great conflagration which spread across western Europe in May 1940 might never have happened. The only other point which Halifax and Chamberlain were insistent on was that Austria should be allowed to choose whether it wanted to remain tied to Germany or regain its independence.

In the midst of all this, the day before Halifax's reply, 16 February, Lady Halifax and son had visited the pope, escorted by Osborne, who wrote about this to Halifax on the 19th: 'He [the Pope] drew me aside at the end of the audience to tell me that the German military circles mentioned in my previous letters had confirmed their intention, or their desire, to effect a change of government.' No doubt showing his frustration at all this talk and no action, Osborne said to Pius: 'if they wanted a change of government, why didn't they get on with it.'

That was the crux of the matter. The British government had indicated that it was willing to negotiate with a new German government. Though there were still differences between the demands of the conspirators and those of the British, these could be dealt with in due course. It was now up to Oster and his co-conspirators to bring down Hitler. On 11 March, the British government re-affirmed that it was willing to discuss peace terms with the Germans providing the following were undertaken:

1. The removal of Hitler
2. The rule of law would be reinstated
3. There would be no war in western Europe
4. Poland should be liberated
5. Other territories (except Austria) should be allowed to determine their own future subject to a plebiscite
6. An armistice would be arranged through the Pope

To help show that the new government had not simply surrendered all the gains Germany had made under Hitler, Britain agreed to allow Germany to hold Austria. This was good enough for the Oster group. But still, they had not come up with a means of assassinating Hitler and for managing the change of regime.

As in 1938, plans were drawn up to seize key locations across Berlin and to round up those who might resist the coup. General Witzleben had been transferred to the Western Front in anticipation of the invasion of France, taking command of the First Army, but Helldorf's police could be counted on to help with the necessary arrests. General Halder arranged for his deputy, Generalleutnant Carl-Heinrich von Stülpnagel, to take charge of the detailed planning of the coup. Once the conspirators had secured control of Berlin, Beck would deliver a broadcast from the captured radio network and notices would be placed in the newspapers, announcing that the Army had taken control of the government and that a state of emergency had been declared and martial law had been imposed. This would be followed by a further announcement that elections would soon be held and that peace talks would be undertaken with the Allies.

All that the conspirators needed now was the support of the Army. The entire secret operation with the pope and the British government, as it had unfolded so far, was laid out by Müller and Oster's deputy, Hans von Dohnanyi, in what was to be known as the 'X-Report' (Müller, remember was 'Herr X'). This report was presented to Brauchitsch by Halder, hoping that it would finally convince the field marshal to back a move against Hitler. Brauchitsch, though, was not impressed: 'You should not have shown this to me,' he told Halder angrily. 'What is happening here is sheer treason. Under no circumstances can we be involved in this. We are at war. In peacetime you can talk about contacts with a foreign power, but in wartime soldiers cannot do that.'[10] All the efforts of Oster, Müller, Osborne, Father Leiber and, especially, the pope, had been for nought.

The truth is that no coup could have succeeded at that time, as Brauchitsch later conceded: 'Of course I could have had Hitler arrested and even imprisoned him,' he told lawyer Otto John, one of the conspirators to have survived the war:

> Easily! I had enough officers loyal to me who would have carried out even that order if given by me. But that was not the problem. Why should I have initiated action against Hitler – tell me that? It would have been action against the German people. The German people were pro-Hitler.[11]

Within the echo chamber of the resistance this was not generally appreciated but the reaction against the perpetrators of the 20 July 1944 assassination attempt, which will later be touched upon, demonstrates just how wisely Brauchitsch had judged the mood of the majority of Germans.

At the same time that Oster was in communication with the British government via the Vatican, others in the opposition were looking elsewhere for external support for regime change in Germany. Ulrich von Hassell was a career diplomat who, in 1932, became the German Ambassador to Italy. He was recalled from Rome in 1938 following disagreements with the newly-appointed foreign minister, von Ribbentrop, but he continued to work for the German Foreign Office, being given the task of reporting on economic conditions across Europe.

Hassell travelled frequently to Switzerland and Italy as well as the German-occupied territories, making contact with like-minded individuals who opposed the regime in Berlin. His anti-Nazi views must have become widely known, as he was approached, unofficially, by James Lonsdale-Bryans, a well-travelled old Etonian and a member of Pall Mall's exclusive gentlemen's club Brooks's. Lonsdale Bryans was a friend or acquaintance of numerous diplomats both in London and abroad and, in November 1939, he approached Lord Halifax with the suggestion that he might be able to use his many contacts to stop a war that no one seemed to want except Hitler. Receiving what he considered to be a cautious approval from Halifax, Lonsdale-Bryans set off on his self-appointed mission to save Europe from catastrophe.

Lonsdale-Bryans had moved to Rome the previous month where he met Count Detalmo Biroli who was just about to marry Hassell's daughter Fey. Over the course of the following weeks, Lonsdale-Bryans met Biroli and his wife dozens of times, and the English gentleman returned to London with an unsigned letter from the Italian aristocrat which contained the peace terms sought by the German opposition as perceived by Hassell.

Halifax was reluctant to meet Lonsdale-Bryans again but, through his friend, Lord Brocket, a close associate of Chamberlain, he did see the Foreign Secretary a second time on 8 January 1940. This time, having read the statement from Biroli, Halifax took Lonsdale-Bryans a little more seriously. He agreed that Lonsdale-Bryans could explore the opposition's proposals further, providing that the Foreign Secretary's name was not mentioned in any of the discussions. Halifax, however, did instruct the British Ambassador in Rome, Sir Percy Loraine, to help Lonsdale-Bryans but he stressed that the latter was acting entirely of his own accord and his mission had no official status of any kind.

Eventually, Hassell and Lonsdale-Bryans were able to meet in neutral Switzerland on 22 February 1940. This must have presented an extraordinary scene, with Hassell acting very cautiously and refusing to name the members of the opposition with whom he was in contact, and Lonsdale-Bryans declaring himself to be the 'English Envoy Extraordinary (if not plenipotentiary) of the First Secretary of State for Foreign Affairs for His Britannic Majesty'.[12]

As with the other representations by the opposition, all that Hassell could offer were vague promises if Britain was to support a regime change. Each of the various representations to the British government sought different terms and always without disclosing how they would dispose of the existing regime or how they would be able to take over the reins of power. It was all too insubstantial for Halifax to take seriously. What was taken seriously, however, was a letter from Lord Brocket in which he informed the Foreign Office that Lonsdale-Bryans was deeply in debt and that he expected a large financial reward for his diplomatic endeavours. He was told by Halifax that his services were no longer required and that if there was to be any further contact with Hassell it would be undertaken by a professional diplomat.

Shunned thereafter by the Foreign Office, Lonsdale-Bryans wrote bitterly:

> True to form, therefore, they let slip this unique opportunity of arriving at a solution of the European problem, provided by the amazing fact that a German of the international stature of Baron Hassell came across the frontier into Switzerland in the first year of war as an Ambassador of Peace.[13]

While Britain was still regarded as the major player in the game, it was the United States which was already selling the UK large amounts of war matériel and, if the war was a prolonged affair, would be likely to become an indispensable element in Britain's capacity to wage war. Washington's influence in London was considerable. An attempt to win over America to the cause of the resistance therefore made much sense.

In October 1939, just weeks after the outbreak of war, Adam Trott zu Solz, a German Foreign Office counsellor travelled to the United States, ostensibly to address a conference arranged by the Institute of Pacific Relations. Trott was an enigmatic character. He was a fervently-nationalistic German who largely welcomed many of Hitler's policies and beliefs. He considered Czechoslovakia to be an artificial state created by the Treaty of Versailles and believed that Germany had the right to annex the Sudetenland region, and that it was Germany's right to take Polish land to allow the expansion of the German empire. One of those who attended the conference was the British academic and historian, John Wheeler-Bennett, who spoke to Trott, and wrote the following: 'To the suggestion that a non-Nazi Germany might, as an earnest of good faith, restore some of the territorial acquisitions of Adolf Hitler, von Trott returned an uncompromising negative.'[14]

It was these sentiments that hindered his diplomatic endeavours. Indeed, he even stated that he thought Britain and France might allow Germany to re-possess its overseas colonies lost in the First World War. Nevertheless, while in the States, Trott met a former editor of the German newspaper *Berliner Tageblatt* who had emigrated to the USA. Together, they compiled a document which outlined, as they saw it, a way in which Germany's needs could be squared with Allied apprehensions.

What Trott wanted was the re-establishment of Germany as a major world power by peaceful means and he saw that war with Britain and

France would destroy both his country and his own aspirations. Somehow, Hitler had to be stopped.

Regardless of the extreme nature of his views, Trott's proposals were passed on to the US Department of State, the Canadian Ministry of External Affairs, and the British Embassy in Washington. Trott also wrote directly to Lord Halifax. He told the British Foreign Secretary that the war being fought was one against fascism and the Nazi Party, not Germany, and that action against Hitler would liberate not only those territories already subsumed by the Third Reich, but also the German people who had been unwittingly subjected to the arbitrary rule of the Nazis.

While the initial response from all sides was negative, and the arrest of Stevens and Best had made the British extremely cautious about engaging with any supposed members of the German resistance, the possibility of being able to bring about a peace in Europe encouraged President Roosevelt to send Sumner Welles, undersecretary at the State Department, on a peace mission to Europe in February 1940 to try to mediate an end to the war.

All these endeavours were simply too little, too late, for, on 9 April, Hitler launched his invasion of Denmark and Norway. Once again, Hitler seemed to have outwitted the Allies, and though the fighting in Norway continued into June, a German victory was assured long before then. Hitler's popularity throughout the Reich soared even higher. The conspirators had waited too long. They dared not now try to topple Hitler.

As for Trott, the FBI had become suspicious of his ability to be able to travel freely during time of war and the Bureau began to monitor his movements. Others became wary of Trott, and his efforts to enlist external support for the resistance in Germany came to nothing.

Among those who had been watching Trott was the Gestapo and, when given free rein to prosecute anyone suspected of opposing Hitler after the failed 20 July assassination attempt, he was one of the thousands arrested, and subsequently hanged in Berlin's Plötzensee Prison on 26 August 1944.

On 26 September 1944, in that round-up of all suspected dissident individuals and groups following the failed Valkyrie assassination, Joey Ox was arrested by the Gestapo and handed over to the SS and taken to their headquarters in Berlin at 8 Prinz-Albrecht Strasse. He had long known such a day would come and had put his affairs in order. Though Müller tried to stick to his story that his visits to Rome had been to elicit information helpful to German military intelligence, he was presented with a large dossier of documents, many of which should have been destroyed by Oster and his co-conspirators, which left no doubt that he was involved in a plot to take down the Third Reich. He was told he would be executed. He expected nothing less.

After the SS headquarters was severely damaged by Allied bombers on 3 February 1945, Müller and the other prisoners were moved out of Berlin to concentration camps. For Müller that meant Buchenwald. On 4 April he was moved again, this time to Flossenbürg.

On 8 April 1945, with the Third Reich crumbling into ruin, Joey Ox, his face swollen and bruised from the beatings he had received, was taken to the execution yard where a gallows stood with a row of hooks from which nooses hung. According to an eyewitness, a Soviet prisoner, Müller looked content, having accepted his fate. As he stood at the foot of the six steps that led up to the gallows, knowing that he was going to die, Kaltenbrunner, the camp's commandant, called a halt to the execution. Looking to Müller's influence with the pope, SS-Gruppenführer Johann Rattenhuber had telephoned Kaltenbrunner and persuaded him that it might be wise to keep Müller alive. It had been Müller's intention to seek a peace deal with the Allies through the pope; maybe, at last, Müller could fulfil his mission to save Germany from complete destruction?

Incredibly, it was Müller's subversive activities which in the end spared him from the gallows – though quite literally, at the last minute. Of course, all of this was far too late, and nothing could change the Allies' insistence that the war would only end with Germany's unconditional surrender which had been announced at Churchill's and Roosevelt's Casablanca Conference on 2 February 1943, nor could this act of clemency save Kaltenbrunner and Rattenhuber when they stood in the dock at Nuremberg. Predictably, Müller ascribed his salvation to the prayers of the pope and God's intervention, calling it 'a miracle'.

Chapter 14

Cologne, Kurt Hammerstein-Equord, September 1939; Warsaw, Polish Army, 5 October 1939

Hitler's defeat of the Polish forces in September 1939 had been his first military victory – and it merited a victory parade in the captured enemy capital. On 5 October Hitler flew to Warsaw-Okęcie Airport (today's Chopin Airport), where he was greeted by Generals Brauchitsch, Blaskowitz and Reichenau and then, in an armed convoy, set off for the centre of Warsaw.

Hitler was under no illusions that he was likely to be a target as his visit had been pre-announced. Consequently, the city centre was sealed off and hundreds of police patrols roamed the swastika-draped streets which had been cleared of civilians. Machine guns were set up on the roofs of taller buildings and only German military personnel were admitted to the places directly adjacent to the parade route. The residents were forbidden to open windows or leave their apartments or houses under threat of death. Additionally, the Germans held twelve high-ranking hostages as security against a potential attack, including the former mayor of the city, Stefan Starzyński, in the basement of the City Hall. Despite all this, the remnants of the Polish Army planned to blow up Hitler's car.

The man organizing the assassination attempt was General Michał Karaszewicz-Tokarzewski, who in the last days of September created the beginnings of the future Polish underground organization which caused the Germans considerable trouble. Along with Major Franciszek Niepokólczycki, commander of the sapper company in the city's Citadel, they planned to place two massive crates (each holding 250kg of TNT) at a point which it was predicted Hitler would pass after he had taken the salute at the victory parade – where two roads crossed, the Nowy Świat and the Aleje Jerozolimskie. One load was placed near the building of Bank Gospodarstwa Krajowego, on the western corner of the crossroads, with the other one in the building of the Railway Directorate on the eastern corner. The crates were covered with earth and the road surface patched over. Warsaw had been heavily bombed during the fighting and an uneven stretch of road would not appear at all suspicious among piles of rubble from the damaged buildings.

The task of laying the explosives was undertaken by the 60th Battalion of Engineers of the Armia Modlin. They were ordered to attach cables to the explosives and run them to the basement of one of the ruined houses in the vicinity and wait for further orders.[1]

Hitler duly saluted his victorious parading troops for more than two hours. According to one Warsaw resident, Józef Małgorzecki: 'The soldiers, shaved, arrogant, rode cars, others sat on fat horses pulling cannons, mortars, heavy machine guns. Heavy and light tanks rode with a creak of tracks. There was a terrible silence on the sidewalks.'

As the last of his soldiers passed his dais, Hitler climbed into his open-top Mercedes for his tour of the city. Standing in the passenger seat, saluting to all who cared to watch, Hitler completed his tour, returned to the airport and flew back to Berlin that evening.

So, what went wrong? It is said that Niepokólczycki (who later operated with the Polish Home Army under the codename 'Teodor') was unable to reach the crossroads to issue the order to detonate the explosives because the Germans had closed the streets where Hitler was supposed to pass. The officer present on the scene was ordered to act on his own initiative, but only in the event that there was no doubt that he saw Hitler himself in front of him. There was too much at stake to be allowed to make a mistake with the hostages in German hands. Not knowing who was taking the parade – Hitler or Blaskowitz or Brauchitsch – he hesitated and did not give the signal to trigger the detonator at the moment when the procession of cars flashed in front of his nose.

The TNT and missile charges were disarmed a few days later and moved elsewhere.

It was during the German invasion of Poland that a longstanding enemy of Hitler saw an opportunity to dispose of the man he had always detested. That man was sixty-one-year-old Generaloberst Kurt Gebhard Adolf Philipp Freiherr von Hammerstein-Equord who had been Commander-in-Chief of the German Army from 1930 until 1934 when he was forced to resign due to his opposition to the new regime. He had repeatedly advised President Hindenburg not to let Hitler into government, calling the Nazis 'filthy pigs' and a 'gang of criminals'. Hindenburg had, as we know, ignored Hammerstein-Equord's appeals. Nevertheless, it was the president, who still had some degree of influence, who shielded Hammerstein-Equord from the Night of the Long Knives purge.

Hammerstein-Equord was stunned with Hitler's ruthless slaying of those he perceived as his enemies in those nocturnal murders (which actually lasted for three days) in the summer of 1934, in particular the killing of his old friend Kurt von Schleiche. From that moment on, Hammerstein-Equord's hatred of Hitler multiplied.

With the outbreak of war in 1939, the former commander of the Army was recalled to military service, being given command of Army Group A during the invasion of Poland. This was not the important position it may sound as Army Group A was not involved in the operations against the Poles. It was positioned along the Westwall (more familiarly known as the Siegfried Line) the string of bunkers, tunnels and tank-traps along the German border which roughly faced the French Maginot Line but also extended farther north along the Lower Rhine as far as Kleve on the border with the Netherlands. Work on this latter section only began with the outbreak of war and was in its primary stages of construction when Hammerstein-Equord arrived to take over command of Army Group A.

Hammerstein-Equord at last saw a chance to get close enough to Hitler – close enough to kill him. He invited Hitler to visit him at his headquarters in Cologne where, he told Beck that 'a fatal accident will occur'. It has been speculated that this accident might take the form of the detonation of a grenade in a concrete bunker during an inspection by Hitler.[2] Hammerstein wanted the British to be informed of his plan to eliminate Hitler beforehand so that they would not try to exploit the chaos that would inevitably occur in Germany following Hitler's death and the dismantling of the Nazi governmental structure. This was all relayed to the conspirators at Abwehr headquarters in Berlin by one of Hammerstein's aides.[3]

Though he repeatedly asked Hitler to visit Army Group A, arguing that the men were missing out on the glory the rest of the Army was experiencing in the great victory over the Poles and that a visit from the Führer would help maintain morale, Hitler did not take up the offer.

It does appear that Hammerstein-Equord would have put his plan into practice if he had had the chance, as he was described by Heinrich Brüning, who had served as German chancellor between 1930 and 1932, as 'the only man who could remove Hitler – a man without nerves'.[4]

As soon as it was apparent that the Poles would be beaten, and that the Allies were not going to undertake any serious incursions into Germany, Hitler transferred Hammerstein-Equord to Defensive District VIII in Silesia, before relieving him of his command due to his negative attitude towards the Nazi regime.

Hammerstein-Equord maintained his opposition to Hitler but was never arrested. He died of cancer in 1943. Due to his former rank he was entitled to an official funeral in Berlin, but this would have meant his coffin would have been draped in the flag of the Reich – the Nazi swastika. This his family could not countenance, and he was buried instead in his family grave at Steinhorst. Hitler sent a wreath, but this was intentionally mislaid by his family and left behind in Berlin.

Two of Hammerstein-Equord's sons, Kunrat and Ludwig, who were both officers in the Army, became heavily involved in the Valkyrie plot but were some of the very few who survived the reprisals that followed the failed coup.

Chapter 15

Bürgerbräukeller, Munich, Georg Elser, 8 November 1939

While Hans Oster and his fellow conspirators talked endlessly about assassinating Hitler, one man put such thoughts into deeds. Georg Elser was a committed communist and he hated Adolf Hitler. He was a skilled and qualified carpenter, making cabinets for a clock manufacturer among the various jobs he had found which had enabled him to leave the unhappy home of his parents. But, along with so many in Germany, the Depression of the 1930s brought with it unemployment and, for Elser, it meant a return to his parents in the village of Königsbronn.[1] He was diametrically opposed to National Socialism and saw communism as the solution not only to his problems, but those of Germany – and he decided to remove the greatest obstacle to a future communist Germany, the Nazi leader himself. As he later admitted, killing Hitler became an 'obsession'.

Like Maurice Bavaud, Elser travelled to Munich to watch the Beer Hall Putsch celebrations. Strangely, it was the very same celebrations, those of November 1938, at which Maurice Bavaud had failed to shoot the Führer, that Elser attended. Unlike Bavaud, Elser was not going to take a chance on trying to hit a moving target. He knew that Hitler always gave a speech in the Bürgerbräukeller to open the celebrations on the evening before the procession and this, he considered, might give him the opportunity to plant a bomb that would take out not only Hitler but many of his closest followers. Elser was able to enter the Bürgerbräukeller at the end of that evening's festivities and examine the hall – and a plan began to form in his mind.

Elser travelled back to Königsbronn and began to prepare for the assassination of the German leader. Elser was a craftsman and he undertook his mission with considerable skill and much guile. He had found work at the Waldenmaier armament factory in Heidenheim, from which he was able to steal fuses and gunpowder. Having decided that he would plant his bomb in the pillar directly behind the speaker's podium he returned to Munich in early April 1939, visiting the Bürgerbräukeller armed with a camera, enabling him to work out the precise details of his plan.

He then found work in the Vollmer quarry in Königsbronn, from where he took explosives and detonators. Knowing nothing about explosives, he practised with the stolen items in the fields around his home until he was satisfied that he knew how to prepare and detonate a bomb with sufficient power to kill many people. He revealed nothing of his plans to either his friends or work colleagues, conducting all his preparations at the home of his girlfriend's parents – the Schmauder family in Schnaitheim – in the evenings and at weekends.

In August he travelled down to Munich with his tools and explosives and clock parts which had been given to him in lieu of wages from his earlier job with the clockmaker.

He registered with the local authorities, found lodgings and sought work just as any normal person would. Once he has settled in, Elser began taking his evening meal at the Bürgerbräukeller. He would arrive at 21.00 hours, eat his dinner, and then sneak up to the gallery of the functions room. He would then hide in a storeroom until the bar closed for the night and everybody went home. Then Elser would start to work.

Behind the dais and lectern where Hitler would be standing to deliver his speech at the next Putsch celebrations was a thick stone pillar that supported an upper gallery. This gallery ran the whole length of the hall. Elser reckoned that if he could bring down the pillar the gallery would collapse, bringing the whole of it down on Hitler and many of his cronies.

Night after night, Elser chipped away at the plaster and the brickwork of the pillar in the dimmed light of a torch covered with a handkerchief, carrying away the debris each morning in a briefcase as he slipped out of the building via a rear door. It took him thirty or more nights to create the cavity for his bomb, which he built during the daytime using the workshop of a local woodworker with whom he had become friends. By the end of October everything was ready and, on the night of 1–2 November, he installed the bomb in the pillar. The annual celebrations were just a week away.

After dropping off his tools with his sister, Maria, in Stuttgart, on 6 November 1939, Elser returned to Munich the next day and that night made his final checks and set the timer for the following evening when Hitler would be delivering his speech to a packed Bürgerbräukeller hall.

The celebrations in Munich that year would be unlike any before. The weather was forecast to be bad and there was some doubt whether Hitler would be able to fly down from Berlin as planned. But to miss this key event in the Nazi calendar was unthinkable, so Hitler flew down to Munich despite the deteriorating weather conditions. However, as predicted, fog closed in on Munich during the day and the airport was closed. Hitler's pilot also advised the Führer that it would be dangerous to take to the air.

As Hitler was heavily involved with the planning for the upcoming invasion of France, he did not want to be stuck in Munich, so he decided to take the train back to the German capital that night. The railway administration saw only one possibility for working Hitler's private train into the schedule – by leaving Munich at 2131 hours.[2] This, though, would mean he would be unable to stay around to listen to the yarns of his old comrades as he usually did.

As with previous years Hitler stood up to deliver his speech to the 'Old Guard' of the Nazi Party, but on this occasion at 2000 hours, thirty minutes earlier than usual. After his hour-long speech, Hitler left the gathering swiftly to catch the train. The time was 2107 hours. Just thirteen minutes later, at exactly 2120, Elser's bomb exploded. 'Suddenly, there was a bright light, and in the same instant we heard a terrible blast,' recalled Emil Wipfel, a member of the SA who was at the time dismantling the sound system. 'I was thrown back two metres, falling into the rubble, whilst all hell broke loose above me. When I came to my senses, I was lying on my stomach with my right arm over the foot of my comrade, Schata. I did not know at the time that he was already dead. I couldn't move my left arm, and my feet were stuck fast… . I realized later that a section of the roof, that had fallen across the Führer's podium, was on me. I suspect it was only held up and prevented from crushing me by a broken table nearby, and perhaps by the body of my comrade.'[3]

Elser's bomb killed three and wounded a further sixty-seven, five of whom later died of their injuries, but Hitler and his acolytes were long gone. Elser was also far away when his bomb exploded; in fact he was heading towards the Konstanz and the Swiss border. When he had checked out the border the previous year, during the planning of his escape route, he found the post unguarded, but that was before the outbreak of war. Now it was manned.

The two border guards on duty were Waldemar Zipperer and Xaver Rieger. A few weeks later, the latter spoke about the night of 8 November:

> Between 8.40 and 8.45, a figure stepped out from behind the building and, after quickly surveying the area, made for the border, moving stealthily, yet very rapidly. The distance between me and the figure was about fifteen to twenty metres. When I saw the figure, I immediately ran quickly and cautiously toward the man, while simultaneously readying my carbine. When I was confident that I would be heard, I shouted at him.[4]

A weak attempt to bluff his way out of the situation he was in by saying that he was looking for a friend did not convince the guards and he was taken into the border post. It was all over for Elser when he was searched. He was carrying a postcard of Bürgerbräukeller with the pillar where the bomb was placed marked in ink with a cross, a fuse, a sketch of his bomb, and a Communist Party badge.

Elser eventually confessed and, the game being up, he proudly explained in detail how he had concocted and carried out his plan. But he was tortured by the Gestapo into revealing his co-conspirators, as Hitler, and in fact most others, refused to believe that he had acted alone. Elser was not a known political revolutionary, despite his left-wing leanings. He was a skilled craftsman, an ordinary hardworking German. He would seem to be exactly the kind of person that, across Germany, had either been won over to the Nazi cause or at least generally approved of what Hitler was trying to achieve for the country. Hitler, and indeed the German press, concluded that Elser must have been encouraged to act the way he did by someone else, blaming especially the British and the Black Front. Though Elser was beaten, drugged and even hypnotized, his story did not change.

The Gestapo arrested over a hundred suspects and known family, friends, and associates of Elser but eventually had to accept that he was indeed simply a rogue male.[5] A number of those who had unwittingly aided Elser by providing him with parts, such as the owner of the quarry where he had stolen the explosives and fuses, were tortured and imprisoned. The village of Königsbronn was dubbed 'Assassinville'.[6]

Elser was sent to Dachau concentration camp. He was held without trial as a special prisoner of Adolf Hitler for over five years until executed there on 9 April 1945.

While the Black Front had been blamed in the state-controlled German press, Otto Strasser claimed that the whole incident was stage-managed by leading Nazis. This was reported in the British newspapers on 23 November 1939: 'I am convinced that the Munich explosion was organized by Hitler and the Gestapo,' said Strasser.

> I have just had definite proof from a very reliable party member. The plot was the idea of Himmler himself, who told Hess (Hitler's deputy) that he needed an attempt on Hitler to let loose a hate offensive against Britain, and in order to have a pretext to attack internal enemies ...
>
> Hess agreed on condition that there were no victims; but Himmler decided he needed victims, otherwise nobody would believe it was a real attempt. Finally, they agreed that there should be victims, but people of no importance.
>
> Everything was carried out according to a prearranged programme. The beer cellar was insured by a Swiss company, and Munich hospital was ordered to be ready. The bomb was placed after Hitler went out. Immediately after the explosion an order was given to say it was an attempt organized by the [British] intelligence service.[7]

Whilst it was evident that Elser had acted alone, such was the outcry in the German media against Britain over the attempted assassination, the SD decided to create 'proof' that the British were involved. As it transpired, the British Secret Service had already fallen into a trap the day after the bombing in what is known as the 'Venlo Incident', which will be related in the next chapter.

The suspicion that the whole incident had been contrived by Himmler surfaced once again shortly after the war. Hans Rothfels wrote that 'the installation of a time bomb would have been impossible without the assistance of the Gestapo'.[8] This view was repeated in a brief article in the *Manchester Guardian* on 28 January 1948. Providing little detail, the article stated that the entire episode was stage-managed by Reinhard Heydrich, head of the Reich Main Security Office (which included the Gestapo and the SD) under Himmler. According to the article, the German General der Infanterie Georg Thomas claimed the bomb was timed to go off after Hitler had safely left the Bürgerbräukeller. 'The scheme was devised, supposedly, by Goebbels and Himmler, the objective of the assassination attempt being designed to shatter an embryo peace movement among high Army officers who distrusted Hitler's Blitzkrieg.'

It was not until the transcript of Elser's interrogations, edited by Lother Gruchman and released in 1969–70, that such conspiracy theories could finally be dismissed. Elser really did plan, prepare and execute the whole operation entirely by himself.[9]

Chapter 16

Venlo, Holland, Sigismund Best & Richard Stevens, 9 November 1939

Britain's Prime Minister Neville Chamberlain has not been treated kindly by history. His laudable efforts to try and avoid war have marked him down as an 'appeaser'. Yet the war he tried to prevent became the most destructive conflict the world has known, resulting in the deaths of more than sixty million people. Though no one could have envisaged the full horror that was unleashed across the world during the Second World War, the experiences of the 1914–18 war served due notice that any future conflict would be unparalleled in its severity. So, even though war had been declared on 3 September 1939, Chamberlain still sought some means by which peace could be restored.

He was aware that senior German figures had attempted to enlist support from his government in opposing Hitler before the outbreak of war and he hoped that MI6, the British Secret Service (SIS) might, therefore, be able to make contact with opposition leaders in Germany. As it transpired, Hitler also had no wish to be involved in war with Britain, a country he much admired, and he, too, wished to find a way to reach a settlement with the UK. But the problem was that neither Chamberlain, who was being widely castigated for his seemingly ineffectual dealings with the German chancellor, nor Hitler who, because of his unbroken series of victories had never been more popular with the German people, could be seen to be openly seeking a peaceful arrangement with the enemy. But if some kind of deal could be arranged that both leaders would accept, maybe the conflict in Europe could be brought to a conclusion without the rest of the world becoming involved.

Hope that a behind-the-scenes arrangement could be reached seemed a possibility through the activities of a British SIS officer, Captain Sigismund Payne Best, who was working under the cover of being a businessman living with his Dutch wife in The Hague, in still neutral

Holland. The SIS were well aware of the dissension in the officer ranks of the German Army and hoped that, if those opposed to Hitler could be assured of British support in the event of a coup, the war could be brought to a speedy conclusion before too much blood had been shed. Best had established contacts within Germany but, by the very nature of his job, he had kept a very low profile. With the outbreak of war, he decided to throw off his cloak of secrecy and work more openly in a bid to reach out to those in Germany who sought to bring down Hitler.

Through a somewhat mysterious German exile, known to Best as Dr Franz Fischer, the SIS had for some time received what it considered to be reliable, and often valuable, information passed to him by a major in the Luftwaffe named Solms. What Best and the SIS did not know was that Fischer was working for the SD.

Franz Fischer had been forced to flee from Germany to escape charges of embezzlement. He had set himself up in Paris where he became friendly with anti-Nazi exiles in the French capital. But he had been unable to escape the long reach of the SD, who offered to quash all charges against him if he worked for them. This he agreed to do, betraying his new friends. After this success, Fischer was sent to the Dutch capital to repeat his trickery.[1]

Fischer let it be known that Solms had some very important news to impart but that he would only do so when assured that Fischer had made contact with a senior figure in British Intelligence. It was made clear that Solms would not say anything further until such contact had been established and that a face-to-face meeting could be held with the British representative.

Best was authorized to meet Fischer at the beginning of September 1939, whom he described as 'a likeable little man' but who was 'very far from a model of discretion'. Best, of course, had no idea he was being played.

Best wanted to meet Solms at The Hague or in Amsterdam, but Solms, so the story went, could only be absent from his post for a few fleeting hours and an aeroplane flight into either of those cities would be impossible for him. He could, however, travel to the Dutch town (now a city) of Venlo which was just a couple of miles from the German border. This was because Germans living near the frontier were still allowed to cross the border to shop in nearby places in Holland.

Best met Fischer and Sohms in a hotel in Venlo. According to Best, the German major was 'a big, bluff, self-confident fellow, a Bavarian and inclined to talk as big as he looked.' Nevertheless, Best believed that Sohms was merely the 'errand boy' for far more important people, and indeed he was – Sohms was acting on behalf of Major Walther Friedrich Schellenberg of the Foreign Intelligence (counter-espionage) section of the SD. Best had swallowed the bait.

A second meeting was arranged, and this time Sohms revealed that there was a 'big' conspiracy to remove Hitler from power in which some of the highest-ranking generals were involved. He said he could not give any further details, and that the leaders of the conspiracy would only talk to Best directly. In textbook spy fashion, they made arrangements to communicate, devising a code which only the conspirators would know.

All this was passed back to London and received approval from the Foreign Secretary. Lord Halifax was as keen as any in the British government to avoid a deepening of the conflict with Germany and he ordered Best to proceed, though cautiously.

Sure enough, a few days later, Fischer allegedly received a phone call from an officer he knew in Berlin, using the secret code. The message passed on to Best was that a German general wanted to meet him but that he wanted to be assured that Best was indeed a British secret agent. Best was given the wording of a news item that the BBC was to broadcast in the daily German News Bulletin. This, Best later wrote, was easily arranged and, on 11 October, the paragraph in question was broadcast twice.

At around the same time Sohms stated that he believed he was being watched by the Gestapo and that he would have to lie low for a while. In reality, Solms had been replaced with two SS-officers, working under the aliases of Leutnant Grosch and Hauptman von Seidlitz. Nevertheless, all this intrigue suggested to Best that he was on to 'a big thing' and that it might be more than he could, or indeed should, handle by himself. He therefore decided to ask Major Richard Henry Stevens, who was working covertly for the SIS as chief of the passport control office at the British Embassy in the Hague, to join him at the next meeting.

There were, though, fears of a German invasion and the Dutch Army had been mobilized. Roadblocks and guard posts had been set up on roads leading to the frontier and anyone wishing to travel to the border had to establish their identity before being permitted to pass. The chances of being able to organize clandestine meetings were slim without approval from the Dutch authorities.

When details of the proposed meetings were presented to the head of the Dutch Intelligence Service, Major General van Oorshot, he saw no reason to withhold his permission. But, as the discussions were taking place on Dutch soil, he considered that he should have full disclosure of what was said between the British and the Germans. For that reason, he instructed a member of his staff to attend the meetings. This officer, Lieutenant Klop, was to see to it that the talks should not degenerate into any violation of Holland's neutrality. The last thing the Dutch wanted was to give the Germans any reason to invade.[2]

The next meeting was to be on 19 October, when the Germans would be at the small village of Dinxperlo on the frontier. Best's party included Fischer, Stevens and Klop who went in the guise of an English officer, Captain Coppens. When Grosch and von Seidlitz arrived at the pre-arranged café they appeared so nervous in such a public place that Best contacted a friend in nearby Arnhem to see if they could talk at that person's house in privacy. This was agreed and Best drove them there in his car.

Despite the precautions, all that the Germans would say was that they had been sent to check out the practicality of crossing the border and meeting the British. They declared that they had found no difficulty in crossing into Holland and that they were certain more senior officers would be attending following meetings.

The first of those following meetings took place on 25 October. This time there had been problems crossing the border and the Germans had tried to cross into Holland through a wood and had been spotted and arrested. Klop was able to clarify the situation with the border guards and the Germans were let through. This time, Hauptman von Seidlitz's place had been taken by Hauptman Schemmel, which was the cover name for nobody less than Walter Schellenberg himself. The cat wanted to see the mouse in person.

Schemmel told Best and Stevens that the Germans had suffered heavy losses in the invasion of Poland and that Germany was not in a strong enough position, both economically and militarily, to continue with the war. The General Staff had explained all this to Hitler, but

The Feldherrnhalle on the Odeonsplatz, where the 1923 Putsch came to a bloody end. (© *Thomas Wolf, www.foto-tw.de*)

1 April 1924. Defendants in the Beer Hall Putsch trial. From left to right: Heinz Pernet, Friedrich Weber, Wilhelm Frick, Hermann Kriebel, Ludendorff, Hitler, Wilhelm Brückner, Ernst Röhm, and Robert Wagner. (*Heinrich Hoffmann, Bundesarchiv, Bild 102-00344A*)

Munich's Hofbräuhaus today. (*Author*)

Inside the Hofbräuhaus. (*Author*)

Hitler enjoying a glass of his mineral water at the Osteria Bavaria on 5 October 1932. (*National Archives at College Par*)

The sharp bend in the road from Berchtesgaden to the Berghof where Otto Strasser claimed Hitler's driver Julius Schreck was killed in a failed assassination bid in 1935. (*Author*)

The former Hanslbauer hotel in Bad Wiessee where Ernst Röhm, head of the SA, was arrested on 30 June 1934. It is now the Hotel Lederer am See. (*Author*)

The point along the route of the procession commemorating the 1923 Putsch as it passes the Heilig-Geist-Kirche where Maurice Bavaud waited in 1939. (*Author*)

The ruins of the Bürgerbräukeller after Georg Elser's bomb had detonated, give some indication of just how close Hitler had been to serious injury or death. (*Historic Military Press*)

The interrogation room in Dachau where Georg Elser would have been interrogated. (*Author*)

Georg Elser's cell at Dachau. (*Author*)

Army Group South headquarters (*Hauptquartier heeresgruppe süd*) in Poltava was located in one of the buildings of the Poltava pedagogical Institute. Now it is the first academic building of the Poltava national pedagogical University named after V. G. Korolenko. It is situated at 2 Ostrogradski Street. (*Author*)

Memorial to the derailment of a train by the Polish town of Strych which it was hoped would be Hitler's *Führersonderzug* on 9 June 1942. (*Author*)

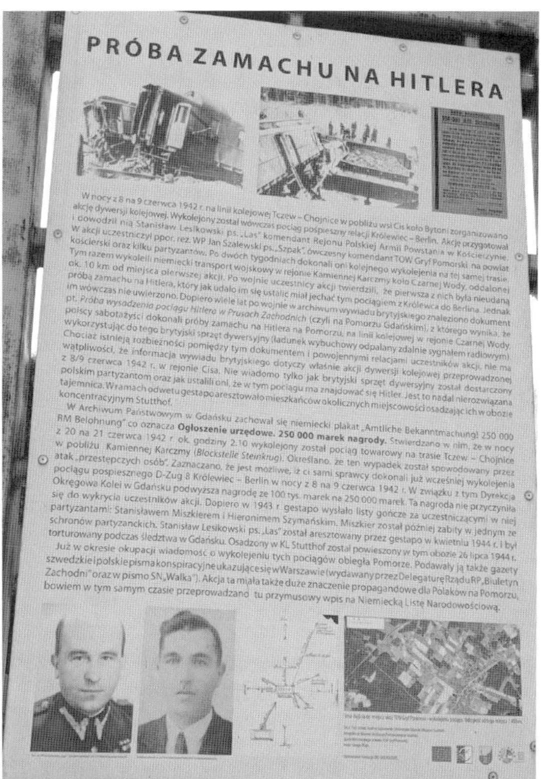

On the approach to Strych centre is an information board relating the derailment, which includes photographs of the wreckage of the train. It is said that 150 Germans were killed in the crash and that posters were displayed offering 250 Reichsmarks for information leading to the arrest of the perpetrators. It is evident that the locals are very proud of their attempt at killing Hitler. (*Author*)

The famous photograph of Hitler with Stauffenberg (standing erect on the left) at the Wolfsschanze 15 July 1944, the day that the *Valkyrie* orders were issued in Berlin before it was known that Stauffenberg had been unable to attempt the assassination. (*Bundesarchiv, Bild 146-1984-079-02 / CC-BY-SA 3.0*)

Though this photograph was taken in 1943 at the Wolfsschanze, one can imagine that this scene would have been very similar to that of 20 July 1944. (*Historic Military Press*)

The ruins of the *lagebaracke* where the assassination attempt of 20 July 1944 took place.

Though basically a reinforced brick and wood structure, like many of the buildings in the Wolfsschanze, concrete was added to the walls and roof in 1943. Though just half-a-metre thick on the walls, the concrete on the roof, as can possibly be gauged from this photograph, was a metre thick. (*Author*)

The still impressive remains of the Guest Bunker (*Gästebunker*) which was where Hitler was living in July 1944 as his own personal bunker was undergoing refurbishment and reinforcement. (*Author*)

On the left of this photograph can be the scant remains of the last checkpoint that Stauffenberg had to pass through before he could leave the Wolfschanze and head for Rastenburg airfield. (*Author*)

Rastenburg airfield is still in use, being known as the Ketrzyn Wilamowo Airport. (*Author*)

Stauffenberg's office in the Bendlerblock where he planned *Valkyrie*.

The courtyard of the Bendlerblock where the wounded Stauffenberg, along with Olbricht, Haeften and Mertz von Quirnheim were summarily executed. (*Author*)

A view from the bottom of the path up to the ruins of the Berghof across the route Hitler used to take to the teahouse each morning. Though the road seen here differs from the original one, the old path through the trees can still be found. (*Author*)

Hitler walking to the outside viewing area of the Mooslahnerkopf Teehaus. (*Historic Military Press*)

This outside area is all that is to be found of the Mooslahnerkopf Teehaus. The view enjoyed by Hitler, though, remains magnificent. (*Author*)

Hotel zum Türken was where the men of the RSD responsible for guarding Hitler lived when the Führer was in residence at the Berghof. (*Author*)

Little now remains to be seen of the Berghof, which was demolished by the Bavarian government in 1952, other than its retaining walls. (*Author*)

The impressive Schloss Klessheim used by Hitler for conferences and to host official guests. It is now the Salzburg Casino. (*Author*)

The railway sidings near Schloss Klessheim. (*Author*)

The ruins of the Reich Chancellery photographed in 1945. (*Historic Military Press*)

Albert Speer and Hitler shown here in happier times. They became close associates, but Speer might have been the last man to plot a scheme to assassinate Hitler. (*Bundesarchiv Bild 183-2004-1103-500*)

he refused to accept what they were saying. The Führer, therefore, had to be removed. But Hitler's popularity was so high among the German people, they believed if they assassinated him there would be widespread anger throughout Germany and chaos would result. Instead, supposedly, the conspirators would take Hitler prisoner and then force him to create a junta of officers who would begin peace negotiations. But, said Schemmel, 'We are Germans and have to think of the interests of our own country first. Before we take any steps against Hitler, we want to know whether England and France are ready to grant us peace which is both just and honourable.'[3]

The best lies are always those closest to the truth, and as discontent among some senior figures in Germany was well known in London, everything Schemmel/Schellenberg said tied in neatly with what people in London believed and wanted to hear, and, of course, had heard in similar guises in the past.

Best, therefore, received approval to continue dealing with the Germans, but to proceed with caution. Regular contact was established by Best and Stevens with the Germans at a certain hour each day. But there were limits on what could be said and, of course, nothing could at this stage be put in writing. Another face-to-face meeting was clearly necessary, and that this time a German general would be present.

The date set for the meeting was 7 November. On the day in question, Best, his driver Jan Lemmens, Stevens and Klop drove to the hotel in Venlo where they had met the Germans previously. Leaving the others at the hotel, Klop went to the border to collect the German delegation. When he got there, the Germans claimed to be very anxious about travelling deeper into Holland and with meeting in such a public place. Klop rang Best to inform him of this and suggested that they all should meet at the frontier. Klop was telephoning from a café by the border called 'Backus' which he said would be suitable for their purposes.

When at last the two parties met up, instead of the high-ranking general Best and Stevens were expecting, only Schemmel and Grosch were there. Though disappointed, they accepted that the Germans were worried about being compromised and the meeting with the elusive general was postponed until the following afternoon, and then again put back to 9 November – the day after Geoge Elser's Bürgerbräukeller bomb. As we know, Hitler and Himmler believed that Elser must have had outside help, and presumed that help came from the UK – and an opportunity to link the attempted assassination to the dastardly British was about to be handed to the Germans on a plate.

On 9 November, the men, armed with Browning automatics, set off from The Hague for the frontier and the café Backus. Best and Stevens were not happy at going so close to the border, but Klop paid a visit to the border office of the Dutch Royal Constabulary, the *Koninklijke Marechaussee*, and it was arranged that a patrol would be sent along the border as a security measure.

During the drive to the border, with Best himself at the wheel of his Buick, and Jan Lemmens merely a passenger, the increased level of precautions against a German invasion were all too obvious, which added to the already tense atmosphere in the car.

As they approached the café, Best admitted that he felt nervous. But the scene before their eyes appeared peaceful enough. There was no one in sight apart from a German customs officer 'lounging' along the road and a little girl playing a ball game with a black dog outside the café. But all was not as it seemed. Best described what happened next in his recounting of the incident:

> I let the car drift slowly along to the front of the café on my left and then reversed into the car park on the side of the building farthest from the frontier. Schaemmel was standing on the veranda at the corner and made a sign which I took to mean that our bird was inside.

Stevens got out of the car first and, as Best was about to follow suit,

> there was a sudden noise of shouting and shooting. I looked up, and through the windscreen saw a large open car drive up round the corner till our bumpers were touching. It seemed to be over-packed with rough-looking men. Two were perched on top of the hood and were firing over our heads from sub-machine guns, others were standing up in the car and on the running boards; all shouting and waving pistols. Four men jumped off almost before their car had stopped and rushed towards us shouting: 'Hands up!'

Klop was quicker on his feet, and he ran round the car and began firing back at the Germans. He shattered the windscreen of the German car, but he was outnumbered and outgunned, and he was hit, mortally wounded. Klop was dragged into Best's Buick, while Best and Stevens were handcuffed and, along with Lemmens, were bundled into the German car. Both cars were then driven off over the border into Germany.

The whole incident was over in so short a time that the Dutch frontier guards, although they were only a short distance away, could not get there in time to prevent it.

Klop died later that day and, as he was only the driver, Jan Lemmens was released by the Germans in November 1940, but Best and Stevens spent the rest of the war in various concentration camps before being freed in May 1945.

The operation achieved everything Hitler and Himmler could have wished for. Not only did it show that the British were trying to overthrow the legitimate German government, reinforcing their declaration that George Esler was a British pawn, but also that the Dutch, in the form of a member of their Intelligence Service, i.e. Klop, were violating their neutrality. This gave Hitler the pretext he needed to invade the Netherlands, which his armies did on 10 May 1940.

Chapter 17

Champs-Elysées, Paris, RAF, 27 July 1940; Champs-Elysées, Paris, Schwerin von Schwanenfeld & Hans von Voss, 21 May 1941; Location unspecified, Helmuth von Moltke, 1941; Paris, Hans-Victor von Salviati, 1942

On 10 May 1940 Hitler launched his invasion of France and the Low Countries which saw the British Expeditionary Force driven off the continent and the capitulation of France just six weeks later. It was an astonishing feat, and it was expected that Hitler was going to celebrate his great success with a victory parade in Paris as he had done in Warsaw. In anticipation of the event, large numbers of German troops were moved towards the French capital to take part in the parade.

This meant that Hitler would, for the first time, be in the open at a known location within easy striking distance of the RAF and in a static position. It was an opportunity that Air Vice-Marshal Donald Stevenson, the Director of Home Operations at the Air Ministry, could not let pass, proposing that the RAF could bomb Hitler at the review. He believed that the saluting platform would be close to the Arc de Triomphe, 'and no one can say what effect a few salvos of 40lb and 250lb bombs would be on an occasion of this kind … from our experience, provided we have good cloud cover, it is a practicable operation.'[1]

It was understood that four *gruppen* of Bf 109s and six of Bf 110s had been earmarked for the defence of Paris during the parade, amounting to around 400 fighters. These would be drawn from Luftflotten 2 and 3. This, though, did not dismay the Air Ministry planners, who reckoned that if there was a significant covering of stratocumulus the German fighters would be flying in groups above and below the cloud. It was thought that it might be possible for waves of single Bristol Blenheims, at that time the RAF's fastest bomber, to 'slip down from the clouds, drop their bombs, and get back with a good chance of escaping interception, even though fighter patrols were in the closest vicinity'. It would be necessary for the Blenheims to penetrate French air space to within twenty or thirty miles of Paris before being detected, so if there was inadequate cloud cover the raid would be out of the question. The timing of the attack would have to be very precise because the parade was to consist of just a band and a combination of sixty soldiers and sailors.

Hitler, though, had never been so close to Britain, and potentially so vulnerable, for the Luftwaffe could not have had time to establish a sophisticated early-warning system for Paris. As Britain had been driven from Europe, an offensive action of this nature would also be entirely unexpected. So, such an attack might indeed have succeeded in bombing the parade but, as aerial bombing at that stage of the war was somewhat imprecise, the chances of striking one individual were extremely remote.

Another drawback was that the French government had declared Paris an open city, after which the Germans did not carry out any bombing attacks. Relationships with the French were already strained after the French fleet had been attacked by the Royal Navy earlier in July at Mers-el-Kébir. But such a raid would be an enormous morale boost at a time when Britain was squarely on the back foot. 'We should … consider the effect of an air raid warning on the parade. A wave of single Blenheim raids routed towards Paris at about the right time … might well prevent the Parade from happening.'

Sholto Douglas, Assistant Chief of the Air Staff at the Air Ministry, put forward a different plan. He considered such an attempt as 'an expensive and rather futile gesture'. He proposed, however, taking advantage of the fact that so many German fighter planes would be concentrated in the Paris area to undertake attacks on other targets that had been denuded of air cover.

After taking all the above factors into consideration, Stephenson decided not to carry out the attack upon the parade, concluding that: 'The Germans have conquered France. The triumphal march through Paris is in accordance with military custom – we did the same thing ourselves after the Battle of Waterloo.'

It was not just the British who saw that Hitler, away from his usual haunts and the security of well-practised protection arrangements, would on this occasion be exposed and potentially vulnerable. Lieutenant Fritz-Dietlof Graf von der Schulenburg and Dr Eugen Gerstenmaier believed that they could shoot the Führer whilst he stood on the reviewing platform during the parade.

Schulenburg was a reserve officer who, as vice president of the Berlin police, had long sought to remove Hitler from power. He was called to active duty in May 1940 and now was in France along with Hitler's victorious troops. Dr Gerstenmaier was an official of the Evangelical Church who worked in the Information Division of the Foreign Ministry. The two had talked earlier in Berlin of organizing a small officers' cadre to arrest Hitler, but nothing came of it; now they saw their chance.

Yet again Hitler confounded the plotters. Whilst one would imagine that Hitler would be unable to resist the glory of watching his soldiers marching down the Champs-Élysées, marking his greatest, and totally unexpected, victory, in fact, that was exactly what Hitler did not want to do. He wanted the French to support Germany in its efforts to fight communism and in the new French president, Marshal Foch, he believed he saw a kindred spirit. The last thing he wanted was German troops parading as conquerors through the streets of the French capital.

Nevertheless, Hitler, understandably, could not resist visiting Paris and he slipped unannounced into, and out of, Paris three days before the proposed review. In a brief sightseeing tour, he saw some of the usual sights, such as the Louvre, Napoleon's Tomb and, inevitably, the Eiffel Tower. He also permitted himself a little journey into the past, visiting many of the battlefields in France where he had served during the First World War.

Yet a similar set of circumstances presented themselves almost a year later, when another review was arranged in Paris. The date was 21 May 1941 and a major parade of Heer and SS regiments was planned. A reviewing stand for Hitler and other dignitaries was constructed near the Place de la Concorde for the parade along the Champs-Élysées as in the previous year. Once again this was seen as an opportunity to assassinate Hitler.

The plan was multi-layered and was to be carried out by staff officers from Field Marshal von Witzleben's headquarters. Witzleben was

Commander-in-Chief West, with headquarters outside Paris, in St Germain. The plan was that Captain Graf Schwerin von Schwanenfeld and Major Hans Alexander von Voss, both of Witzleben's staff, and Captain Graf von Waldersee of the Paris staff would be able to get close to Hitler, giving them the chance to shoot the Führer at point-blank range. If something went wrong and these men were not able to get close enough to kill him, then a fourth officer was assigned to throw a bomb or hand grenade at him. Something did indeed go wrong with this plan as, it seems at the last minute, Hitler decided not to make the trip to Paris. Other versions of this account state that Hitler never intended to visit Paris in the first place.[2]

It is interesting to note that, regardless of Hitler's runaway success in 1940, there were people in Germany at that time who still believed that Germany would eventually lose the war and who were planning for a restoration of democracy in the country after Hitler. This was, no doubt, due to the Luftwaffe's defeat in the Battle of Britain and the UK's resilient response to the Blitz. Britain, it seemed, could not be beaten in the air, and with the Royal Navy dominant at sea plus the resources and manpower of its worldwide empire and arms and munitions being supplied by the USA, there must have appeared little chance of Germany ever defeating the UK – and with the pugnacious Winston Churchill now installed in No. 10 there was no possibility of a negotiated peace deal. It was not that those opposed to Hitler did not want to get rid of him, it was that they saw no need to take pre-emptive action as Hitler would eventually be toppled when his regime collapsed.

This was expressed after the war by the widow of the leader of one of the main groups of these disaffected individuals, Freya von Moltke. Her husband, she said 'looked at National Socialism as a poison which not only existed in Germany, but which you can find all over the world in human beings. And he felt the only way to really get rid of the poison was to let National Socialism defeat itself.'[3] But von Moltke and his group could never have envisaged how Hitler would take their country to the point of almost total annihilation before National Socialism met its demise.

If, therefore, Germany did not win the war and the Third Reich collapsed, it made sense to plan for a post-war, post-Hitler Germany.

This was what prompted Helmuth James Graf von Moltke to gather round him like-minded people to prepare for that future Germany.

Moltke was born into what was one of the most, if not the most, prestigious military families in Germany. He was the great-grandnephew, and namesake of Generalfeldmarschall Helmuth von Moltke, who had been instrumental in the creation of Germany during the Austro-Prussian War and the later Franco-Prussian War. This also meant that he was the grandnephew of another of his namesakes, Generaloberst Helmuth von Moltke, who was Chief of the Great German General Staff during the First World War. In spite of such a pedigree, the youngest of the Helmuth von Moltkes had little interest in the military, instead devoting his time to international law, setting up his own practice. In his work he travelled a great deal and had numerous contacts in various countries, including the UK where he undertook training in English law. With the outbreak of war in 1939, Moltke was drafted into the Abwehr where his skills would be most useful.

Throughout the 1930s, as the Nazi Party strangled all forms of free expression, Moltke had strived to re-establish a more equitable and just society and in doing so had formed a loose association of trade union leaders, economists, moderate politicians, religious leaders, historians, civil servants and fellow lawyers. The outbreak of war gave their activities added impetus.

They met infrequently in Berlin in small numbers but held three major meetings at Moltke's Kreisau estate (today's Krzyżowa in south-west Poland), in July 1941, October 1942 and June 1943; hence the group became known as the Kreisau Circle. The circle included representatives of both the Catholic and Protestant churches, and the main reason for the meetings was to devise a new and wholly Christian post-war German constitution.[4] Such views were in stark contrast to those of other opposition groups. Ulrich von Hassell, for example, wanted a monarchical authoritarian state which he saw as 'a safer path to a sound society' than the parliamentary route.[5] The communist opposition, though driven underground, still had many adherents who sought an entirely different future for Germany. As one historian has commented, the opposition groups 'had little or nothing in common except their hatred of the regime'.[6] One of the few conspirators to have survived the war was Hans Gisevius and he was well aware of these differences:

> Some wanted Socialism, others considered that to be the root of all evil. Some supported Collectivism, others felt that it was difficult even to tone it down, since we were already up to our necks in it. Some wanted a centralist Germany, others a federal state. All of them were concerned about the education and upbringing of the young generation, but opinions diverged widely on even the most fundamental aspects, such as Christianity and the school.

However, it was a generally held belief among the conspirators that the Weimar regime had proven a dismal failure and that democracy was a flawed concept.[7]

Had Hitler been removed from power Germany might well have seen a return to the political turmoil that followed the First World War which had effectively propelled him into power in the first place.

Though the Kreisau Circle was opposed to removing Hitler by force, both on pacifist religious grounds and for fear of making Hitler a martyr, Moltke had a long association with Ludwig Beck through what was known as the Wednesday Club, which was a small group of right-wing conservatives, composed of academics, industrialists and civil servants. They used to meet on Wednesdays in Berlin to discuss history, economics, and politics, which inevitably led to discussions concerning the end of the Nazi regime and what might follow.

These meetings, in turn, gave Beck the confidence to persist with his plans of removing Hitler by force in the knowledge that there were many high-ranking people ready to support a change of regime.

Moltke himself discussed this very point with Baron Hans Christoph von Stauffenberg, cousin of the man who came closest of all to killing Hitler:

> We are not conspirators, we're not capable of being, we've not learnt how to do it, we shouldn't try to make a start now, it would go wrong, we would make an amateur job of it.
>
> What we ought to devote some thought to is what is going to happen if someone takes it into their head to throw Adolf over or what is going to happen if he has an aeroplane accident. An event like that mustn't find us unprepared.[8]

As a result of such considerations a draft 'shadow', or post-Hitler government, was drawn up on paper.

One slightly detached member of the Kreisau Circle was Albrecht Georg Haushofer. He was the son of General Karl Haushofer who in turn was a friend of the Deputy Führer, Rudolf Hess. His maternal grandmother, however, was Jewish which, under the Nuremburg Laws, should have prevented him from being classified as a Reich citizen and precluded him from any official office of the state. But through his father's friendship with Hess, he was declared an 'honorary Aryan'.

Haushofer was a professor at the Faculty for Foreign Studies at Berlin University and became an assistant to Foreign Minister Ribbentrop and personal advisor to his protector, Hess. In these positions, Haushofer tried to influence the Reich's foreign policy, striving to moderate Hitler's ambitions in the vain hope of preventing war. When his hopes were dashed in 1939, Haushofer told one of his colleagues in the Foreign Office that he knew Britain would fight to the bitter end and that he despaired of deposing Hitler now that the country was at war: 'The pressures exerted on all Germans, the Gestapo terror and the indecision of political generals made it appear impossible that any internal action for the removal of the Hitler regime could succeed during the war.' He also knew that 'Germany's chances of an understanding with the opponents would only present themselves after Hitler's downfall'.[9]

Nevertheless, it was Haushofer who offered up the Duke of Hamilton as the most likely person of influence in Britain to contact when Hess began planning his bizarre flight to the UK in the spring of 1941. Though Hess in no way sought to oppose or undermine Hitler, whom he idolized, the Führer saw Hess' action as a betrayal and, from that time onwards, Haushofer was treated with even greater suspicion than before. He was jailed for a number of weeks and thereafter kept under surveillance by the Gestapo, yet he was still able to keep in contact with the Kreisau Circle as well as the Red Orchestra and had come to accept that the only possible way to save Germany from ruin was with the forceable removal of Hitler. But only the Army could make this happen, and in July 1941, its generals were too heavily engaged in Operation BARBAROSSA, the invasion of the Soviet Union, to contemplate a change in Germany's leadership.

According to Ulrich Hassell there was still a belief in the early months of 1941 that Britain would be amenable to a peace deal on 'a rational basis', but 'not for much longer'. Even when it was clear that Hess' mission had failed, opposition members continued to try and contact the British government indirectly, and it was said that a representative of Himmler had approached Carl Burckhardt, a Swiss politician and a leading member of the International Committee of the Red Cross, to see if Britain would be willing to make peace with Himmler instead of Hitler.[10] Some of Himmler's covert efforts to oust Hitler are discussed in a later chapter.

There might have been an earlier flight by a German officer that mirrored Hess' 1941 solo endeavour, but it is shrouded in mystery. This took place on 1 November 1940. At 1800 hours a Messerschmitt Bf 109, painted bright yellow, crashed to the ground just to the west of the Medmerry Windmill in an area occupied by the Royal Artillery on the edge of the Salt Marshes on Selsey Bill, near Chichester.

There was no sign of smoke or flame coming from the aircraft which appeared to be completely undamaged. On examination it was found to be pilotless too – adding further intrigue to the strangely coloured aircraft. However, a few minutes before, a German parachutist had drifted down from the sky and landed at Hilsea Barracks football ground near Portsmouth – right in the middle of an evening match between Portsmouth Constabulary and the Royal Army Ordnance Corps.

The parachutist, a Luftwaffe colonel, claimed to be on a mission from Göring to meet Churchill and seek a peace deal. Of course, there was no possibility of this happening and the man was whisked away to Mimico PoW camp in Ontario, Canada. Though a report and photo of the crashed plane did appear in the next day's *Daily Sketch*, just who the officer was and how much truth there is in the story remains undetermined.[11]

The strange case of Hess, which has provided fertile ground for conspiracy theorists, almost became even stranger. Towards the end of the war, as the Special Operations Executive contemplated a means of killing Hitler codenamed FOXLEY (which will be outlined later), Major General H.L. Manderstam submitted the following 'Top Secret' memo dated 18 December 1944:

> Has the possibility of using Hess for FOXLEY II [the assassination of leading Nazis] ever been considered?
>
> Hess might either be bluffed into doing it with the reason given to him that it might open a way for peace negotiations or, alternately, be hypnotised into doing it.
>
> Hess is known to be an extremely nervous individual and should be very susceptible to hypnotic treatment.[12]

Astonishingly, this suggestion was followed up by Major General Gerald Templer, head of SOE's German Section, who sought access to Hess' files. Nothing, of course, came of this.

In due course, it would be the atrocities carried out during the invasion of the Soviet Union, and the disasters which befell the Army in Russia, which would eventually drive the officers of the Army to take the step they were so reluctant to take, and plan the assassination of Adolf Hitler.

Moltke, likewise, had come to accept that waiting for Hitler to fall from power was unrealistic, and he sought a method of disposing of Hitler by any means. Having reached this decision, in the summer of 1941, Moltke said to Baron von Stauffenberg: 'You have a cousin in the Führer's headquarters. Can any use be made of him?'

Hans Christoph replied that he had not seen his cousin Claus for some time, but he promised to make contact with him and put forward Moltke's suggestion. Some weeks later, Claus responded. He stated that first of all the war had to be won: 'During the war one must not try anything of that kind, above all not during a war against Bolshevism. Afterwards, however, when we arrive back home, we will get rid of the brown plague.'[13]

Predictably, Helmuth Moltke's activities eventually became known to the Gestapo and, in January 1944, he was arrested with many others of the Kreisau Circle, whose membership had risen to twenty individuals, and sent to Ravensbrück concentration camp. Out of respect for his grand-uncle, he was treated moderately well. He was transferred to Tegel prison in Berlin for his trial in the People's Court. Though there was no evidence uncovered which suggested he wanted to overthrow the Third Reich, his plans for a post-Nazi Germany were considered treasonable, for which the penalty was death. He was executed at Plötzensee Prison on 23 January 1945.

While the generals engaged in the fighting in the East were too heavily occupied to find time to contemplate devising a means of taking down Hitler, that was not the case for those in the comparatively peaceful West – and they made one final attempt at luring Hitler to Paris to kill him. In 1942 SS-Sturmbannführer Hans-Victor von Salviati, the adjutant of Generalfeldmarshall von Rundstedt, who had replaced the unwell Witzleben as Oberbefehlshaber West, along with Hans Oster, invited the Führer to the French capital. Rundstedt himself did not agree with assassinating Hitler. He was approached to lend his support for a coup and, though he had no love for Hitler, he believed that such an act would be 'base, bare-faced treachery'. Had he supported the plot, he said, 'I would have emerged and been considered for all time the greatest traitor to my Fatherland.' He also believed that 'The Army and also the people still believed in Hitler at that time, and such an overthrow would have been quite unsuccessful'.[14] Nevertheless, though fully cognizant of the plan to remove Hitler, he did not betray any of those involved.

By this stage of the war, though, Hitler confined his trips beyond Berlin, his *führerhauptquartiere* in the East and the Berghof to a minimum and, predictably, he declined the offer.

Security had also been tightened whenever Hitler moved, and this included the car he travelled in. The man who had replaced Julius Schreck as his chauffeur, Erich Kempka, had long been concerned that Hitler's car was vulnerable to attack and that he suggested to the Führer that his vehicle should be armoured. Hitler turned down the idea, saying that he was loved by his people and was therefore in no danger. Nevertheless, Kempka went ahead with the construction of an armoured Mercedes-Benz 770k. He applied to Bormann for the money to build the car but was refused. So he approached wealthy friends and supporters, raising enough cash for the car to be completed. The windshields were of 45-mm multi-layer glass, the sides were of 35 to 40mm thick hardened armour plating, while the floor had between 9 and 11mm plate as protection against land mines or bombs. The vehicle was bulletproof against hand guns and explosives up to around half a kilogram. After the Elser experience, Kempka again spoke to Hitler and showed him his armoured car. Hitler was hugely impressed: 'In future I will use only this car,' he told his proud chauffeur, 'for I can never know when some idiot might throw another bomb in front of my vehicle.' Much to Kempka's amusement, Hitler ordered Bormann to pay Kempka the money for the car.[15]

Chapter 18

Lympne, England, Hans Baur, 25 March 1941

On 21 February 1941, Air Marshal Arthur Harris, at that time Deputy Chief of the Air Staff, sent a remarkable memorandum to Air Marshal Sholto Douglas, Command-in-Chief of the RAF's Fighter Command. It was marked 'Most Secret' and went under the label of 'German Deserters: Enemy Aircraft Landing in UK'. What the memo revealed was that one such deserter who planned to land in the UK was Hitler's personal pilot – and that he would be bringing the Führer with him![1]

This proposal had been put to Harris earlier that month when a Bulgarian by the name of Kiroff had approached the British Air Attaché in Sofia claiming to be the father-in-law of Johann Peter Baur, more commonly referred to as Hans Baur, who was Adolf Hitler's personal pilot.

A First World War veteran and holder of the Iron Cross First Class, Baur, who enlisted in 1915, had claimed six victories with a further three unconfirmed by the Armistice. Post-war he flew for Lufthansa, becoming one of the first of their pilots to fly 1,000,000 kilometres. It was as a result of this experience that Baur was personally selected by Hitler to be his official pilot in February 1933.

According to Kiroff, Baur had become disaffected with the war and, evidently, with the Nazi regime – seemingly to such an extent that he was prepared to defect to the United Kingdom whilst flying his Focke-Wulf Fw 200C Condor. More importantly, the aircraft was Hitler's personal transport and it was said that Baur intended to carry out this action when the Führer was on board. One document in the file adds: 'Baur, who is of Austrian extraction, had lost two brothers flying in this war, and being almost continuously on duty as Hitler's pilot, had become "fed-up" and was prepared to attempt to make a forced-landing in England.'

Harris had checked out Kiroff's story which, 'with one or two exceptions', seemed quite genuine, especially as Kiroff had not asked for any money or sought any advantages for himself. Even if Kiroff was wrong about his son-in-law, the possible consequences of capturing Hitler were so enormous that it could not be ignored, and every effort had to be made to facilitate Baur's defection.

Consequently, Harris issued specific instructions which were passed to Kiroff for onward transmission to Baur as to how his momentous flight to Britain should be conducted. Those instructions read as follows:

1. Aircraft must approach coastline and make steep descent to Lympne aerodrome with wheels down. The exact position is seven miles due west of Folkestone.
2. Pilot should fire not less than four red flares at thirty second intervals when approached by British fighters.
3. As soon as aircraft lands engines should be stopped and put out of action.

The reason why Harris had informed Douglas was to ensure that Baur's aircraft was not engaged by RAF fighters as it approached England. Almost immediately, HQ Fighter Command issued the following orders to its fighter squadrons:

> An aircraft [of this type] seen approaching Lympne during daytime is at once to be closed on by our fighters. If accompanied by enemy fighters these are to be destroyed or driven off. The aircraft itself is not to be attacked unless: i) it fails within five minutes to fire four red flares, or ii) it proceeds inland beyond circuit radius of Lympne, or, iii) it attempts to get away towards the French coast in which case it is to be shot down.
>
> During its approach and landing the aircraft is to be held covered by the AA defences. Directly it lands, it and all its crew are immediately to be seized. Opposition may be encountered. Our fighters are to remain airborne and patrol over the aerodrome until the aircraft has been seized. The aircraft is on no account to be allowed to take off again. If this is attempted, it is to be disabled or destroyed by the AA defences or by fighters should it take to the air.

On the ground, too, there were naturally preparations to be made for the arrival of this very important visitor. RAF Lympne, which had been selected as Baur's place of arrival in Britain, was not exactly a frontline station albeit that it was very much *on* Britain's front line, being situated close to the Kent coast. As with all operational RAF airfields it had its ground defence forces along with anti-aircraft protection, though the RAF officers involved in planning for the arrival of the Fw 200 quickly realized that the existing defensive measures might not be adequate to deal with the eventuality of Hitler's arrival. Consequently, the arrangements for providing armed defensive personnel and equipment were considerably increased for what was, in effect, a relatively quiet airfield that otherwise demanded no particularly elaborate measures.

It would seem that the identity of the individual who would be arriving at Lympne was kept strictly on a 'need to know' basis and this did not include Squadron Leader D.H. Montgomery, the station commander. All that he was told was that the new security arrangements were being put in place for an anticipated defection.

Back in Sofia in early March 1941 the British agent or official there had had further contact with Kiroff. The Bulgarian claimed to have been to Vienna to meet with his son-in-law. The German pilot had understood perfectly his instructions from the British, stated Kiroff, and had passed back some information relating to his proposed flight.

Three aircraft, Baur claimed, always accompanied the Fw 200 on its flights; they flew at a distance from the passenger aircraft unless Baur or his co-pilot signalled them. For that reason, he preferred not to fire flares but had instead prepared a number of yellow metal plaques bearing the initials 'A.B.' (possibly intended to be 'H.B.' for Hans Baur, although specified as 'A.B.' in a memo from Harris on 7 March 1941) which he would drop over Lympne.

Continuing with the planning, Baur had also asked that one red light should be shown on the aerodrome. The mission, he added, was likely to take place on or after 25 March 1941, between 0500 and 0600 hours, or later the same day between 1800 and 2000 hours. The timings, it was concluded, were Central European Time since blackout ended at 0623 hours GMT on 25 March and began again at 1921 hours that evening.

On the ground at Lympne in the early part of 1941 the ground defences comprised four Bofors guns as anti-aircraft and ground defence weapons.

In addition, the RAF airfield defence force included one Armadillo Mk III armoured car equipped with a COW 37mm gun – although on 1 March this was noted as being 'unserviceable'.

The RAF defenders also held twelve .303 rifles and one revolver (with a further twelve revolvers ordered in early March) and operated four Hispano 20mm gun posts. Assistance was provided by seven officers and one hundred and fifty other ranks of the 70th Battalion, Royal East Kent Regiment. Deployed on 'inward defence', these soldiers were equipped with sixteen .303 Browning machine guns, seven Vickers machine guns, two Boys anti-tank rifles, one Bren gun, three light automatics and twelve .303 Lewis guns. Other army units in the locality were also instructed to provide three Bren carriers and six 25-pounder field guns to supplement the airfield's defences.

This was quite a formidable force to protect an otherwise relatively insignificant and little-used airfield. There was little doubt that if the Focke Wulf Condor did arrive then it would be quickly disabled and its occupants taken.

Quite what the depth of involvement of British Intelligence was in this whole saga is unclear from the National Archives file, and nothing from a security service source is included in the file. At the same time, whilst all of the pages in the file are consecutively numbered, there are gaps – a fact which suggests that some papers may been weeded out before the file was downgraded to open status in 1972 and eventually released to the public.

One intelligence officer who was involved was Air Commodore Archibald Boyle, then head of the RAF Intelligence Branch (Boyle was also involved in the 'Double X' Intelligence Committee which specialized in passing disinformation to the Germans). In one letter Boyle described the plot as 'a fantastic story'. There was also a degree of realism expressed by Harris, who remarked: 'This is an event we hope for, but do not expect.'

On 19 March 1941, Sholto Douglas wrote to Air Chief Marshal Sir Trafford Leigh-Mallory, within whose group command Lympne was located, setting out some detail as to how Hitler was to be transferred from Lympne to London. In his communication, which was copied to Squadron Leader Montgomery, Sholto Douglas avoided any mention as to identity of the expected occupants of the German aeroplane. They were simply 'persons of importance'. These instructions read thus:

> All persons taken from the enemy aeroplane are to be promptly put under guard and removed from the precincts of the aerodrome to safe custody. Any persons of importance, to a maximum of two, are to be removed immediately under the charge of the senior officer with an armed guard by car direct to Air Ministry, Whitehall, where report is to be made to DCAS or Director of Intelligence (Air Commodore Boyle) or to Director Ground Defences (Air Commodore Sanders).
>
> A car for this purpose is to be kept ready and a spare car and motor cycle to proceed in company with it. The Air Ministry … is in the meantime to be notified of the action taken. A further report to sector and Group is then to be made.

For the purposes of transporting Hitler to London, Squadron Leader Montgomery had been provided with a Ford V8 Touring Box Car and two motorcycle outriders from the RAF's No. 4 MT Section, which was based in Abbey Road, London. All these were kept on twenty-four-hour stand-by for what would be their epoch-making assignment, albeit that their task remained unknown to them.

Throughout March and April, and then into May, watch was kept at Lympne for a mysterious German arrival which, as we know now, never came. By mid-May it was agreed that the plan would be kept in place until the end of the month. In correspondence to Leigh-Mallory on 19 May, it was stated that the special arrangements were to be kept in being for another fortnight from 17 May.

Then, on 28 May 1941, the incoming Deputy Chief of the Air Staff, Air Marshal Norman Bottomley, wrote the final memo in the whole saga. In this he issued the instructions that stood down the operation at Lympne. What would have been the most astounding kidnap attempt of all time was evidently not going to take place.

Baur remained as Hitler's personal pilot throughout the war, and was even with him at the very end when he committed suicide in his Berlin bunker – by which time he had been promoted to the rank of SS *Gruppenführer*. Trying to flee the city, Baur was shot and injured, after which he was captured by the Russians and taken prisoner. This marked the start of ten years of captivity – Baur was of great interest to his captors, who insisted on believing that he had flown Hitler to safety before the fall of Berlin.

Released in 1955, Baur then wrote a book entitled *Hitler at my Side.* With such a title and subject matter it is perhaps unsurprising that no mention is made of any planned defection to Britain. In his writings Baur is also vague about day-to-day events, and his part in them, during the period of late 1940 and early 1941.

When questioned by aviation historian Andy Saunders at his home near Frankfurt in 1991, Baur denied that he had ever been involved in a plot to kidnap Hitler. His elderly wife – his third – said that her husband was 'a good and true German' who would never defect to the enemy. She also claimed that neither of Baur's other wives had been Bulgarians. All three were from Bavaria.

If there was anything to this story at all, then the full facts behind it were taken to the grave by Hans Baur when he passed away, aged ninety-five, at his Herrsching home, in Upper Bavaria, Germany, in March 1993.

Had Hitler been taken to England, he would have been whisked away to London and sent straight to the gallows. There would have been no lucky escape from the public executioner.

Chapter 19

Moscow, Lev Knipper, October 1941; Orsha, Belarus, Soviet Air Force, 13 November 1941

The Molotov-Ribbentrop pact between the Soviet Union and the Third Reich came to a very abrupt and bloody conclusion on Sunday 22 July 1941. Hitler intended to give his people the promised living space – *Lebensraum* – for the expanding German nation, taken from the territory of the Soviet Union. This was no new concept. It was first proposed in the 1890s and popularized at the start of the twentieth century, becoming a fundamental part of Nazi Party policy from the 1920s. It entailed the removal of the indigenous populations of Central and Eastern Europe, either by extermination, enslavement or deportation, and the repopulation of those areas by ethnic Germans.

Hitler's belief in such a policy was expounded in *Mein Kampf* but what he also wrote in that book was that one of the reasons for Germany's failure during the First World War was because of fighting on two fronts – against Russia in the East and France and Great Britain in the West – at the same time. It was knowing that Hitler was about to embark on just such a potentially disastrous policy which drove Hess to undertake his failed mission to Britain two months earlier. But, such had been the spectacular success of every operation Hitler had undertaken, he believed that he could contain Britain and still have the strength to crush the Soviet armies.

The invasion of the Soviet Union was to be like no other campaign the German soldiers had fought before. This was made clear to officers before the start of what was codenamed Operation BARBAROSSA with the issuing of the *Decree on Exercising Military Jurisdiction in the Area of Barbarossa and Special Measures by the Troops* issued by Generalfeldmarschall Wilhelm Keitel, head of the OKW, on 13 May 1941. In a preamble Keitel explained that the vast extent of the operational areas and the enormous populations they embraced meant that it would not be possible for all those civilians in conquered territories suspected of acts against the German forces to be held and tried in civilian courts. The officers themselves would have to become not only judge and jury, but also, if necessary, executioners as well. But, as Keitel pointed out, the officers must focus on their main task of defeating the enemy on the battlefield and not become embroiled in civilian affairs. 'This is possible,' Keitel wrote, 'only if the troops themselves ruthlessly oppose any threat from the enemy population.'

He then spelt out how this would be done. Partisans were to be liquidated ruthlessly by the troops and if any civilians opposed German troops or any of their support services they were to be wiped out in their entirety. Where such measures were not taken or could not be carried out, the persons suspected of the act were to be taken to an officer who would decide whether they were to be shot. If the circumstances did not permit a quick identification of the culprit or culprits in a locality 'collective coercive measures' had to be applied immediately. In other words, people were to be rounded up and shot until the perpetrators were given up. Keitel also said that no action should be taken against a soldier who committed an offence against a Soviet citizen, regardless of the crime.

Keitel did recognize that, when a district had been secured and pacified, civilian German authorities would move in and take over judicial responsibility. But he pointed out that 'there is no rule of international law that guerrillas be brought to trial before a court,' and that, consequently, 'the arbitrary decision of an officer is therefore not illegal.'

These instructions legitimized summary executions by Germans against any civilians they deemed posed a threat to the Wehrmacht without any fear of being called to account. Many tens of thousands of Soviet and Polish civilians would be murdered because of Keitel's order.

That the war against the Soviet Union would be conducted along lines never seen before was explained by Hitler to his officers less than three months earlier at the Chancellery, when he told them that it would be a 'struggle of annihilation' and that 'In the East harshness is kindness to the future', telling the officers that they should 'demand of themselves the sacrifice of overcoming their scruples'.

The officers were shocked with what they heard and Halder, the Army's Chief of Staff, told Brauchitsch, the Army's Commander-in-Chief, that they should both immediately resign. But Brauchitsch told Halder that he had already protested to Hitler and it had done no good. Hitler was going to carry out his barbaric scheme against the Soviets regardless of what the Army commanders thought. So, both men remained at their posts, hoping, like Hitler, for a speedy victory which would enable them to return to Germany, leaving the savagery that was certain to follow in the hands of the Gestapo and the SS.

With the older, senior figures unwilling to take action to prevent the German Army becoming embroiled in these inhuman acts, it was the younger generation that was to come to the fore in the Army's opposition to Hitler. In early June, just weeks before the invasion of the Soviet Union, Oberstleutnant Henning Hermann Karl Robert von Tresckow, an operations officer with Army Group Centre, and the army group's intelligence officer and member of the Abwehr, Christoph Freiherr von Rudolf von Gersdorff, went to speak to the group's commander, Generalfeldmarschall Fedor von Bock to insist that he should tell Hitler that Keitel's orders would not be carried out.

The two young men tried to persuade Bock to fly to the other army group commanders – Generalfeldmarschalls Rundstedt (Army Group South) and Leeb (Army Group North) – and then together the three commanders would confront Hitler. Tresckow, who was Bock's maternal nephew, told his uncle that he had made his plane ready and said to him: 'You must put a pistol to Hitler's chest and demand the immediate revocation of the orders.'[1]

But Bock would not take such a bold step. His only response was to send Gersdorff to Berlin to voice his objections. But Gersdorff did not get to see Hitler, being told that Brauchitsch had already tried to have the orders rescinded without success and there was nothing more that could be done.

With the older generals unwilling to move against Hitler, it was to be the group of younger men which formed around Tresckow and Gersdorff who would lead the Army's opposition to Hitler. As with so many Army officers, Tresckow initially had been a supporter of the Third Reich but had become increasingly disgusted with the regime as its true colours were revealed. Through Fabian von Schlabrendorff, who, having joined the Army, held the rank of *leutnant* and took the post of Tresckow's adjutant, he had contact with the Abwehr which meant that he was in touch with the Canaris/Oster group in Berlin and therefore knew that there was a team in place to take over the reins of government should Hitler be assassinated.

Treschow cautiously drew more like-minded officers into his resistance cell. These included, as well as Gersdorff, Treschow's cousin Generalstabsoffizier Alexander Stahlberg and Rittmeister Eberhard von Breitenbuch. As the war in Russia later stumbled and stuttered from defeat to defeat, this group became ever more emboldened and finally committed itself to take that irrevocable step and carry out an assassination attempt. That, though, was in the future, and meanwhile there was a more pressing enemy to defeat. Though many may have been repelled by the practices of the Nazis, none wished to see Bolshevism re-appear in Germany. Now that the war in the East had begun, it had to be won for the very survival of the Reich.

While the invasion of the Soviet Union had temporarily postponed any thoughts of assassinating Hitler among the Army officers, the start of BARBAROSSA immediately meant that the German leader could become a legitimate target of the Soviets and, once the initial shock of the German invasion had receded somewhat, murderous thoughts in the Kremlin turned to practical means of assassinating Hitler.

Just as Hitler had told his generals that the war against the Soviets was a war of annihilation, Stalin warned his officers that the Soviet Union faced utter destruction if Germany was not defeated and that they must respond to the brutality of the Germans in an equally ruthless fashion. Not only would the Red Army fight the enemy on the front line, but partisans must operate behind the German lines. Special stay-behind groups were formed under General Pavel Sudoplatov to continually harass the invaders. This included arrangements to kill high-ranking Nazis.

Such was the seemingly unstoppable advance of the German armies through the western Soviet Union in the late summer of 1941 it appeared that Moscow would fall to the invaders. Believing that if it was captured by the Germans, they would occupy the city's principal buildings, so the Metropole and National hotels were mined as was the huge foreign ministry. Under an elaborate plan, ballerinas and circus acrobats were armed with grenades and pistols and ordered to assassinate German generals if they attempted to organize concerts and other events. Booby traps were laid in the orchestra pit of the Bolshoi theatre as well as around the Kremlin and Moscow's best-known cathedrals.[2]

As Hitler had visited Warsaw and Paris after his troops had occupied the Polish and French capitals, it was thought that he would not be able to resist travelling to Moscow if it was taken by the Germans. Stalin saw this as an opportunity to eliminate the Führer and, in October 1941, an autonomous group led by the classical music composer Lev Knipper and his wife Mariya Gsriknova was formed to kill Hitler and his close associates if they entered Moscow. They headed an eleven-man 'battle group' which included a radio operator. Arms caches were placed around the city which held remote-controlled grenades, explosives, and ammunition. Knipper was of partial German descent and he looked every inch the ideal Aryan. He could speak fluent German with a mastery of its regional dialects. He would be able to pass as a German officer and conduct his subversive tactics without suspicion. Lev Knipper was also tasked with sabotaging the city's water supply.[3]

As it transpired, Hitler failed to take Moscow, but the Kremlin was not finished with Lev Knipper, nor with the idea of assassinating Hitler. Knipper was the brother of Olga Chekhova. Olga, a budding actress, had moved to Berlin in 1920 and had become something of a star, appearing in numerous films and becoming quite a favourite of the leading Nazis, including Himmler and the Goebbels family. She was also photographed in May 1939 sitting on the front row immediately next to Hitler at a lavish garden reception for the diplomatic corps – a photograph which appeared in the German press. This gave Lavrentiy Pavlovich Beria, the head of the Soviet secret police (NKVD), the impression that she had close, possibly even intimate, contact with Hitler and that she could help her brother Lev get close enough to the Führer for him to assassinate the despised Chancellor – for Olga had been a spy for the Soviet secret police since the 1930s.

The first hurdle that Lev faced was getting to Berlin in a world torn apart by war. So, Beria planned for Knipper and his wife to 'falsely defect' to Germany to rejoin his sister in Berlin. He first travelled to Iran, ostensibly to research Iranian folk music. Indeed, he gave credibility to his cover story by writing two Iranian-themed preludes.[4] The next part of the plan was that he was to defect to Germany from Iran or Turkey, both of which were pro-Axis countries, and then on to Bulgaria. But, as the war ground on, the plan was not put into practice.

The Kremlin, at least in the early stages of the war, was still interested in killing Hitler but, from the start of the invasion of the Soviet Union, he spent most of his time – some 800 or more days – at his headquarters in East Prussia, the Wolfsschanze, only leaving there on a small number of occasions before his eventual withdrawal to his final days in the Chancellery bunker in Berlin.

The Wolfsschanze, which would be the scene of the most memorable of the assassination attempts on 20 July 1944, was situated inside the forest of Gorlitz, five miles to the east of the town of Rastenburg, which is today's Polish town of Kętrzyn. It had been in the autumn of 1940 that Dr Fritz Todt, a construction engineer, who in March of that year had been made Reich Minister for Armaments and Ammunition, was instructed to find a suitable site for the establishment of a headquarters complex close to the border with the Soviets from where the Führer and his staff could direct the assault upon the USSR. Shortly after the Gorlitz forest had been selected work began on what would become the most sophisticated of all Hitler's field headquarters.

The forest was cleared of inhabitants and buildings and a forbidden zone with a radius of ten kilometres extended around the site surrounded by barbed wire and fences. Inside this was a minefield approximately 150 metres wide. The site was constructed with three security zones. The outermost of these was Security Zone III (*Sperrkreis* III). This outer perimeter was surrounded by land and fencing, and defended by the Führer-Begleit-Bataillion (FBB) with a strength in 1941 of 1,277, who manned slit trenches, guard houses, watchtowers, and checkpoints. The area in and around the forest was noted for its numerous lakes and swampy ground, which in itself was an excellent defensive feature against any attack on the Wolfsschanze from the land.

Security Zone II (*Sperrkreis* II) was the area inside the outer security zone. There could be found the buildings of the Wehrmachtführugsstab, the Armed Forces Joint Staff, and the headquarters of the Commandant of the Wolf's Lair, Oberstleutnant Gustav Streve, and his staff.

Security Zone I (*Sperrkreis* I) was the most secure area of the Wolf's Lair. It was ringed by steel fencing and guarded by the RSD.

Only those persons with the correct identification and a valid pass were permitted to enter the Wolfsschanze and these were scrutinized at every checkpoint and entrance, only those with the highest security clearance being permitted into Security Zone I.

There were normally approximately thirty anti-aircraft guns deployed around the Wolfsschanze along with seventy light and two heavy machine guns, up to twenty-one anti-tank guns plus armoured cars and tanks.[5]

These arrangements made any direct attack upon Hitler almost impossible, which meant that the only chance the Soviets had of killing Hitler was when he was on the move to visit any of the fighting fronts or the headquarters of the various army groups.

With communications across the western part of the Soviet Union severely disrupted by the German invasion, and the tight security measures enforced by Gruppenführer Rattenhuber, the only reliable source of information on Hitler's movements available to the Soviets came from the now famous Enigma intercepts deciphered at Bletchley Park. As the transcripts were shared with only a few trusted people on the Anglo-US side, there were understandable concerns about revealing this information to Stalin. But needs must, and it was decided that details of Hitler's whereabouts should be passed on to Moscow but with no indication from where the information had emanated, and in November 1941 just such a piece of information fell into the hands of British intelligence, from a 'most reliable source'.

It was learned that, on 8 November, all the army commanders on the Eastern Front were told that a meeting would be held with the German High Command at Orsha in Belarus on 13 November. This was clearly a very important meeting and, almost certainly, it meant that Hitler would preside over the conference. The meeting was to commence at 08.00 hours with quarters and food available for the attendees from the afternoon of 12 November until 14 November.

A telegram was sent to the British Military Mission in Moscow, which read as follows: 'Most reliable source reports conference to be held in special train [presumably the Sonderzug *Afrika*] at ORSHA during daylight 13th November … If daylight attack impracticable suggest night attack on 12th or 13th.'[6]

Accordingly, on the night of 12 November, a force of around twenty Ilyushin Il–4 bombers of the Long-Range Bombing Division attacked the railway station at Orsha where it was supposed the special train would be stationed for the conference.[7] The Soviets claimed they lost one aircraft during the mission. Michael Moorhouse has cast doubt on whether or not the raid took place, but one thing is certain: between 10 and 20 November Hitler was safely ensconced in the Wolfsschanze.[8]

On 29 March 1942 the Foreign Office received a report from the Moscow Mission stating that Stalin was 'extremely anxious to see Hitler dead and he proposed to use every effort to bring this about'. It was of the 'utmost importance' to the Soviet leader that he was informed of where Hitler and his general staff might be.

The report went on to say that a 'week or so ago' Stalin had heard that Hitler was at Minsk and so Minsk had been heavily bombed, and then the German General Staff had moved to Vilna three days previous to the report and the Soviet bombers had been sent to Vilna. It was then believed that Hitler had returned to Minsk and that very day the unfortunate city was being bombed again in the vain hope of killing Hitler, who had divided his time between the Wolfsschanze and Berlin during this period.

The Foreign Office replied on 1 April to say that it had no information available on Hitler's whereabouts but that they would 'certainly' pass on immediately any information it received.[9]

In the end, Stalin, ever suspicious of the Western Powers, contrived to convince himself that if Hitler was killed the Allies would agree a separate peace deal with Germany, leaving the Soviet Union facing Germany alone and without the vast amounts of military and other materials the Allies had been sending to Russia, and he ordered all attempts on Hitler's life to be suspended.

Chapter 20

Dirschau to Konitz Railway, Polish Home Army, 9 June 1942; Bydgoszcz, Bernard Drzyzga, 22 May 1943

The invasion of Poland in 1939 created almost an entire nation of would-be assassins. Germany's dismemberment of Czechoslovakia the previous year had received a degree of international acceptance, but the attack upon Poland was a step too far. Just two days after German troops had crossed the Polish border, Britain, and then France, had declared war.

International relations no longer had any moral force. All that counted now was victory, for it was the victors who would hold the moral high ground when the war was ended. With the usual moral constraints removed, the Germans did as they pleased with the Poles, whom they regarded as sub-humans. The brutal ill-treatment they received from the occupiers of their country very rapidly led to an underground resistance movement, which Britain quickly sought to support. Through the SOE, Britain's secret sabotage and espionage organisation which was formed in the summer of 1940, the Poles received parachute drops of weapons and personnel. It is said that a total of 318 secret agents were flown into Poland during the war and that 485 airdrops were made delivering 600 tons of arms, ammunition and explosives (the RAF losing seventy-five aircraft on these missions).[1] It was with some of this material that the Poles fought back.

The more the Germans bore down on the Poles, the more they retaliated. Poland became a very dangerous place for German officials of all sorts. In 1943, in Warsaw alone, one policeman was killed, on average, every day and this figure continued to rise until around ten a day were being murdered. More than 750 Gestapo agents were assassinated in the first half of 1944 and it is recorded that the Germans suffered more than 1,000 casualties every month across the country.[2]

Amongst the thousands of planned assassinations there were at least two to eliminate Hitler by attacking his train. Over the course of the war the Polish resistance movement, led by the Polish Home Army, accounted for approximately 6,000 train derailments and one of these may have been inspired by the SOE in the autumn of 1941. Conducted by a Polish group, supplied by the SOE, the intention was to derail any fast trains, not necessarily Hitler's, passing through the former Polish Corridor in West Prussia.

As it happens, the Home Army was informed that Hitler's train, the *Führersonderzug*, was due past the spot where one of its detachments had laid several kilos of explosives. Hitler's personal train, codenamed 'Amerika' until 31 January 1943 when it was renamed 'Brandenburg', was originally presented to him by a group of powerful industrialists and, over time, developed into not just a means of transporting Hitler on official visits to heads of state of other Fascist countries but also as a mobile headquarters when visiting theatres of war, when it became a *Führerhauptquartier*.

The Home Army was organized into detachments of twelve men, with one being a radio operator, six being responsible for the actual sabotage – in this case the laying of charges – and the remaining five providing local protection. The detachments were armed with a variety of weapons from pistols to machine guns. The shortwave radios of the radio operators were not only used for communicating with HQ and other detachments, but also for firing the electronic charges.[3]

The charges were laid some twenty to thirty minutes before the train was timed to pass by. As the train rushed by the charges were detonated by an electric current controlled by a receiving set, which received the signal over the air from the transmitter which was approximately 400 metres away from the track.

Everything, then, was set to derail Hitler's train at the anticipated place and time, but once more the German leader rode his luck, as the *Führersonderzug* made an unscheduled stop at a nearby station, allowing another train to pass ahead of the Führer's. It has been said that when the train stopped, Hitler talked to a group of Danish volunteers who were on their way to the Eastern Front. The twenty-two minutes he spent there quite possibly saved his life.

Just how close Hitler came to serious injury or death can be gauged by the fact that the train which overtook the *Führersonderzug* was derailed at speed, in what was described as a 'devastating' crash, killing 430 of the Germans on board. It took two days to clear the mangled wreckage from the line.

A more specifically recorded attack on Hitler's train took place in the summer of 1942. By this time the Polish Underground had built up a highly effective operation, but Hitler's visits to Poland were brief and infrequent and his travel arrangements were kept a closely guarded state secret. Nevertheless, the Home Army had seemingly got wind of the Führer's movements. It was understood that, on the evening of 8 June 1942, Hitler would be travelling by train from the Wolfsschanze to Berlin.

Hitler's train was not an easy target. *Amerika* was built entirely of high-grade welded steel panels. It was powered by two locomotives and included a communications car and two anti-aircraft cars. It was always heavily guarded by dedicated SS troops which meant that it would not be possible to attack it whilst stopped at a station. The Poles' only chance was to derail it, and this was something at which the Home Army had become very proficient.

Captain Stanislaw Leslkowski's Home Army group operated in an area through which a stretch of the Königsberg to Berlin line passed. Under the codename *Viennese Blood*, Lieutenant Jan Szalewski would command two teams, one of which would cut the railway track whilst the other secured the surrounding area.

Dressed in stolen Waffen-SS uniforms, the Poles positioned themselves close to the track to await *Amerika*. It was known that a dummy train always preceded the *Führersonderzug* in case obstructions had been placed on the line. At approximately 0245 hours on 9 June what was believed to be the dummy train, but was in fact the usual scheduled service, sped by. The Poles then quickly dismantled the track and retreated into the nearby woods as what they thought was the *Führersonderzug* rushed into view.

The train flew off the track and down an embankment. When the train finally slithered to a halt, the surviving German soldiers scrambled clear only to be engaged by the Poles. The Germans, thought to be members of the *SS-Leibstabdarte*, Hitler's bodyguard, proved too strong for Szalewski's men who were forced to retreat.

The Poles believed that they had succeeded, and that Hitler had been killed, though they had no evidence to support this. Whilst a large number of Germans were killed in the crash and the subsequent firefight, Adolf Hitler was not one of them.

Exactly what happened that night is far from clear. There was most certainly a crash on the track between Dirschau (Tczew) and Konitz (Chojnice) on the night in question. It is also a fact that Hitler was intending to travel to Berlin that night. This was because he was due to attend the state funeral of Reinhard Heydrich who, coincidentally, had been attacked by SOE-trained Czech agents who had thrown a bomb at his car, dying as a result of the injuries he sustained on 4 June.

Yet once again Hitler had narrowly escape death by a fortuitous change of plan. He had, seemingly at the last moment, decided to break his journey at Marienberg to meet the *Gauleiter* (provincial governor) of Danzig (today's Gdansk), Albert Forster.[4]

A little more information regarding this crash was provided by Bruno Zwarra. His story reads as follows. He was due to travel by train to Danzig shortly after the attack and went to the ticket office to claim the free ticket that he was authorized to receive. The route the lady in the ticket office advised him to take was a circuitous one through Stettin (Szczecin). This meant that Zwarra would not arrive in Danzig until after midnight. Zwarra asked to be re-routed, but the cashier 'looked at me with a rather strange expression and quietly advised me to go via Szczecin due to the other route being dangerous. I was completely surprised but, judging from the woman's young face, I guessed she wasn't joking.'

Zwarra then realized why he had been warned not to travel on the shortest route. 'Everyone was talking about an assassination attempt on an express train which took place during the night of the 8th and 9th of June 1942, in the village of Strych … It was not just any attack but on Hitler himself!'

The mystery surrounding this attack is how the Poles got wind of Hitler's movements. The number of railway employees who knew the route and the departure and arrival times were kept to an absolute minimum and, at the end of the journey, all the written orders, timetables, and documents that had been distributed to the authorized parties were collected, counted and then destroyed, to make sure that no one could plan a future attack on the same route.[5]

Despite these precautions, a telephone switchboard operator, Zofia Ryszkowska, at the Kościerzyna railway station claimed that she had read a secret message warning the railway police, who guarded all tunnel entrances and exits, underpasses, bridges and stairways, to be ready for the passage of the *Führersonderzug*. Zofia passed this information onto Stanisław Lesikowski; thus the trap was laid.

In typical Nazi fashion, the Germans arrested almost all the men in Strych (a total of about 100 people), some of whom were sent to the Stutthof concentration camp, even though none of the residents were involved in the incident. The day after the incident, a special commission of the General Security Office of the Reich offered a very high reward (sums variously are given as 100,000 to 250,000 marks) for the perpetrators. Some indication of the seriousness which the Germans regarded the incident can be gauged by the fact that, at the time, the average family house cost around 15,000 marks.

Only one man has ever been named as having confessed to the Germans that he participated in the attack, Maksymilian Drobiński. He admitted (probably under torture) to have been one of those Poles dressed in stolen Waffen-SS uniforms. He was hanged. Stanisław Lesikowski met the same fate for his partisan activities, dying on the gallows in the summer of 1944 in Stutthof. A memorial to the derailment can be seen by the track at Strych and on the main road approaching the town.

It is also said that another plan to destroy the *Führersonderzug* in Poland took place near Bydgoszcz in the spring of 1943 by a special branch of the Polish Home Army, called *Zagra-Lin*, whose task was to conduct sabotage and subversion in Germany as well as in the Polish territories incorporated into the Reich. This unit achieved considerable acclaim for planting bombs in Berlin, including an attack on 10 April 1943 at Friedrichstrasse railway station. The bomb exploded when two German military trains were stopped at the platform. Fourteen people died and sixty were injured. Hitler ordered Himmler to take personal supervision of the investigation and a reward of 10,000 marks was offered for the head of each of the perpetrators, but no one was ever arrested.

The deputy commander of *Zagra-Lin* was Bernard Drzyzga, who lived in Bydgoszcz. He had been born in Berlin, knew German well, and he maintained many social contacts with Germans in the town, including some of those who held prominent posts in the district. In May 1943 he was informed by an SS officer, Rudolf Teschke, that Hitler was due to pass through Bydgoszcz in two days' time.

Drzyzga realized he had to act quickly if he was to be able to mount an attack upon Hitler's train. He knew that if he sought permission to act against Hitler from Home Army headquarters the opportunity would be gone, so he decided to carry out the attack without consulting his superiors.

He chose a site, eight kilometres from Bydgoszcz Hauptbahnhof, on a bend in the railway track just ahead of a dense grove. Two powerful explosive devices were buried under the tracks at a depth of about forty centimetres, some six metres apart. These devices were to be ignited remotely through an electric wire. A Polish railway official at a railway crossing eight kilometres from Bydgoszcz Hauptbahnhof and one kilometre from the target site was to give an agreed signal when the *Führersonderzug* approached.[6]

At the time and on the day in question, which appears to have been 22 May, Drzyzga saw the lights of a train approaching but there was no signal from the railway official. It was a freight train. Drzyzga waited for another hour or so, but there was no sign of Hitler's train. Once again, if the details of this story are correct, the Führer had changed his travel plans and cheated death.[7]

Chapter 21

Smolensk, Henning von Tresckow, 13 March 1943

The war on the Eastern Front was just as barbaric and bloody as Hitler had predicted, and his generals had feared, with little mercy shown by either side. In what would become the largest military confrontation in history, around thirty million would lose their lives through combat, starvation, exposure, disease, and mass murder.

Most of those deaths were suffered by the civil population of the Soviet states and Poland, being the victims of arbitrary deportation and summary execution on a vast scale. Orders were issued to German commanders that 'partisans are to be ruthlessly eliminated in battle or during attempts to escape', and all attacks by the civilian population against *Wehrmacht* soldiers were to be 'suppressed by the army on the spot by using extreme measures, till [the] annihilation of the attackers'. The instructions issued by the *Oberkommando der Wehrmacht* included the statement that 'Every officer in the German occupation in the East of the future will be entitled to perform execution(s) without trial, without any formalities, on any person suspected of having a hostile attitude towards the Germans.'

These measures, and the treatment of innocent, unarmed civilians and of helpless prisoners of war, appalled many German officers. Some, who had reluctantly tolerated the extremes of the Nazi Party, now found themselves being repelled with what they witnessed. Ordinary decent men also saw themselves being implicated in these excesses by association.

An example of the scenes that so shocked many of the Germans was witnessed by Major Axel von dem Bussche in the autumn of 1942 when he was out riding past an airfield near a village called Dubno to the west of the River Dnepr in the Ukraine:

> Naked people stood in front of the pit, men, women, the aged, children. They lined up in a perfectly regular queue, like lining up for milk and bread. The queue was around 600 metres long. At the edge

> of the pit sat an SS man. He let his legs dangle and held a machine gun in his hands. He gave a sign, and the queue started to move forward. The people climbed down the steps dug into the earth and laid down in the pit, one next to the other, face down. The SS man fired, immediately waved again and the queue moved forward … Naked women carried naked toddlers. Men led children by the hand or supported faltering old people. Families stood embraced. Nobody was screaming or crying, nobody was praying or begging for mercy, and nobody tried to flee. Between the shots total silence prevailed. There were eight SS men … The operation at the airport lasted two days, and three thousand people were shot.[1]

It was the officers of the Army, the *Heer*, who saw that it was up to them to put a stop to these horrors or they would be as guilty as those who had issued the orders, and the only way this could be achieved was by assassinating Hitler. It was at this point in the story that one promising young officer comes to the fore – Oberstleutnant Hermann Henning Karl Robert von Tresckow.

Born in Magdeburg, Treschow was the son of a cavalry general and was steeped in the Prussian military tradition. Initially impressed with Hitler's militarism, by 1938 Treschow was another of those who saw the Nazi leader was going to drag his country into a calamitous war. There was, of course, no means by which he could influence events and, once the fighting began in 1939, as a patriotic German, he put all his endeavours into securing a German victory.

As first General Staff officer (Ia) of Army Group Centre in Operation BARBAROSSA, Tresckow was well aware of the crimes that were being perpetrated against the Poles and the Russians. Serving at Headquarters also meant that he had contact with the senior officers of the Army Group and was able to quietly learn which of them were as shocked as he was at what was happening throughout the occupied Soviet territories, and who was willing to put an end to the horrors by killing Hitler.

Tresckow had the support of his adjutant, Leutnant Fabian von Schlabrendorff, and fellow intelligence officers Count Hans von Hardenberg, Leutnant Heinrich Graf von Lehndorff-Steinort, Oberstleutnant Berndt von Kleist and brothers Philipp and George von Boeselager. Though they sought to end the war by assassinating Hitler, there was little point in them taking such action if the Nazis remained in power. Tresckow had been one of those who had voiced his concerns over Hitler's policies in 1938 and he was aware of the opposition in the Army which had existed at that time. Sohe sent Schlabrendorff to Berlin to see if Ludwig Beck, or anyone else of such standing, was still willing to act against Hitler.

Schlabrendorff did indeed find that the group around Oster and Canaris continued to seek a means by which Hitler could be deposed. He later discovered that General der Infanterie Friedrich Olbricht, Chief of the General Army Office in the Oberkommando des Heeres (OKH), also wished to see Hitler, whose strategic decisions were proving increasingly disastrous, removed from power. Knowing that there were such powerful figures willing to support him, Tresckow felt confident that he could make a move against Hitler that just might precipitate the collapse of the entire rotten Nazi regime.

Tresckow could not take such action unless his commanding officer was in league with the conspirators. Generalfeldmarschall von Bock, though, was not prepared to be drawn into such an act, especially as Hitler remained immensely popular across Germany.

A reversal of German fortunes on the battlefield, as many believed was inevitable, gave Tresckow his opportunity. During the winter of 1941–42, the Soviets mounted a counter-offensive which saw the German army suffer its first defeats of the war. Buoyed by expectations of continued success, the sudden setback in the East came as a severe blow to the people of the Reich. This had two beneficial effects for the conspirators. The first was that Hitler's popularity waned for the first time in many years and the second was that von Bock was replaced by Generalfeldmarschall Günther von Kluge who had been against Hitler's occupation of the Sudetenland in 1938 and had argued against the attack upon France and the Low Countries in 1940. Though Kluge was unwilling to plot against Hitler in the midst of a titanic struggle against the Soviets, Tresckow knew that he was free to plan the demise of Hitler without fear of being denounced.

The fortunes of war once again swung back in favour of the German armies in the East in the summer of 1942 and, likewise, Hitler's popularity rose accordingly. It did not last long. The winter of 1942–43 saw the Soviets return to the offensive, and German casualties mounted to unprecedented levels, and Hitler's orders to his generals became increasingly unrealistic, causing mounting resentment against the Führer – a mood the conspirators sought to exploit, as Carl Hardenberg later explained:

> Already the first meetings we had with the individual field marshals and colonel-generals had shown that not a single one of them was willing to step in against us. Almost all had toyed with the idea, accepted its necessity, and expressed their willingness to join in against Hitler, if someone else took on the responsibility.[2]

The conspirators knew that the moment had come. All were agreed that, unless Hitler was assassinated, Germany faced utter ruin. How, though, could the conspirators kill the most closely-guarded man in Europe? And as the opposition circle grew so did the chances of its discovery by the Gestapo.

To make the conspirators' task even harder Hitler had become increasingly reclusive and an audience with him either in Berlin, at the Wolfsschanze or at the Berghof was practically impossible. The only likely way that the conspirators could get close to Hitler was if he could be persuaded to leave the safety of his various *Führerhauptquartiere* and travel to Army Group Centre headquarters at Smolensk. Tresckow made repeated suggestions to Hitler's staff that the Führer should visit the front to assess the situation for himself. Eventually, Hitler agreed. He would indeed visit Army Group Centre.

The worsening military and logistical situation at the front had also forced Kluge to change his mind. He wanted to see the end of Hitler, but was understandably worried about the repercussions, particularly if any attempt on Hitler's life failed and all those involved were arrested. A painful death was certain. He told Tresckow that he would join the conspiracy, but only after Hitler had been killed. Nevertheless, this was an important step forward for the conspirators for it meant that the leader of an entire army group would support them, making it impossible for the SS to stand in the way of the new government which would declare itself immediately it was known that Hitler was dead. A 'shadow' administration had already been decided upon, with Beck as the new head of state. Backed, therefore, by an army in the field, a senior figure at the OKW in Berlin as well as in the Abwehr, any opposition to the new government would find itself facing a formidable organization. This was essential if any solid advantages were to be gained by killing Hitler. Nothing would be achieved if the likes of Himmler or Goebbels stepped into Hitler's shoes. The assassination would have to be followed by a fullscale coup and the displacing of the Nazi Party. The stakes could not have been higher.

The conspirators knew that Hitler had been enticed into their trap; all they had to do now was work out how they were going to carry out the murderous task. Like Kluge, they feared failure more than anything else. They had to conceive a foolproof method of killing Hitler. Many ideas were proposed. The most obvious to Army officers was to shoot Hitler. A sniper would be able to choose his moment and even the place where he could easily target Hitler. The problem with this method was that Hitler's bodyguard, who would willingly sacrifice their lives for the Führer, would form a barrier around Hitler making him a difficult prey. The most certain way would be for an individual to get close to the Führer, draw a handgun, and shoot Hitler at an unmissable close range. Few men were willing to attack the Führer in this way. Many regarded Hitler as a liability but they still saw him as their leader, their Führer. They had also sworn an oath of allegiance to him as Army officers and such an act would mean breaking that oath. It also seemed an underhand and cowardly method, hardly befitting German officers. It was somewhat hypothetical, anyway, as Hitler would be surrounded at all times by a strong bodyguard and the chances of getting anywhere close to the Führer without permission were extremely remote. Another take on this, and a more honourable one in the eyes of Georg von Boeselager, was to overwhelm the SS bodyguard and kill Hitler in a 'fair' fight. In this attack, all those who had committed themselves to the conspiracy would take part, much the way that Caesar had died at the hands of the Roman senators. It would be all for one and one for all. This was vetoed by Kluge who did not want to see large numbers of Germans fighting each other. This evolved into all the conspirators attacking Hitler as he sat down to the pre-arranged lunch that was to be prepared for his visit. This plan was also dropped; allegedly Kluge disapproved of killing a man at dinner – possibly not the least factor being that he would be seated next to Hitler. The true reason was, no doubt, that Kluge would forever be stigmatized as being complicit in murder.[3]

It was Tresckow himself who conceived the plan that was finally adopted by the conspirators. He had seen that Hitler usually travelled long distances by aeroplane. All he needed to do, therefore, was plant a bomb on the Führer's plane. As Hitler would be flying over areas where Soviet partisans were known to be active, all Tresckow had to do was set the fuse for around thirty minutes after placing the bomb and the aircraft would be brought down in hostile territory. Not only would the perpetrator of the incident be unidentifiable, and most likely attributed to the Soviets, thus allaying Kluge's personal concerns, it would most likely be days before the wrecked plane was discovered. The conspirators could then have quickly formed a new government with all the trappings of legitimacy, untainted with the stain of usurpers and murderers.

With the help of Gersdorff, Tresckow gathered together the necessary explosives and fuses for the assassination attempt. This was no easy task, as the timer had to be silent (a loud hissing or a ticking noise within the confines of an aeroplane would be certain to cause alarm) and the explosives had to be both compact and therefore easily hidden or disguised, whilst being powerful enough to cause damage that would bring the aircraft crashing to the ground. This is where Gersdorff proved invaluable. The Abwehr's Section II dealt with, amongst other things, sabotage, and here he was able to obtain all that Tresckow desired. Gersdorff gave as his reason for needing such items was that he wanted to equip a White Russian (i.e. anti-Communist) partisan unit that was being formed under George Boeselager, known as the 'Boeselager Brigade'.[4]

Section II duly handed over the items Gersdorff requested. This included a powerful plastic explosive from stock captured from the British. The RAF had been dropping large quantities of explosives to the SOE and resistance movements across Occupied Europe, some of which had been seized by the Germans. A comparatively small amount of this substance would be quite adequate for the job. He was also given some British fuses. These were more sophisticated than the German fuses, and they worked by the release of acid from a capsule. When the fuse was set, the acid ate through a wire which then released a spring which drove the firing pin on to the detonator.

There were three different types of trigger mechanisms with differing time delays. One set off the explosion after just a few minutes, another after half an hour and the third after two hours. To make sure that they gauged the correct length of time for the operation of the fuse and the amount of explosive, and how it could be carried and contained, Tresckow and Schlabrendorff practised in fields close to the front line where explosions would not attract any especial attention.

For these field trials Gersdorff was able to obtain a variety of explosives, including a special small British bomb called a 'Clam' which was attached to its target by magnets. Filled with plastic tetryl and TNT, it had the power to penetrate 2cm steel plate.[5] According to Schlabrendorff, these 'Clams' were 'extremely powerful, but not bulky. A package no bigger than a thick book was capable of tearing apart everything within the space of a fair-sized room,'[6] The two men rehearsed the arming procedure so many times that they could perform it with their eyes closed.

Worryingly, not every trial was a success, with some detonations occurring far later than should have been the case. Possessing no technical knowledge, the two officers assumed that the severely low temperatures in Russia were the problem as heat can speed up a chemical reaction just as cold can slow reactions down. But with the bomb sitting in the warm cabin of Hitler's heated plane this was unlikely to be an issue.

Tresckow also made contact with Captain Ludwig Gehre, a member of the Oster group in Berlin, and asked him to obtain drawings of Hitler's aircraft. Through a fellow conspirator who worked for Lufthansa, Otto John, Gehre learned that Hitler's aircraft was always closely guarded and anyone who approached it, even the usual mechanics who worked on the plane, was searched. John reckoned it would be impossible to plant a bomb inside the aircraft. He did, however, manage to obtain drawings of the plane which were passed onto Treschow.[7]

This aircraft, a Focke-Wulf Fw 200 Condor, named *Immelmann III* in honour of a famous First World War German fighter ace, was well protected. The walls, floor and ceiling were lined with 0.47-in (12mm) thick armour plate and the windows were of 1.96-in (50mm) thick bulletproof glass. Hitler also had his own specially-insulated cabin with a parachute harness fitted into the cushions at the back of his seat. In front of his seat was a spring-loaded escape hatch. In an emergency, Hitler would have been able to don his harness, pull on a lever to open the hatch, and float safely down to earth. To be certain, therefore, of killing Hitler, the bomb had to be powerful enough to utterly destroy the aircraft and kill everyone on board. It would not be enough to simply bring the

Condor down. As the dreadful consequences of failure were always on the conspirators' minds, they decided to use two bombs to make doubly certain of destroying the aircraft.

All that Trescow and Schlabrendorff now had to do was think of a way to get the bombs onto the carefully guarded aircraft. The plan they devised was to fashion the bombs into a parcel which looked like the shape of two bottles of Cointreau, the only brandy that came in square bottles, and then have one of Hitler's entourage unwittingly carry the parcel onto the Condor. The wrapping was arranged in such a way that the fuse could be triggered from the outside without disturbing the package.

As a precaution, in case placing a parcel on Hitler's plane was impracticable, Tresckow had other schemes prepared. The first of these was that of putting a bomb in Hitler's parked car during his visit. The second was to have Boeselager's Brigade ready to open fire on Hitler and his retinue if the opportunity arose, despite Kluge's desire not to see Germans fighting and killing each other.[8] Tresckow had arranged for Boeselager's men to stand by the SS troopers as 'additional security' for the Führer. He knew that he might never get another chance to eliminate Hitler and he was determined that, one way or another, the Führer would never leave the East alive.

Meanwhile, back in Berlin, Beck and his co-conspirators put in place the method by which they would seize control of the reins of government as soon as word was received that Hitler's plane had crashed. The public statement that would be released would declare that the Army had taken control of the government on the grounds of national security. One of the conspirators' principal concerns was with the Reserve or Replacement Army which was the principal armed body in the Reich, its main purpose being to recruit and train troops for the frontline divisions. Among its secondary roles, the Replacement Army was also responsible for internal security and, if this force refused to accept the change of regime, the conspiracy would be certain to fail. While the conspirators knew they had Army Group Centre on their side, that body was hundreds of miles away and engaged with the enemy. Kluge could not, realistically, simply disengage and march back to Berlin to provide military support for the coup. Army Group Centre, however supportive of the conspiracy its officers might be, would never contemplate fighting fellow German soldiers. A minimum requirement, therefore, was that the Reserve Army would be mobilized to enforce the regime change during the initial stages of the coup. With this in mind, approaches were made to Generaloberst Friedrich Fromm, who had command of all Army troops inside Germany, by his subordinate General der Infanterie Friedrich Olbricht who headed the Allgemeines Heeresamt (General Army Office) of the Army High Command in Berlin and who had become one of the leading figures in the conspiracy.

Despite the growing disenchantment with the Führer throughout the Army, Fromm refused to be drawn into the plot but, although he was now fully aware of the conspiracy, he did not betray his fellow officers to the Gestapo. The likelihood was that Fromm would wait on the turn of events before committing himself to supporting or opposing the coup. That would, at least, give the conspirators time to put their plans into place in the key cities.

The most important of these cities was, of course, Berlin, where the Brandenburg Division was stationed. Providentially, this division was undergoing re-organization and awaiting a new commander, which enabled Oster and Canaris to use their influence to secure the appointment of Generalmajor Alexander von Pfuhlstein to the vacant post in the spring of 1943. A friend of Oster, Pfuhlstein was willing to help secure the capital and prevent the SS division at Jüterbog to the south of Berlin from entering the city.

It was Olbricht who, as early as the winter of 1941–42, devised the method by which control of Berlin could be achieved by the Reserve Army. He had urged Canaris to send a series of reports to Hitler warning of the risks posed by the large numbers (some four million) of forced, and potentially rebellious, labourers in Germany. This worked, and instructions were issued to develop a contingency plan to use the Reserve Army to supress internal unrest. Olbricht set his staff to work on a variety of plans which were given Wagnerian names such as 'Rheingold' and 'Valkyrie'.[9] The latter became the codeword for the conspiracy which gave the plotters the freedom to discuss Valkyrie as, should their conversations be overheard, it would be assumed they were referring to the quite legitimate plan to protect the Reich in the event of an uprising.

The Valkyrie orders were to be signed by Hitler personally unless he was incapacitated, in which case the commander of the Reserve Army – Fromm – was authorized to issue the orders. These orders were constantly updated to reflect troop movements, bomb damage to buildings, newly-created bodies and changes to command structures and personnel (altogether they were reworked at least 220 times).[10] Along with the genuine Valkyrie arrangements were a number of secret additions to ensure complete control of the main administrative, public and military installations, similar to the plans made by Brockdorff-Ahlefeldt and Gisevius in 1938, as soon as confirmation had been received of Hitler's demise under the guise of protecting such establishments from sabotage.

It was also essential that the SS in general were kept in the dark about the death of Hitler until after the new administration had taken over all the key government positions. This meant delaying knowledge about the plane crash both in reaching Hitler's advanced headquarters at the Wolfsschanze, and of that information being passed to Berlin. To cut telecommunications in and out of the Wolf's Lair, fellow conspirator General der Nachrichtentruppe (General of Communication) Erich Fellgiebel was to ensure that signal stations and telephone exchanges were occupied by men loyal to him who would ensure that Rastenburg was temporarily isolated from the outside world.

The conspirators would then be able to dictate the message that would be broadcast to the German nation. The people would be told that Hitler had been murdered by a cabal inside the Nazi Party seeking power for their own ends and the Army had been forced to intervene to save the country by arresting and/or executing those responsible for killing the beloved Führer. This, it was hoped, would ensure public support for the new administration and avoid civil war.

As far as possible, every contingency had been taken into consideration by the conspirators. There was a growing belief amongst the troops in general, especially those on the Eastern Front, that if the war continued to be prosecuted in the manner it was being fought, Germany was heading for certain defeat. On the Home Front the situation was equally depressing with the RAF and the USAAF bombing Germany day and night and systematically destroying one city after another. If Hitler was to die, seemingly at the hands of the Soviets, his death might be symptomatic of Germany's declining fortunes, and few, other than hardened Nazis, would be opposed to a change of government. At last, after a number of cancellations, on 13 March 1943, it was announced that the Führer would visit Army Group Centre Headquarters for a briefing on the current situation on his way from his *Führerhauptquartiere* at Vinnitsa to the Wolfsschanze.

Three Focke-Wulf Condor aircraft of the Fliegerstaffel des Führers flew into Smolensk airport where, on the morning of 13 March, Tresckow waited in person to greet the Führer. Tresckow had prepared the bomb for the aircraft and at the controls of Hitler's plane, coded D-2600, was his personal pilot SS-Gruppenführer Hans Baur. 'We knew Hitler's plane was equipped with special devices designed to increase its safety,' conceded Schlabrendorff. 'In spite of all this, Trescow and I, judging from our experiments, were convinced that the amount of explosive in the bomb would be sufficient to tear the entire plane apart.'[11] With Hitler now in their presence, the codeword could be sent to Berlin to advise the other conspirators that the assassination was soon to take place. Schlabrendorff therefore telephoned Gehre, whom Oster had designated as the contact in Berlin, with the words 'Operation Flash', receiving the reply that, 'the ignition can be switched on'.

The party drove to Army Group Centre Headquarters for the briefing in Kluge's barracks and then went to the nearby officers' mess for lunch. Of course, rather than risk all the dangers of trying to put the bombs on Hitler's plane, it would have been far easier to have detonated the bomb in the mess, but that would have meant killing all those inside. So, they had to continue with the original plan.

Tresckow learned that Lieutenant Colonel Heinz Brant was due to give a presentation to Hitler during the flight back to Rastenburg, so he made a point of sitting next to Brant during the meal. Here one witness described the scene: 'Hitler was sitting with his head hunched over his plate, shovelling in his vegetables, when Tresckow turned to Brandt, who was seated next to him, and asked if he minded taking two bottles of Cointreau back to headquarters on the flight.'[12] Brant happily agreed to take the liqueur back to the Wolfsschanze, with Tesckow explaining that the bottles were part of a bet he had made with Colonel Helmut Stieff, who was Chief of Organization at the OKH (but who was not part of the conspiracy). He told Brant that the package containing the Cointreau would be handed to him at the airport before he boarded the Condor.

After the meal, Hitler took his leave. As so often with the highly suspicious and unpredictable Führer, he took a different route back to the airport and invited Kluge to travel in his car with him. This meant that any attempt at bombing Hitler's car or of an attack by Boeselager's Brigade was out of the question. Everything now, the whole course of the war and the future of Germany, and indeed that of Europe, depended upon the package Heinz Brandt would carry onto the plane.

At Smolensk airport, Schalbrendorff pushed the detonator into the explosives which were parcelled up ready for Brandt and, just before handing the package over, he pressed down hard on the acid detonator with a key. The bomb was expected to ignite thirty minutes later which, Treschow and Schalbrendorff calculated, would see the aircraft flying over the area around Minsk.

D-2600 duly departed Smolensk with the other Condors in the flight, plus the usual fighter escort. Schalbrendorff duly telephoned Berlin once more to indicate that 'Flash' was underway. As it happened, Brandt did not carry the package with him, but he placed it in the cargo hold, which was considerably colder than the main cabin.

The conspirators waited anxiously for news of the 'accident', expecting one of the escorting fighter aircraft to report the crash, and were shocked and stunned when they received word that the Führer's plane had landed safely at Rastenburg airfield. Their most immediate concern was that the package with the bomb inside would be discovered or that, even worse, it would explode and kill their brother officers at the Wolfsschanze. Either way, Treschow's and Schalbrendorff's involvement would be obvious. The quick-thinking Tresckow telephoned Brandt at the Wolfsschanze. Luckily Brandt still had the package which remained intact. Tresckow told Brandt that there had been a mix-up and he had been given the wrong package. He asked Brandt to hold on to the item which Schalbrendorff would collect from him and exchange it for the correct one.

Schalbrendorff flew to Rastenburg on the daily courier flight the next day, hoping to be able to continue on to Berlin to report to the conspirators in the capital. He met the unsuspecting Brandt and made the exchange, which was two genuine bottles of Cointreau. 'I felt my blood running cold,' Schalbrendorff admitted,

> for Hitler's aide, serenely unaware of what he was holding, handed me the bomb with a grin, juggling it back and forth in a way which made me fear a belated explosion. Forcing myself to display an outward calm which I most certainly did not feel, I took the bomb

> and immediately made my way to the nearby railroad junction at Korschen.[13]

Schalbrendorff boarded the waiting train to Berlin and, once inside a closed compartment, he opened the package and the reason for the failure was quite obvious. What he found was that the acid had eaten its way through the wire holding the firing pin which had duly struck the detonator. Even the percussion cap on the detonator seemed to have worked but for some reason the detonator had not ignited. It was a dud. It has been suggested that this might have been because the temperature inside the Condor's cargo hold was too low for the detonator to ignite – as had happened a few times during Treschow's and Schalbrendorff's trials. It was not unusual for the heater in the aircraft's hold to fail. Hitler's life might have been saved through nothing more complex than a faulty heater.

Chapter 22

The Armoury, Berlin, Rudolf von Gersdorff, 21 May 1943

Surprisingly, the failed bomb attempt in no way diminished Treschow's resolve. Just eight days later, on 21 March, another opportunity presented itself and Treschow did not hesitate. Hitler was scheduled to view an exhibition of captured Soviet equipment and weapons at the Armoury in Berlin, and Army Group Centre was asked to send a representative who could answer any questions the Führer might have. This was an unexpected chance to get close to Hitler and an ideal assassin stepped forward to sacrifice himself for the sake of the Fatherland.

The aristocratic Rudolf von Gersdorff, who had supplied the explosives for Treschow's Cointreau bombs, had come to the conclusion that Hitler must be eliminated, whatever it took, whatever the risk. Being connected to the Prussian royal family, and an intelligence officer with Army Group Centre, he was perfectly suited to the task of explaining the tactical application of the enemy weaponry and the context in which they had been captured.

The display of the Soviet weaponry was to form part of the celebrations for Heroes' Memorial Day (a holiday honouring German dead of the First World War) and was scheduled to take place in the Zeughaus – the old Armoury – on the Unter den Linden, where Hitler was also due to deliver a speech to the faithful. Usually, the Memorial Day was celebrated on 16 March but, on this occasion, was delayed because of Hitler being unavailable due to the situation on the Eastern Front. Nevertheless, not only would Hitler be present, but also a number of top Nazi and military officials, among whom would be Göring, Himmler, Keitel and Grand Admiral Karl Dönitz. Gersdorff knew that he would not be allowed into Hitler's presence with a firearm and that his only chance would be with explosives.

Gersdorff travelled to Berlin on 19 March, two days before the celebrations, with Generalfeldmarschall Walter Model, one of Hitler's most ardent supporters. The following day, Model asked Hitler's adjutant Rudolf Schmundt about the exact time of Hitler's visit to the Zeughaus because he wanted to squeeze in a quick visit to his wife before returning to the front. Schmundt answered that on security grounds he could not give out that information – leaking such details could cost him his life. Model persisted and the adjutant finally relented. All this time, of course, Gersdorff was listening intently. But Schmundt pointed out that Gersdorff was not on the guest list. Model explained that he was not an expert on Soviet weaponry and that he needed the intelligence officer with him to answer any questions the Führer might pose. Schmundt accepted Model's reasoning and added Gersdorff to the list.

Now officially invited to the event, Gersdorff could legitimately walk around the Armoury on the pretext of familiarizing himself with the exhibits. 'I spent March 20 at the Armoury to examine the possibilities for an assassination attempt,' he later wrote in his memoirs.

> Labourers were at work everywhere, in the yard of the museum, where the ceremony was to take place, and in the exhibition halls themselves. A speakers' stand had been set up, and a stage for the philharmonic orchestra. The entire area had been festooned with wreaths of flowers. SS and SD troops roamed ceaselessly among the workers ... guarding the place day and night.[1]

Gersdorff could see that there was no possibility of concealing a bomb anywhere in the exhibition hall. Not only were the security precautions too tight, the hall was also very large, and there was no way of knowing where Hitler would be at any particular time. The only place he could be certain that the Führer would be standing for any length of time was at the podium where he would be delivering his speech but, after what had happened at the Bürgerbräukeller in 1939, this too was under heavy SS guard.

Determined to carry out his mission, Gersdorff decided that the only way he would be able to assassinate Hitler was to carry the bomb in his pocket and detonate it as he stood by the Führer. Gersdorff was to become the *Valkyrie*'s suicide bomber. Gersdorff was handed the bomb in his room at the Eden Hotel on the evening of the 20th by Fabian von Schlabrendorff. It had a ten-minute fuse.

With the time of Hitler's arrival at the Zeughaus still largely a secret, the guests began gathering at around 1100 hours on the morning of the 21st. Two hours later the event began.

Gersdorff had no idea how long Hitler would talk for, so he could not activate the fuse until the speech ended. Gersdorff, who to acquaintances appeared 'dreamy', waited anxiously for Hitler to finish. At last, the Führer stood down from the podium and headed towards the exhibition. Gersdorf activated the fuse of the bomb in his pocket and approached Hitler to begin his description of the Soviet weapons. Hitler's visit was scheduled to last thirty minutes, but he rushed through the display without stopping to inspect any of the exhibits. Gersdorff tried to draw Hitler's attention to some of the items but the Führer hurried on, paying no attention to either Gersdorff or the weapons. Hitler was through and out of the Armoury and into the street in, it was reported, fifty seconds. There was no point in Gersdorff following Hitler into the street (which he was not authorized to do in any case, his duties being confined to the exhibition) as the effect of the blast would be vastly reduced, and a failed attempt by an officer of Army Group Centre would have thrown suspicion on all of Gersdorff's associates.[2] Poor Gersdorff then suddenly remembered that he was holding a bomb that was due to explode! He dashed into a toilet and removed the detonator with just moments to spare.

Though yet another plan had failed, the conspiracy remained undetected. Its chance would come again.

Chapter 23

Heinrich Himmler, Stockholm, 1943; Egon Hanfstaengl, Berghof, 1943

Despite the rebuffs the resisters had received from Britain, and the failures of the pope's endeavours, efforts at persuading the UK government to support their aim of disposing of Hitler continued as the war progressed. Approaches were made again through ecumenical avenues, but rather through the Protestant Church than the Catholic one.

In May 1942 the Bishop of Chichester, Dr George Bell, was sent to Stockholm by the Ministry of Information to maintain contact with the leaders of the church in neutral Sweden on behalf of the Allied powers. On learning of Bell's visit to Sweden, Oster saw an opportunity to try yet again to convince the UK that the German resistance was ready to act against Hitler if given the necessary guarantees it sought.

Oster arranged for Dr Hans Schönfeld, the research director of the World Council of Churches, to visit Sweden and urge Dr Bell, a longstanding friend of Schönfeld, to present the resistance's appeals to the British government. After so many earlier promises by the resistance to remove Hitler had not been fulfilled, it was most improbable that the British would listen to any further proposals. Nevertheless, the war against the Soviet Union had not been the quick victory Hitler had promised and had resulted in alarmingly high casualties among the German soldiers, and the Führer's aura of invincibility was starting to fade. There had not been a better time since Hitler re-militarized the Rhineland in 1936 to bring down the Third Reich.

Schönfeld met Bell on 28 May and tried to convey the impression that the resistance in Germany had in the previous months become better organized and more capable of taking positive action than previously. Schönfeld also wanted to show the British that it was not just the Catholic Church that was involved in planning the overthrow of the Nazis, but all denominations. He also reiterated that the resistance leaders needed to know that the Allies would not take advantage of an internal struggle inside Germany, which would most likely be the situation if Hitler was assassinated, to gain militarily. Without such assurances there was little chance of the resistance deposing Hitler.

Bell was also a friend of the Lutheran pastor and theologian Dietrich Bonhoeffer who had long been a very vocal critic of Nazi Party policies and he, too, travelled to Stockholm quite independently of Schönfeld, though also at Oster's behest, to explain to George Bell the position of the resistance movement from his perspective. Unlike the more cautious Schönfeld, Bonhoeffer wanted to see the end of Hitler and his poisonous regime whatever it took, even if that meant the defeat of Germany. Indeed, Bonhoeffer believed that only through defeat could Germany atone for the terrible wrongs it had committed. Bonhoeffer sought no retention of any of the territories seized by Hitler; he wanted nothing to stand in the way of destroying the Nazis and rooting out every aspect of their ideology.

This was a lot for Bell to absorb and a heavy burden for him to carry when he returned to the UK on 11 June. The potential collapse of the Nazi Party, the defeat of Germany and a rapid end to the war lay in the manner in which he conveyed the messages from the resistance to the British government. The messages which Bell had received, though, were mixed. While Oster, no doubt, thought that by sending two high-ranking clergymen whom Bell knew and trusted it would reinforce the conviction that the resistance was strong and widely-spread, but instead it had the opposite effect, showing clearly that there was no common agreement among the resistance groups.

Bell met Lord Halifax's successor at the Foreign Office, Anthony Eden, at the end of June. The meeting did not go well for the cause of the resistance. As Eden pointed out, there had been numerous previous approaches by the opposition over a number of years, all of which had come to nothing. The impression must have been that there were people in Germany who wanted to get rid of Hitler, but none willing to risk their lives to assassinate him. This view was reinforced by the fact that the names of the leading Army officers involved in the plots were never revealed. Nor could Britain alone be seen to be negotiating with the Germans. She was a signatory to the Declaration by United Nations which contained only two clauses, the second of which was that each government pledged itself 'not to make a separate armistice or peace with the enemies'. If the Germans wanted rid of Hitler, they should do this of their own volition and accept the consequences.

Correspondence between Bell and Eden continued until 4 August when the Foreign Secretary ended the dialogue by repeating part of a speech he had delivered in Edinburgh on 8 May that year:

> If any section of the German people really wished to see a return to a German state based on respect for law and the rights of the individual, they must understand that no one would believe them until they had taken active steps to rid themselves of their present regime.[1]

Eden told Bell that:

> I realise the dangers and difficulties to which the opposition in Germany is exposed, but they have so far given little evidence of their existence and until they show that they are willing to follow the example of the oppressed peoples of Europe in running risks and taking active steps to oppose and overthrow the Nazi rule of terror I do not see how we can usefully expand the statements which have already been made by members of the Government about Germany.[2]

And there was the rub.

Hans Gisevius saw the folly of all these attempts to persuade the British to commit themselves to any formal agreement with the opposition groups. The repeated approaches to HM Government did, in his opinion, more harm that good: 'The enemy secret services were so swamped with reports from reliable sources that they no longer knew whom to believe,' he later wrote.

> Indeed, the task of intelligence on the other side was complicated by the fact that some of these peace rumours were spread by agents of the Sicherheitsiienst or the Abwehr, in order to test the enemy's firmness, or by Gestapo spies who hoped to get on the trail of the Opposition … Since all of these conversations naturally awakened certain hopes on the other side, the disappointment abroad was all the greater afterward. In the end various people had cried wolf so many times, had announced revolts and named dates so often, that the very existence of an Opposition to Hitler was no longer believed.[3]

There was one senior figure in Germany, however, whose position in the Nazi hierarchy was such that he believed the British would take his opposition to Hitler very seriously indeed. As early as October 1939, Reichsführer Heinrich Himmler, the head of the SS and one of Hitler's closest associates, was covertly conspiring to remove Hitler. This can be gleaned from Chamberlain's assistant private secretary, John 'Jock' Colville, who wrote in his diary that:

> Two Englishmen, called [Group Captain M.G.] Christie and [Philip] Conwell-Evans, have been talking to high-placed Germans, of whom one is Prince Max von Hohenlohe, in Switzerland about the possibility of getting rid of Hitler with … [a] new Government under Göring on the basis of restoring independence to Poland and Bohemia, disarming all round and agreeing to leave inviolate the unity and boundaries of Germany proper.[4]

Prince Hohenlohe was known to be acting as Himmler's emissary, and he would act in this capacity again in the future, but what is intriguing from this note by Colville is that the proposal set out by the prince was not for Himmler to become the new German leader, but Göring. Did this mean that there was a conspiracy at the very top of the Nazi Party, or was this just a ploy by Himmler to deceive the British government into believing that the removal of Hitler would be welcomed by the prime movers in Germany, thus ensuring a peaceful transition to the new regime in Berlin and that he (Himmler) was acting entirely altruistically?

This offer was not pursued by the British Government, mainly because of the Venlo Incident in November of 1939, mentioned earlier, and by the attack upon France and the Low Countries in the spring of 1940. As we have seen, Hitler's popularity reached its peak after the fall of France and Himmler would not have dared try to oust the Führer, nor seen any advantage in doing so, as the feared defeat at the hands of the French and British had actually been turned into a resounding victory. Even so, Himmler still believed that Britain might negotiate with Germany if it was he rather than Hitler in the Chancellery.

On 11 May 1942 Britain's military attaché in Madrid, Brigadier Torr, met Hohenlohe at the home of Colonel Juan Beigbeder, the former Spanish Minister of Foreign Affairs. The prince had flown to Spain four days earlier, sending a message to the British Ambassador Extraordinary in Madrid, Samuel Hoare, that he wished to meet him urgently as he had a 'matter of utmost interest' to discuss. That matter was the overthrow of Hitler. 'He revealed that he has been sent here by Himmler, who wants to know whether we would be willing to treat with him as an alternate leader of Germany.' Hoare informed Foreign Secretary, Anthony Eden, 'Hohenlohe stated Himmler has the support of Germany's leading industrialists, who want rid of Hitler as he has led Germany into a very damaging war of which there is no end in sight.'[5]

This offered the Allies, and the Political Warfare Executive (PWE) in particular, an opportunity to destabilize the Nazi machine. This was coupled by an approach made by Monsieur Visser't Hooft, General Secretary of the World Council of Churches in Geneva, on behalf of Moltke's Kreslau Circle. He arrived in the UK in early May 1942. Hooft met a senior member of the British Foreign Office who had previously been first secretary at the British Embassy in Berlin, Ivone Kirkpatrick, revealing to him that he represented a group which had support from all sections of German society, including the Army, which sought to depose Hitler and the Nazis. The purpose of Hooft's visit was to try and gain Great Britain's willingness to negotiate a peace deal with the new German government, should the Nazis be toppled. PWE had no desire, indeed no remit, to aim for such a settlement. Its function was to do as much damage to the enemy as possible and nothing could suit its objectives better than an internecine war in Germany. In its efforts to create as much chaos as it could in Germany, PWE had arranged for millions of replica ration cards – including coupons for clothes, fuel and food – to be dropped during air raids resulting in shops being wiped out of goods by those fortunate enough to pick up the cards and leaving others in states of considerable distress. It had also passed on to foreign workers thousands of travel permits which allowed them to escape Germany back to their own countries.[6]

Such opposition to Hitler was therefore to be encouraged, but without any embarrassing commitments. The response was, as had been the case with all the previous approaches from the German opposition, that any such group should act first before HMG would consider any peace offers from a new regime in Berlin.

In March 1943 contact with the British authorities was again initiated by Himmler, not directly, of course, but through his friend and lawyer,

Carl Langbehn, who travelled to Stockholm. There he met the highly influential Swedish banker and business manager, Marcus Wallenberg, who facilitated a meeting for Langbehn with the British Ambassador, Victor Mallet. 'I was invited to Marcus Wallenberg's home last evening,' Mallet wrote, 'where to my surprise, he presented a visiting German named Karl [sic] Langbehn, who he revealed was Himmler's agent. Langbehn wanted to know under what circumstances H.M.G. would treat with Himmler as an alternate leader of Germany, and repeatedly referred to the "Himmler Solution".'[7] According to the diaries left by Hassell, Langbehn claimed that even some of the highest-placed SS officers were, by 1943, contemplating the removal of Hitler.[8]

With reference to such approaches from Himmler, Sir Stewart Menzies, the head of MI5, laid down a number of conditions that would have to be met before any discussions could take place. These were that Hitler must be placed under house arrest away from political interference – the Berghof was suggested as a suitable place – a de facto government should then be installed comprising a 'Council of Twelve' led by Himmler. Only when this had been done would the British government agree to armistice negotiations.[9]

With arrangements with the British proving difficult, Himmler and his co-conspirators turned to the USA. Langbehn went to Switzerland where he met Gero von Schultz Gavernitz, a German who had gone to the US at the beginning of the Second World War and who was assisting Allied intelligence. Gavernitz, an ardent anti-Nazi, was on good terms with Allen Dulles the head of the Office of Strategic Services (OSS) – the predecessor organization to the CIA – in Berne.[10]

Dulles was naturally cautious and non-committal, so Prince Hohenlohe was despatched to Switzerland to add his royal credentials to the appeal made by Langbehn. Despite this, and even though Dulles – who had known Hohenlohe before the war – would appear to have been amenable to pursuing negotiations with Himmler's group – he was discouraged by his superiors in Washington from continuing talks with Himmler's associates.

After the war, J. Edgar Hoover, head of the FBI, reflected wistfully on the decision not to engage further with Himmler: 'I felt sure that if Himmler tried to arrest Hitler, he would fail; [however] the effect on the morale of the Nazi Party and the German Army would be shattering.' If a split between Hitler and Himmler could have been achieved, he believed that 'the resulting disorganization might have resulted in the collapse of Germany before it did, in fact, occur. The lives of at least a million people would have been saved.'[11] According to one source, in 1943 elements inside the conspiracy had at one time or another not only considered Himmler 'as the head of a large and dissatisfied force of men [the SS] both inside Germany and on the battlefronts abroad which might well be prepared to take action where the generals themselves were either too weak or too unwilling', as a possible catalyst to bring about regime change, but also Göring because of his 'well-known antipathy to Hitler's war policy'.[12]

It is also said by one German source that Stauffenberg sent a representative to Madrid to try and make contact with General Eisenhower, the Supreme Allied Commander in Europe, hoping to 'exploit mutual hostility to the Bolshevist enemy in the East'. How far this representative got is not clear.[13]

There is another strange affair connected with the USA in 1943. This involves Egon Ludwig Sedgwick Hanfstaengl. Egon's father, Ernst, had become one of Hitler's closest adherents in 1920s Bavaria. After the failed putsch of 1923, it may be recalled, it was Hanfstaengl's house where Hitler sought shelter and it was his wife, Helene, who had dissuaded Hitler from committing suicide when the police came to arrest him. Hanfstaengl helped fund the publication of *Mein Kampf* and he became head of the Foreign Press Bureau in Berlin. He stated that he was the originator of the verbal salute *Sieg Heil*. So close was Hanfstaengl's relationship with Hitler, the Führer became his son's godfather.

Over time, Hanfstaengl fell out of favour and he defected to Britain and later the USA where he took over the management of the American branch of his father's business, the Franz Hanfstaengl Fine Arts Publishing House. He was a regular at the Harvard Club of New York where he met both Franklin and Theodore Roosevelt.

Egon, who had been a member of the Hitler Youth before following his father to America, began work on a book on the Hitler Youth and, astonishingly, President Roosevelt dictated several paragraphs for a foreword to the book.

With the passage of time, Egon Hanfstaengl appears to have reconsidered his views of the Third Reich and, in 1943, he made an astonishing comment to anthropologist Henry Field, an Oxford-educated expert on the Middle East and a member of the Special Intelligence Unit of the White House: 'The death of Hitler would shorten the war. I believe I can kill him. I have unique qualifications.'

Hanfstaengl had clearly given such a project some thought, as he outlined his plan to Field, in the belief, no doubt, that his suggestion would be passed on to the President. He said that he would travel to Berchtesgaden, which he knew well from his childhood visits, at a time when Hitler would be in residence at the Berghof.

He told Field that he saw two possible ways of killing Hitler. He could grab a rifle from a guard and fire at Hitler through the huge plate-glass window behind which he used to pace up and down at sunset. Alternatively, he could bluff his way into the Berghof by telling the guards that he had a secret message for Hitler from his father, Ernst, who, of course, was extremely well known in Hitler's circle.[14]

Because of his longstanding relationship with Hitler, who after all was his godfather, he believed that the Führer would be unable to resist meeting him again. 'If I can get close enough to shake his hand,' said Egon, 'I can kill him.'

Ludicrously, he stated that he believed he would not get gunned down before claiming prisoner status under the Geneva Convention by announcing that he was 'an American sergeant acting under direct orders of enemy assassination from the commander-in-chief [i.e. the President]'.

There was, of course, no possibility of Hanfstaengl either killing Hitler or surviving the attempt, yet his suggestion was taken seriously enough by Field for him to pass it on to Roosevelt. The President turned down Hanfstaengl's offer.

But Hanfstaengl's 'unique' knowledge of Berchtesgaden and the Berghof was not to go unused entirely. It was believed that the Third Reich would make a stand in a rumoured 'Alpine Fortress'. Though such a place existed more in the imagination of Nazi leaders than in reality, it was considered possible by the Allies that this might include the Berghof. Egon Hanfstaengl was therefore asked to advise US Army Air Forces officers on the practicalities of attacking Hitler's Alpine retreat. With the aid of a sand model of the Berchtesgaden area, Hanfstaengl instructed the American pilots how to avoid the anti-aircraft defences and which buildings were the homes of Hitler and the other leading Nazis. As will be related later, bombing the Berghof did indeed occur towards the end of the war in Europe.

Chapter 24

Poltava, Ukraine, General Hubert Lanz, 17 February 1943; 'Werwolf', Vinnytsia, Dimitri Medvedev, 1942

Anger and frustration with Hitler's handling of the war was spreading throughout the Army and, for one officer, Karl Hubert Lanz, enough was enough – the Führer would have to be removed from power. On 26 January 1943 Lanz had been promoted to the rank of General der Gebirgstruppe (General of the Mountain Forces) and placed in command of the Army Detachment Lanz (Armeeabteilung Lanz). His task was to hold the city of Kharkov in north-east Ukraine.

On 2 February the Soviets launched Operation STAR aiming to retake Kharkov. The Red Army's Central Front was able to deploy 210,000 men for the operation. Lanz had less than a third of that number. As usual, Hitler told Lanz that he must hold Kharkov whatever the cost. That cost would be the loss of Lanz's entire corps as had happened at Stalingrad just days before when Generalfeldmarschall Paulus's Sixth Army had been forced to surrender. Lanz knew that his force would suffer the same fate for no discernible advantage. So, after holding on until the middle of February, Lanz withdrew and the Soviets entered Kharkov on 16 February. The next day Hitler was due to visit Lanz's headquarters in Poltava and Lanz had his plan ready to end the Führer's faltering regime before it was too late, and the German forces were utterly destroyed.

Along with his Chief of Staff, Generalleutnant Hans Speidel and Oberst Hyacinth von Strachwitz, Lanz had worked out a scheme whereby von Strachwitz's Panzergrenadier Regiment Großdeutschland would overpower Hitler's SS bodyguard and then take the Führer prisoner. Though the group did not want to kill Hitler, if capture became impossible, then they would not hesitate to take that step. They hoped, instead, to be able to arrest Hitler and then have him tried by the Army's senior staff for war crimes. Hans-Heinrich (Jonny) Herwarth von

Bittenfeld, a cousin by marriage of Claus von Stauffenberg and an early and persistent opponent of the Nazis, believed Hitler would have to be killed as merely arresting him would be futile:

> the general conviction [was] that German troops would never be willing to accept a different command as long as Hitler lived, but the news of his death would instantly bring about the collapse of the myth surrounding his name. Hence there was no way of gaining the support of large numbers of German troops without eliminating Hitler.[1]

As it transpired, Hitler, once again, changed his travel plans and instead of going to Poltava, he flew down to Generalfeldmarschall Manstein's headquarters at Zaporozhye.[2]

Though Lanz had been unable to carry out his scheme, the significance of his plan was that it demonstrated just how widespread the Army's disillusion was with Hitler, despite Herwath's misgivings. It is said that Lanz's plan was known in certain military circles, including the leadership of Army Group B which had become Army Group South (rather confusingly, on 12 February, Army Group Don and the existing Army Group B were combined and re-designated Army Group South. A new Army Group B became a major formation elsewhere), and no one opposed the plan nor betrayed the plotters.

As for Lanz, he was dismissed from his post for disobeying Hitler's orders, but was reinstated in command of XXII Army Mountain Corps in Greece in September that same year. He survived the war.

The Ukraine was the scene of another plan to assassinate Hitler, but this time by the Soviets. On 16 July 1942 Hitler and his entourage left the Wolfsschanze and flew south to the Luftwaffe air base at Kalinovka (Kalynivka) in the Ukraine to take up residence in what would be the most easterly of the Führer's field headquarters, the 'Werwolf' some seven miles north of the city of Vinnytsia. The war on the Eastern Front had reached a critical period and Hitler wanted to be as close to the fighting as was practical.

Being deep inside what had recently been enemy territory and potentially at risk from local partisans and fifth-columnists, security was of paramount importance and when Hitler arrived at his latest

Führerhauptquartier he was met by Oberstleutnant Thomas, head of the Führer-Begleit-Battalion and HQ commander, who showed him round the site. The area was surrounded by a defensive strip of bunkers linked by an underground tunnel, anti-aircraft guns and tanks, as well as anti-tank ditches and minefields. These positions were manned by a well-armed detachment of Thomas' FBB plus the 4th Heavy Company, 5th Panzer Company, and the eight batteries of Flak Regiment 604.[3] In addition, Gruppenführer Johann Rattenhuber, head of the RSD, had formed a special group of men whose job was to watch the approaches to the HQ and to keep an eye on the local population.

Though small compared to the Wolfsschanze, the Werwolf was still a sizeable complex. In addition to Hitler's personal accommodation, of a modest log cabin built around a private courtyard with its own concrete bunker, there were three small bunkers and a total of eighty-one wooden cottages and barracks. Among the buildings was a tea house, a barber's shop, a sauna, a cinema, a bathhouse and three air-raid shelters. There was also a personal swimming pool for Hitler and, though he never used it, others did.

While those local inhabitants and the Soviet PoWs who helped to build the Werwolf had been murdered to try and preserve secrecy, its existence, and the influx of the senior generals and their staffs could not be disguised, and before long word of Hitler's presence reached the NKVD.

A group of partisans was sent to establish the exact location of the new German headquarters and to try and discover if, or when, Hitler would be there. As luck would have it, a detailed plan of the Werwolf was found in the possession of two captured German officers. All that was needed was a plan.

The one that was devised went under the codename Operation MÜNCHEN. Such was the degree of security around the Werwolf, and so strong the German forces in the Ukraine, no direct assault was practical. The aim of MÜNCHEN was to infiltrate a Soviet agent, posing as a German officer into the Werwolf.[4] That agent was the legendary Dimitri Medvedev. Medvedev had worked for the NKVD in the Ukraine and had served as an intelligence officer abroad for two years before the war. He retired in 1939, but a few days after the German invasion in 1941 he was re-instated with the NKVD and began to raise partisan groups in the western regions of the Soviet Union. Then, in the spring of 1942, Medvedev was given a new assignment – to organize partisan units deep behind the enemy lines in the Nazi-occupied Ukraine.

In the spring of 1943 Medvedev began to study the Werwolf but, as with Alexander Foote, he had missed his chance. Hitler had paid the second of his three visits to the Ukraine on 13 March 1943. He returned again, for the last time, on 27 August, but stayed for less than three weeks.

Though Medvedev was unable to move against Hitler, he achieved remarkable success. In more than 100 actions, his group named Pobediteli (Winners) liquidated up to 2,000 German soldiers and officers including eleven generals and other high-ranking officials.

Chapter 25

Axel Bussche-Streithorst, Wolfsschanze, 16 November 1943

Kurt Freiherr von Plettenberg was a descendant of a Westphalian aristocratic family, who had resigned his position as *Oberlandforstmeister* in the Reich Forestry Office in 1937 because he could no longer bring himself to work in an official capacity under the Nazis. Two years later he was drafted into the Army, serving with distinction with the 9th Infantry Regiment. At the end of 1941 Plettenberg became the general representative of the former Prussian royal family, the House of Hohenzollern. He had also become an important member of the resistance, using his considerable influence to help link the civilian and military branches of the movement and, since 1942, had considered the possibility of killing Hitler himself.

Plettenberg's plan was a simple one. He revealed this to Baroness Marion Dönhoff. Each year, on 21 March, Hitler attended the wreathlaying ceremony at the Tomb of the Unknown Soldier at Die Neue Wache (the New Guardhouse) on the Unter den Linden to commemorate those who died in the First World War. The baroness wrote:

> As general agent of the Hohenzollern family he lived in the so-called Dutch Palace on Unter den Linden opposite Die Neue Wache next to the armoury. When I visited him there one day, he had just returned from big game hunting, the telescopic rifle was still lying on the table. 'Look', he said, picked up the weapon without aiming it and pointed to Die Neue Wache … 'when he [Hitler] makes his appearance there, I could easily shoot him'.[1]

But, as his friend Axel von dem Bussche-Streithorst observed, Plettenberg doubted the wisdom of committing such an act. He asked Bussche if the killing of Hitler at that time would turn the Führer into a martyr? Was the German populace ready to accept the overthrow of Hitler's regime?

Plettenberg's doubts served to restrain him from shooting Hitler. Such fears had probably been planted in his mind by Kurt von Hammerstein who, despite his attempt to lure Hitler to his death in Cologne, told Plettenberg on his deathbed earlier in the year, that 'we should guard against overthrowing Hitler prematurely. First the entire populace must have realized. A new stab-in-the-back legend must not arise … do not do it too early, the people have to go along.'[2] Plettenberg decided to bide his time, using his considerable influence to widen and strengthen the conspiracy.

There were, though, increasing numbers of Hitler's officers who wanted to see him removed as soon as possible, partly through concerns over the atrocities being committed by the German forces in the East, both military and paramilitary, and also because of the looming prospect of humiliating defeat and with it the destruction of Germany.

When the German armies had rolled across Poland and overran France and the Low Countries, even the most sceptical military men had to concede that Hitler's seemingly reckless rush into war had achieved results far beyond anything the more conservative generals had imagined possible. At that time the atmosphere at the headquarters of the OKW was one of great optimism. But things had changed enormously in little more than three years. Defeat was in the air and no one knew how Hitler would react. The growing opposition amongst officers to Hitler was prompted as much by fear of their own fate as much as that of Germany. The all-intrusive Gestapo, well aware of the growing disenchantment with the Führer, had already begun to probe deeply into the affairs of some of those officers suspected of treasonable intentions. That there was a group of officers actively conspiring against Hitler was known by Himmler and possibly even by Goebbels.[3] He had told Canaris that 'he knew full well that leading circles in the army were considering plans for a coup. But it would never come to that. He would intervene.' Himmler also professed to know who was 'actually behind it', mentioning names that Canaris knew were key players in the developing resistance movement.[4] What Himmler was telling the Admiral was that if the conspirators did not cease their plotting they too would be arrested.

This had what Himmler must have regarded as the desired effect of disrupting the plans of the conspirators. To enforce his message a party led by senior judge advocate Manfred Roeder and SS-Untersturmführer

Franz Sonderegger marched into Canaris' office to arrest one of the conspirators at Abwehr headquarters, special agent Hans von Dohnanyi, on the grounds of currency violations. Dohnanyi whispered to Oster that he wanted him to send a note to his wife, but all Oster heard was the word 'note' which he assumed referred to an incriminating slip of paper amongst the documents Roeder had seized. Unfortunately, Roeder also heard Dohnanyi mention the note and demanded Oster surrender the paper. As it happened there was nothing of any importance in the paper, but Roeder's suspicions had been aroused and he referred the matter to Generalfeldmarschall Keitel. Oster was suspended from duty and dismissed from the Abwehr, later being transferred to the *Führerreserve*, a pool of temporarily unoccupied high-ranking military officers awaiting new assignments.

This was an immense shock to the resisters, as Oster was considered to be the 'managing director' of the movement. As might be expected, the officers of the Abwehr had covered their tracks well, and Roeder was unable to uncover anything other than questionable foreign currency dealings, poor financial accounting and a number of cases of bogus exemptions from military service (which was widespread across the upper echelons of the Nazi Party). Though suspected, the conspiracy went unproven. Nevertheless, the implications of the move against the conspirators were clear. Either they abandoned their efforts against Hitler, or they acted quickly to remove him.

The initial sentiment amongst the conspirators was one of despondency, particularly as the group suffered a further setback around this time, with Beck undergoing a serious operation for cancer of the stomach. Despite the reverses being suffered by the army in the East, Hitler's standing was still high amongst very many Germans and just how the people would react to his assassination could not be predicted. When four of the leading conspirators, businessman Erwin Planck, Himmler's friend Carl Langbehn, former ambassador to Rome Ulrich von Hassell, and General der Infanterie Georg Thomas, met, they accepted that 'Hitler's prestige is still solid enough that if he's left standing he'll be able to launch a counter-attack that will end in at least chaos or civil war.'[5]

Hitler did indeed mount a counter-attack, but it was on the battlefield. Operation ZITADELLE was launched in the summer of 1943 against the Soviets. It proved to be a disaster, with more than 200,000 men being killed, wounded or taken prisoner. In addition, the Germans lost around 1,400 tanks and artillery pieces whilst some 800 aircraft were destroyed or severely damaged. Any lingering belief in Germany emerging from the war victorious died along with its young men on the bloody fields of Kursk, 280 miles to the south-west of Moscow. Winter brought with it a Soviet counter-offensive which saw the German forces being pushed back for 500 miles.

Far to the south, British and US forces had invaded Italy, and Hitler's once-favourite ally, Mussolini, had been overthrown. German troops had been sent into Italy to halt the Western allies, and with the very real prospect of an imminent invasion of northern Europe, Hitler was faced with fighting a war not on two, but three fronts. The conspirators knew that Hitler had to be removed, and quickly, before Germany was destroyed. As German fortunes declined the conspiracy had gained not only a renewed momentum but many new adherents.

Another member of the conspiracy was lost at this time. Because of his contact with Dulles in Switzerland, Carl Langbehn was arrested by the Gestapo in September. Langbehn had been in an unusual position as a friend and representative of Himmler in his attempts to get Allied backing for the overthrow of Hitler and an important player in the Oster group. Interestingly, Himmler did not save his friend, possibly because he wanted to distance himself from any hint of opposition to Hitler, and Langbehn was executed on 3 October 1944.

It was one thing wishing to see the end of Hitler and his dysfunctional regime, but how to accomplish such an objective was something altogether different. The conspirators had devised schemes to take over the government of the country upon Hitler's death, but what they needed was both someone in Berlin who could activate these schemes under the guise of the official Valkyrie arrangements and a person to assassinate the Führer. This they found in one person – the now famous, or infamous, Oberst Claus von Stauffenberg.

Stauffenberg, the son of a count, fought loyally for his country and its fascist regime throughout the early part of the war, and it was only around the turn of the year 1941–42 that he first began to express negative views about the leadership of his country. This was when he was talking to his cousin, Hans Christoph Stauffenberg, who had cautiously reached out to him on behalf of the opposition led by Count

Moltke. Hans reported that 'I have spoken to Claus. He says that we have to win the war first.'

This was supported by General der Panzertruppe Hermann Black, who had frequent personal and official contact with Stauffenberg: 'As long as I was a member of the High Command of the Army, Stauffenberg was to my knowledge no opponent of the system. He strove, like the rest of us, to bring matters to a good end.'

We can possibly identify the precise day that Stauffenberg decided that unless the conduct of the war was taken out of Hitler's hands Germany was doomed to catastrophic defeat. On 20 January 1942, Stauffenberg noted in his diary that the organizational department of the general staff announced a shortage of 93,000 men for the Eastern Front army. As some 800,000 reinforcements had been sent to Russia, this meant that Germany had lost almost 900,000 men since the invasion of the Soviet Union on 22 June 1941. If that trend was to continue the German army would be wiped out. Stauffenberg was also aware that there were only around 200 serviceable tanks on the Eastern Front. By August of 1942 Stauffenberg was speaking openly of making peace while Germany was still in a strong bargaining position.

Stauffenberg was serving with the Organizational Department of the OKH for the invasion of the Soviet Union but, at his own request, was transferred to the staff of Tenth Panzer Army in North Africa and, on the morning of 7 April 1943, the vehicle he was in was attacked by US aircraft. Stauffenberg was badly wounded, losing his left eye, most of his right hand and two fingers of his left. For some time, his life hung in the balance, but he recovered from surgery and was transferred to a clinic in Munich. After further operations he was discharged, returning to duty on the staff of the Reserve Army in Berlin. It is interesting to note that Stauffenberg told his uncle that he felt his survival from his terrible injuries was not mere good fortune, but that he had been saved for some special purpose. That purpose would soon be revealed not just to Stauffenberg, but to the world.

One grave concern that was being felt throughout the upper echelons of the Army was that Hitler, believing in his own infallibility, blamed his generals for the defeats the Wehrmacht was experiencing. Hitler had no love for the aristocratic Prussian officers, as he had demonstrated so ruthlessly in the past, and there was an aura of mounting tension amongst the officer ranks. Many feared another 'Night of the Long Knives', of mass arrests and executions, with the generals being accused of deliberately conspiring against the Führer.

There was, therefore, no time to lose. The sooner the attempt could be made, the greater the impact, and there was still hope that the death of Hitler would enable the new administration to renounce the policies of the Nazi Party to the world as an aberration and beg the Allies to save Germany – a new democratic and peaceloving Germany that had finally thrown off the shackles of a detested dictator. This could not happen if the leading Nazis stepped into Hitler's shoes. There had to be a complete overthrow of the existing regime. The only chance, the only possible chance, of avoiding a complete calamity was to depose Hitler without delay.

During August and September 1943, Tresckow took extended sick leave in Berlin to try and salvage what he could from the remains of the conspiracy after losing Oster and (temporarily) Beck. In the War Ministry building he put his energies into re-drafting the details of the Valkyrie plan along with Stauffenberg whom he met for the first time, the latter taking up the post of Chief of Staff in the General Army Office. Together they produced precise timetables for the hours and days after the coup as well as the proclamations which would accuse the Nazi Party of killing Hitler and therefore justifying the Army's seizure of power and the arrest of leading Party members.[6]

The Valkyrie plans were arranged into three phases. The first was the issuing of the legitimate instructions to the Reserve Army in the event of an uprising across the Reich. These instructions could be issued, though not acted on, when it was known that the assassination was about to take place. The second stage was the rounding up of the Gestapo and SS in Berlin and the seizure of the key locations. These instructions could be signed by Fromm after Hitler had been killed. Stage three was the announcement in the name of General Witzleben of the introduction of a state of emergency and the temporary imposition of martial law.[7]

However, having finalized these plans, following his sick leave Tresckow was re-assigned to command Grenadier Regiment 442 on the Eastern Front, ending his central role in the conspiracy – creating a void into which Claus Stauffenberg enthusiastically stepped.

The first scheme in which Stauffenberg was involved was in November 1943, and it was Major Axel Bussche-Streithorst, who had been drawn into the conspiracy after witnessing the Dubno massacre, who volunteered to undertake a mission that could not fail to kill the Führer – a suicide mission.

The German troops had suffered terribly from the weather during the first two winters of the war in the Soviet Union, having been ill-equipped for the harsh conditions. In particular, they lacked suitable clothing, many having to fight, and freeze, in their summer uniforms. The design of new winter uniforms for the *Heer* was therefore of interest to Hitler and he was to be given a personal viewing of the clothing at the Wolfsschanze, and the man who would model the uniform for Hitler was Major Bussche. It was understood that both Himmler and Göring would also attend the viewing, allowing for the possibility of eliminating the top three Nazis with a single blow.

Axel Bussche was regarded as exemplifying the true 'Nordic' racial type so beloved by Hitler and the Nazis. He was over two metres tall, blond, and blue-eyed and had served with distinction on the Eastern Front, being awarded a cluster of medals including the Iron Cross First Class. He was the perfect model for the new uniform.

Stauffenberg arranged for Bussche to join him at OKH Headquarters Mauerwald, ten miles from the Wolfsschanze, where he handed Bussche one of the British 'Clam' bombs. The Clam contained approximately 200g of TNT in a plastic body with a No. 27 detonator. The advantage the Clam offered was that its fuse was silent compared with the hissing noise made by the German counterpart. Its main disadvantage was that it was activated by acid from a vial which took ten minutes to eat through the fuse before it detonated the explosive. Such a time lapse was considered too great a risk. Hitler changed his plans so frequently and unpredictably, that he might well have left the room long before the bomb detonated, just as he had in the Bürgerbräukeller in 1939. An alternative had to be found. What was needed was a device which detonated almost instantaneously. This was found in the form of the German hand grenade which exploded in 4.5 seconds after activation. In those few seconds, Bussche believed he could muffle the unavoidable sound of the hissing by coughing or clearing his throat.

Having decided on the detonator, explosives had to be obtained. A staff officer could not simply ask for a quantity of explosives without questions being asked. So, through a somewhat convoluted process, another of the conspirators, Major Gerhard Knaak, managed to procure a 1kg charge which he handed to fellow plotter Leutnant Albrecht von Hagen who passed it on to Leutnant Helmut von Gottberg of Infantry Regiment No. 9. Gottberg took the explosive and a hand grenade casing to Bussche who was in Potsdam. Bussche, with the help of Gottberg, then constructed a suitable fuse mechanism, as described by Peter Hoffman:

> He sawed the haft of the grenade in two, leaving the part containing the fuse, and he unscrewed the primer. He shortened the draw thread which ran down inside the haft, leaving the pull-button so that there was very little play between the button and the haft. In this way only a very small pulling motion would be required instead of the more extensive movement normally necessary. The hand grenade fuse fitted well into the pioneer charge. The whole thing could well be concealed in one of the deep pockets of the wide trousers then normally worn.[8]

Bussche planned to pull on the button, count a few seconds and then leap forward and grab Hitler as the bomb exploded.

Everything was then set for the modelling of the new uniform for 16 November, but once again circumstances saved Hitler. The night before the demonstration, it is said, the rail truck destined to carry the new uniforms to the front was destroyed in what some have described as a 'heavy' bombing raid on Berlin. However, the only RAF raid around this date was on the night of 13/14 November when the German capital was attack by just nine Mosquitoes.[9] Depending on the author, the train was destroyed in a siding in Berlin or to the east of the capital on its way to the Wolfsschanze.[10] For the next two days Bussche remained nervously at the Wolfsschanze, fearing that his bomb would be detected, before, on the 18th he was allowed to return to his unit.

As the plot had not been uncovered, when the viewing of the uniforms was scheduled for 11 February 1944, Bussche volunteered again to carry out the bombing. But in January he was seriously wounded, losing one of his legs. Undeterred by this setback, another officer stepped forward. Captain Ewald von Kleist volunteered to take Bussche's place. However, the situation on the Eastern Front became increasingly critical for the Germans and, with more pressing matters to deal with than uniforms, the demonstration was repeatedly postponed and finally cancelled.

Chapter 26

Berghof, Eberhard von Breitenbuch, 11 March 1944; Platterhof, Herr Wirth, July 1944

The greatest problem that faced those German Army officers plotting to assassinate Hitler was that of getting close enough to be certain of killing him. A failed attempt would be worse than no attempt at all. Not only would it bring down a torrent of retribution, giving Hitler the opportunity to execute all those he suspected of disloyalty, but it would also lead to further tightening of the Führer's security provision, making any subsequent efforts even more problematical.

It was because of such considerations that Captain Eberhard von Breitenbuch, personal aide to Generalfeldmarschall Ernst Busch, who had taken over command of Army Group Centre on 28 October 1943 from Kluge who had been injured in a car accident, decided that he would shoot Hitler at point-blank range, fully aware that he would be gunned down himself. Breitenbuch knew that when he joined the *Heer* he might have to lay down his life for his country. He can hardly have imagined that this would be through killing the German Chancellor.

Breitenbuch's plan was to arrange for Busch to take him along on one of his visits to Hitler. Just such a chance presented itself when Busch was told to attend a conference at the Berghof on 11 March 1944.

He told von Trescow of his plan who offered to provide him with explosives, but Breitenbuch said he was an excellent shot and would require only seconds to draw his pistol, aim at Hitler's head, and fire off at least one shot, before he was killed by Hitler's bodyguards.

With a 7.65mm Browning pistol in his trouser pocket, Breitenbuch flew down with his chief to Salzburg and was then driven up to the Berghof. As usual, before entering the Führer's presence, the officers were obliged to remove their caps, belts and side-arms, Breitenbuch having hidden his Browning in his trouser pocket. The men then filed into the conference room with Breitenbuch being the most junior officer, bringing up the rear. Once again, a sudden change in routine saved Hitler. Earlier that day the SS guards had been told not to allow any aides into the meeting and Breitenbuch was stopped at the door. Although Busch remonstrated, saying that he needed his aide with him at the conference, Breitenbuch was not allowed to enter.

Not being aware of the change of instructions, Breitenbuch feared that somehow his plan had been leaked and he waited nervously in the anteroom, expecting at any moment to be marched away. He felt he was being observed and he wondered desperately how he could dispose of his pistol.

The conference ended and Busch and Breitenbuch walked away unmolested. The experience was a harrowing one for Breitenbuch and it was one that he did not try to repeat. Afterwards he confessed that he would sooner face a Russian division that go through another afternoon like that one in the Berghof. Breitenbuch survived the war, dying from cancer on 21 September 1980 at the age of seventy.[1] The attempt in March may have been Breitenbuch's last effort, but it was not the last time that the Berghof would feature in the plans of the opposition.

Though the suicide attempts had not proved possible, the conspirators still sought to assassinate Hitler, and they still had the explosive in their possession. This 1kg of British haxonite was hidden at Mauerwald. Obviously, it was dangerous to be found in possession of such material and the risk of discovery was high, given the high level of security that was maintained at the OKH headquarters. Rather than leave such incriminating material at Mauerwald, two other members of the conspiracy, Major Joachim Kuhn and Lieutenant Albrecht von Hagen, decided to bury the explosive and detonators in the woods under a wooden watchtower (where its location could be easily remembered) within the boundaries of the Wolfsschanze. The reasoning behind this move was that, should another attempt on Hitler become likely, the conspirators would not need to smuggle the explosive into the Wolfsschanze close to the date of the assassination. Hitler's security was frequently reviewed and there was every likelihood that, ahead of any important meeting at which any of the conspirators might attend, searches might become mandatory. Buried in the grounds of the Wolfsschanze meant that the explosive was near at hand – and its ownership anonymous.

As it transpired, on the night they tried to bury the explosive, the two men were spotted digging in the dark by a guard patrol of the

631st Geheime Feldpolizei. A tracker dog was let off its leash and the explosive was discovered. Fortunately, Kuhn and Hagen escaped unrecognized. The 631st Geheime Feldpolizei turned the explosive over to the Heerwesenabteilung (the Army Department) to complete the investigation. Astonishingly, Lieutenant Colonel Werner Schrader was put in charge of the investigation by Oberst Albert Radke. Schrader was a close friend of Hans Oster, and thus a conspirator was put in charge of investigating the conspiracy.[2] Schrader succeeded in delaying and hampering the investigation and he ensured that the perpetrators were never identified. In fact, he even managed to split the explosive into two, with one half being returned to Major Kuhn and the conspirators.

It is also claimed by one pair of historians,[3] that Tresckow gave two officers the task of concealing a large quantity of explosives for use against Hitler in the grounds of the Wolfsschanze. They buried them under a wooden water tower to wait for a suitable occasion to present itself. Inexplicably, it is said, for no known reason, the material exploded, causing 'consternation' amongst the SS guards. As a consequence, security measures around the Wolfsschanze were increased. It is possible the authors have confused this event with the above incident involving Kuhn and Hagen.

With the military situation becoming ever more serious, efforts were once again made by the conspirators to seek some kind of help from the Western Allies. Though all forms of travel outside the Reich were heavily controlled, Hans Gisevius managed to meet Allen Dulles in Switzerland in April 1944. It seems this time Gisevius was able to provide much more detail about the scheme to overthrow the Nazi regime and how the Allies could play their part. In his report Dulles wrote that as long as the Germans would be allowed to continue to hold the Eastern Front against the Soviets, the British and Americans would be permitted an unopposed advance into Germany as follows:

[1] three Allied airborne divisions should land in the Berlin region with the assistance of the local army commanders,
[2] major amphibious landings should be undertaken at or near Bremen and Hamburg
[3] landings in France should follow, although Rommel cannot be counted for cooperation,

> [4] reliable German units in the area of Munich would isolate Hitler and other high Nazis in Obersalzburg. The opposition group is reported to feel that Germany has lost the war and that the only chance of avoiding Communism in Germany is to facilitate occupation of as large a section of Europe as possible by American and British forces before the collapse of the eastern front.[4]

The summer of 1944 brought further setbacks for German forces. In the East, the Soviets continued what appeared to be an unstoppable advance towards the Reich, and on 6 June – D-Day – the expected invasion of France by British, US and Allied armies began. As the war situation continued to deteriorate, fears grew amongst the Führer's retinue that an attempt would be made to remove Hitler from power.

The worry was that too many of those who formed Hitler's bodyguard and entourage knew too much about the Führer's routines – information that could be used by either home-grown assassins or the enemy. Consequently, some of those closest to Hitler and other top-ranking Nazis who had regular contact with the Führer were frequently dismissed and sent to the most deadly battlefronts – usually in the East. This was the fate of Hitler's chief adjutant, Wilhelm Bücker, and his long-serving valet, Karl-Wilhelm Krause, as well as the major-domo of the Berghof, Herbert Doring.

Concerns over the loyalty of the staff in the Berghof estate proved well-founded. On 4 July 1944 Hitler was scheduled to give a speech to the heads of the war economy at the Platterhof. This building, which had been a hotel before the war, was taken over by the Nazis as a national people's hotel, where the common people of the Third Reich could stay when visiting their Führer. But it never served that purpose, becoming a luxurious retreat for high-ranking Nazi dignitaries and other important visitors. In 1943 the necessities of war turned the Platterhof into a military hospital and rest home, though still used for meetings, such as that in the first week of July 1944.[5]

This gave the house manager of the Platterhof, who like so many Germans had by this time become disillusioned with the Führer, Herr Wirth, what he hoped would be an opportunity to kill Hitler. For reasons no longer known, Wirth did not carry out his plan. But, knowing that his involvement in the resistance movement would be uncovered after the failed assassination attempt on 20 July just over two weeks later, Wirth killed himself and his family in his own official apartment.[6]

The D-Day landings in Normandy did give the conspirators one bonus. The man who had become probably Germany's most popular general, Generalfeldmarschall Erwin Rommel, had been driven into the conspiratorial camp by Hitler's irrational handling of the war.

In November 1943 Rommel had been made General Inspector of the Western Defences to prepare for the inevitable cross-Channel invasion by the British, Canadians and Americans. When he took up this post, he was shocked at how minimal the defences of the much-vaunted Atlantic Wall actually were. Though he improved the fortifications along the Channel coast, the Allies were able to land and drive inland from the beachheads. Finally acknowledging that the war was now lost, on 15 July, Rommel wrote an 'ultimatum' to Hitler demanding that peace terms must be sought without delay.

From early 1944 efforts had been made by Stülpnagel and General der Infanterie Alexander von Falkenhausen, the Military Governor of Belgium, to draw Rommel into the plot against Hitler. Initially, Rommel was opposed to killing the Führer but, it would seem, he finally accepted that the only way to save Germany was by eliminating the man to whom he had once been so devoted. Once he had decided on such a course of action, he sounded out other generals, receiving much encouragement.

Rommel's participation in the coup would certainly help sway the German people, he having acquired an almost legendary status, unlike many of the comparatively unknown Army conspirators. Just how far Rommel would have been prepared to go can only be speculated upon however, for, on the morning of 17 July, he was badly hurt when his car was strafed by an RAF fighter and he was hospitalized with a serious injury to his head.

Chapter 27

Claus von Stauffenberg, Wolfsschanze, 15 July 1944

At this point, with the end of the war and German defeat an inevitability, the conspirators wondered whether or not they had left it too late. Beck certainly believed so, mournfully declaring in May, 'It is no use. Nothing can save us.' Others were of a similar opinion. With defeat inevitable, they questioned whether either the Army or the people would support a revolt which was likely to hasten Germany's demise.[1] The answer was provided by Tresckow:

> The assassination must be attempted at all costs. Even if it should not succeed, an attempt to seize power in Berlin must be undertaken. What matters now is no longer the practical purpose of the coup, but to prove to the world and for the records of history that the men of the resistance movement dared to take the decisive step. Compared to this objective, nothing else is of consequence.[2]

Kunrat von Hammerstein agreed that killing Hitler at this stage of the war was little more than a 'gesture' but told Schulenburg it was nevertheless 'a very important gesture. To have cleansed ourselves from within is most important for us and our place in the world, even at the last moment.'[3]

Graf Molke, and others, doubted the wisdom of killing Hitler at this late stage, believing it would be better if Hitler was forced to 'drink the bitter dregs of Germany's utter defeat and surrender', rather than the new regime. The great obstacle was the Allies' insistence on unconditional surrender. Whether Hitler lived or died, the outcome for Germany was the same.

The only difference might be that the war could be brought to a close earlier if Hitler was removed from power. The German historian Joachim Fest saw that, by July 1944, the conspirators' sole remaining ambition was to save as much of Germany's 'substance' as was possible from the impending catastrophe.[4] Olbricht was clear on this point: 'So many brave soldiers are dying on all fronts, ultimately for nothing. We too must be prepared to die for Germany.'[5]

But if they were then to continue with their plot, they would have to act quickly, especially as it was feared that Himmler was likely to gather all those involved in his Gestapo net when it suited his personal ambitions (though it was more likely that Himmler was waiting for the conspirators to remove Hitler before making his own bid for power). Indeed, already rumours were rife throughout Berlin society of an attempt at overthrowing the regime – the conspiracy had simply dragged on for so long that too many people now knew about it.

Fortunately for the conspirators, on 1 June 1944 Stauffenberg was transferred from Obricht's staff to that of Fromm, becoming the Chief of Staff of the Reserve Army. As commander of the Reserve Army, Fromm frequently attended Hitler's military conferences to report on the status of his troops and his chief of staff usually accompanied him. This meant that Stauffenberg would have close, direct contact with Hitler. From the date of his appointment Stauffenberg knew that it was he who would be the assassin.

What kind of Germany would follow Hitler's death remained unresolved, as became evident at a meeting of the civilian leaders of the conspiracy at the Hotel Esplanade in Berlin on 16 June 1944, when the conspirators argued over the form of government and the kind of society they wanted to see after the war. Despite the wide divergence of views, by 19 June a memorandum had been drawn up which was to be presented by Trott zu Soltz, who was to be the leading negotiator with the Allies, to the British representatives in Stockholm. It set out the expectations of the resisters following the imminent coup. It comprised ten points and can only be described as a fudge, designed to appeal to each of the factions that formed the conspiracy. The key points, which would never be accepted by the Allies, were that the new regime 'could under no circumstances co-operate with the Allies on the basis of an "unconditional surrender".' that there would be no invasion of Germany territory by any Allied forces for several weeks or months after the change of regime to allow the new government to 'stabilize its internal and external authority'; and war crimes must only be judged by German courts on German soil.[6]

For the plan to succeed, the coup had to be enacted quickly to ensure the new regime was fully in control of Berlin and other important cities before any contrary information leaked out about who had really murdered Hitler. It was essential, therefore, that Hitler was assassinated when out of Berlin. As Stauffenberg could not simply go up with a pistol and shoot Hitler, as Breitenbuch had discovered, the only possible way to kill the Führer was by planting a bomb; and planting it so close to him that his death was a certainty.

When he was informed that Hitler wanted to see him at the Berghof to discuss the movement of fifteen newly-formed grenadier divisions to the Eastern Front to try and hold back the Russian advance he knew that his chance had come. On 11 July Stauffenberg flew down to Berchtesgaden with explosives in his briefcase, notifying his co-conspirators that he was about to act. Consequently, Olbricht summoned Generalfeldmarschall Job Wilhelm Georg Erdmann Erwin von Witzleben, the highest-ranking member of the conspiracy, and Erich Hoepner to Berlin to be ready to undertake their roles in the coup. Twenty signals officers were also alerted that they would be required for 'special duty'.

Everything was set; all were prepared. Stauffenberg had taken explosives with him to the Berghof five days earlier, on 6 July, possibly to see how practical an assassination attempt might be. At that meeting there had been only a handful of men, including Himmler and Göring. His bulging pigskin briefcase had aroused no particular interest and had not been searched.

This time he fully intended to carry out the task he had been destined to perform. Nothing happened. Stauffenberg, after discussions with some of the other conspirators, decided that Himmler and Göring must also be eliminated at the same time as Hitler so that there was no possibility of either of these characters being able to mount a successful claim to the leadership of the country. Neither were present and Stauffenberg, and his explosives, returned to Berlin.

But Stauffenberg had seen that he had become a trusted individual and that he could carry explosives in his briefcase without being searched. He also knew that another opportunity would present itself in time. Time, though, was what the conspirators did not have and there was a degree of desperation in their efforts to kill Hitler.

On 15 July Stauffenberg flew to another meeting with Hitler, but this time at the Wolfsschanze. Once again he carried his briefcase in which were two 1kg slabs of plastic explosives hidden under a spare shirt.

After breakfast with Generalfeldmarschall Wilhelm Keitel he attended a succession of short meetings in Hitler's conference room but, as on 11 July, Stauffenberg was unable to carry out the assassination. The reason for this, it would seem, was the setting of the fuse. Before setting the fuse – another of the British-made devices – Stauffenberg had to ensure that not only would Hitler be present, but also that he would still be there when the bomb exploded. Part of this problem was, as we have seen, that the fuse worked far more quickly in warmer weather than cold, making it difficult to determine exactly when the bomb was likely to be detonated.

Once again neither Himmler nor Göring were present, so, when he had the chance, Stauffenberg slipped away to call Berlin, where the conspirators were waiting to receive the call that Hitler was dead. His call was taken by Oberst Mertz von Quirnheim who asked Beck and Olbricht what Stauffenberg should do. Stauffenberg was told to stand down, but by this time the pressure of repeated aborted efforts was proving too great a strain on the brave officer and he asked von Quirnheim what he personally thought, and received the reply 'Do it'.

Stauffenberg returned to the conference room determined at last to blow Hitler to Hell only to find his suitcase missing! As he frantically looked round the room fellow conspirator Generalmajor Helmuth Stieff walked in with the briefcase. There was now no time to set the fuse, and Hitler left the room to live for another few days.

It had been decided that the Valkyrie orders should be issued two hours before the anticipated assassination to make sure the Army units were in place and Berlin sealed off. So certain had the conspirators been that this time the assassination would happen, the orders for Phase One of *Valkerie* ('Internal Unrest')[7] had been issued as planned, instructing the troops of the Reserve Army to mobilize. These orders had to be quickly cancelled before any of Hitler's acolytes learnt of it.

Though a single incident could be explained away as an exercise to test the effectiveness of the genuine Valkyrie measures, the conspirators knew that they could not risk another such failure. Fortunately, on 19 July, Stauffenberg was ordered to meet Hitler the following day at the Wolfsschanze, this time to bring the Führer up to date with the state of preparedness of the fifteen new divisions he had earlier been told to cobble together from the shrinking number of available troops. After the debacle of 15 July, it had been agreed that the assassination would take place whether Himmler or Göring were present or not. Due to the short notice Stauffenberg had received, there was not the time to make the thorough preparations in Berlin that were needed for the coup to be effected smoothly. The consequences of this would prove fatal, though not for Hitler.

Chapter 28

Claus von Stauffenberg, Wolfsschanze, 20 July 1944

Stauffenberg woke early on the morning of 20 July 1944 to prepare for the momentous day ahead. The previous day most of the leading figures in the conspiracy had been alerted that the assassination attempt would go ahead this time for certain, and Stauffenberg's staff had issued instructions to those with vital roles to play in the coup.

Once washed, shaved, and dressed, Stauffenberg was met by his driver, Corporal Karl Schweizer, who had delivered not one but two identical bomb-laden briefcases to Stauffenberg the previous afternoon from their place of safekeeping in the hands of Colonel Fritz von der Lancken. This time there could be no mistake.

Along with Stauffenberg's brother, Berthold, the two men were taken by Schweizer in the staff car to Rangsdorf airport where they were met by Stauffenberg's aide, and fellow conspirator, Werner von Haeften and his brother, Bernd. They boarded the courier plane of the Quartermaster General of the Army (Kurierflugzeug des Generalquartiermeisters des Heeres). Also taking the flight to the Wolfsschanze were Generalmajor Hellmuth Stieff and his aide, Major Roll, who were on their way to Mauerwald. The aircraft took off a little after 0700 hours.[1]

The Heinkel He 111 landed at Rastenburg shortly after 1000 hours, and the party on board were taken by staff car to the Wolfsschanze. Stauffenberg then had breakfast with the adjutant of the camp commandant, Captain Leonhard von Möllendorff, in Casino 2 (Dining Room 2). Stauffenberg carried only the papers he needed for the reports he would have to give. The two bombs were hidden in Haeften's briefcase, the plan being that the two men would meet up before the briefing with Hitler and exchange cases.[2]

At 1100 hours Stauffenberg attended his first meeting of the day which was with the Chief of the Organizations Section of the OKW

General der Infanterie, Walther Buhle, and others, before briefing Keitel, at 11.30, on the state of the fifteen new divisions in the OKW bunker in the Restricted Area of Sperrkreis I.

Kurt Salterberg claims to have been on duty that morning at the entrance of the Führer Restricted Zone. He remembered that Stauffenberg and a number of other officers arrived at his post along with Keitel who 'showed me his valid permanent ID from about three metres away, after which the entire group could enter the inner restricted area'. Salterberg's post was just twenty to thirty metres away from the conference barracks.

The next meeting was to be in the presence of the Führer at 1300 hours but, during the conference with Keitel, Stauffenberg was told that Mussolini was due to visit Hitler that afternoon and the meeting with Hitler had been brought forward to 1230 hours.

Stauffenberg now knew he could set his fuse with confidence. Five minutes before the meeting was due to begin, Stauffenberg asked Keitel's adjutant, Major John von Freyend, if there was somewhere where he could change his shirt, explaining that this was necessary due to seepage from his wounds. Exactly which room Freyend ushered Stauffenberg to is unclear. It is variously described as the lounge in Keitel's bunker, the laundry room which was opposite the room in which Haeften was waiting, and Freyend's own quarters.[3] Whichever room it was, Stauffenberg entered, being joined by von Haeften (ostensibly to help the one-handed colonel with his change of clothes) who was carrying the second briefcase with the bombs.

It has been assumed, though not known for certain, that Stauffenberg had decided to take the two bombs into the conference room to ensure a massive explosion that was certain to kill most, if not everyone, inside. But before he could activate both bombs, FBB Oberfeldwebel Werner Vogel opened the door. He saw Stauffenberg and Haeften 'busy with the same thing' and he noticed that papers had been taken out of one of the briefcases. Vogel informed Stauffenberg that he was wanted on the telephone; General Fellgiebel demanded to speak to Stauffenberg on an urgent matter. At the same time, Freyend was heard calling out from the front of the building: 'Herr Oberst Stauffenberg, *do* come along now.'[4] With the sergeant standing at the door there was only time for Stauffenberg to break the capsule of the chemical timer on one of the bombs with the pair of pliers he had become accustomed to using with the three fingers of his remaining hand. With the other bomb and the papers back in von Haeften's briefcase, Stauffenberg walked out in his fresh shirt to cover the short distance to the concrete encased brick-and-wood briefing barracks which stood behind a high wire fence in the innermost security zone to meet Hitler himself.

The Wolfsschanze was being redeveloped with many of the buildings being converted into the massive concrete bunkers, the remains of which can still be seen today.[5] Work on Hitler's bunker had not been completed and he was residing instead in the bunker normally set aside for important visitors, the Gästebunker, with military conferences being held in the nearby *lagebaracke*, or barracks hut.

A ten-minute timer had been used and in the warmth of late July there was nothing to stop the bomb from exploding. But it was just one bomb. Had Fellgiebel called just a few moments later, Stauffenberg would have had time to arm the second bomb and the consequences of that might indeed have proved fatal to Hitler – such again was the Führer's astonishing good luck. On the walk to the conference hut, Stauffenberg was joined by General Buhle and Freyend. Both these men offered to carry the disabled Stauffenberg's briefcase for him, but he declined.

The officers attending the meeting were stood chatting at the entrance to the building until Oberst von Below, Hitler's Luftwaffe adjutant, asked them to go in. Shortly afterwards Hitler appeared. The conference room was at one end of the *lagebaracke*. To get to it from the entrance one had to walk along the central corridor past the telephone room and the cloakroom, taking about eight paces to the right and then entering through a double-winged door.[6] Hitler's position was in the centre of the table where a chair had been placed for the Führer and his polished spectacles laid ready on the table.

Just before entering the hut Stauffenberg agreed to Freyend's repeated offer and handed him the briefcase, asking the major to put him as near as possible to Hitler so that 'I catch everything the Führer says for my briefing afterwards'.

The much-respected Stauffenberg, badly wounded in action but undeterred in his efforts against the enemy, looked, according to the deputy chief of the OKW, General der Artillerie Walter Warlimont, the very model of a General Staff officer: 'the classic image of the warrior through all of history. I barely knew him, but as he stood there, one eye covered by a black patch, a maimed arm in an empty uniform sleeve, standing tall and straight, looking directly at Hitler.'[7] The Führer shook Stauffenberg's hand 'wordlessly, but with his usual scrutinizing look'.[8]

General Adolf Heusinger was giving an assessment of the Eastern Front, which cannot have been very positive, to the assembled officers stood around the room's large oblong table. It was an uncomfortably hot summer day, no breeze being able to penetrate the trees of the Gorlitz forest in which the Wolfsschanze stood. All the windows were open but covered with mesh to keep out the mosquitoes which tormented those who had to live and work there.

At this point accounts differ. It is said that Freyend placed the briefcase against one of the table's thick wooden supports near Heusinger and his assistant, Colonel Brandt, who were both standing on Hitler's right in the eighteen-by-forty-foot room. Stauffenberg tried to edge closer to Hitler but the only space available was at the corner of the table – and his briefcase remained beyond his immediate grasp and, more significantly, on the opposite side of the wooden support from Hitler.

As Heusinger delivered his inevitably gloomy report, Keitel broke in, suggesting that it would be a good idea to listen to the statement that Stauffenberg was going to give about the fifteen new divisions upon which Hitler placed so much hope, and that Heusinger could continue with his assessment afterwards. According to one source, Hitler was sitting on a stool halfway along the rectangular desk.[9] But Hitler said he would hear Stauffenberg later and told Heusinger to carry on. Stauffenberg saw that this was his chance to get away, as attention was focused once more on Heusinger and he left the room, whispering to Keitel that he had to take an urgent phone call from Berlin for an update on the numbers available for the Russian front. It was not unusual for men to be going in and out during briefings, and Stauffenberg's departure attracted little attention. He deliberately left his cap and belt in the lobby of the hut to feign his imminent return to the briefing.[10]

Another version of events is that, upon his arrival, Stauffenberg had slipped his briefcase as close to Hitler as he could and it was only after he left the briefing room that Colonel Brandt moved the briefcase behind the right outer wooden table support. Brandt leaned across the table to examine the map more closely and, as he did so, he kicked over Stauffenberg's briefcase. He bent down, picked up the briefcase and, in doing so, moved it behind the wooden support.[11]

There is, however, no divergence of views at what happened next.

Stauffenberg went straight to the signal officers' room in the Wehrmacht adjutant's building where Haeften was waiting. Also there was fellow conspirator Fellgiebel and Lieutenant Colonel Ludolf Gerhard Sander, one of Fellgibel's communications officers. But the car which had brought the party from Rastenberg had been driven back to the car parking area. Sander was asked to order a car for Stauffenberg who said that he had urgent business to conduct.

While waiting for the car to arrive, Stauffenberg heard that Hitler was requesting Stauffenberg's briefing and already General Buhle had set out to find him. The time was 1240.

Two minutes later, at precisely 1242 hours, Heusinger was outlining the dire situation facing Army Group North: 'West of the Dvina, strong Russian forces are driving northwards. Their spearheads are already south-west of Dvinsk. Unless at long last, the Army Group is withdrawn from Lake Peipus, a catastrophe … .'[12] Hitler stretched out across the table to look more closely at the large-scale map in front of him just as there was a blinding flash followed instantaneously by a deafening roar. Bluish-yellow flame shot out of the windows, hurling with it glass and splinters, and a cloud of choking black smoke

When he recovered from the shock of the blast, General Warlimont was able to take in the scene around him, and saw 'nothing but wounded men groaning, the acrid smell of burning and charred fragments of maps and papers fluttering in the wind'.[13]

Stenographer Heinz Buchholz was sitting at the opposite end of the table:

> I remember it as a clap of thunder connected with a bright yellow flash and ever-increasing thick smoke. Glass and wood splintered through the air. The large table on which all the situation maps had been spread out and around which the participants were standing – only we stenographers were sitting – collapsed. After a few seconds of silence … shouts and screams of pain arose.[14]

Nicholas Below was standing a little to one side discussing the agenda for Mussolini's visit with the other three adjutants:

> Heusinger made a point which interested me, and I moved to the opposite side of the table to obtain a better view of the map. I had

> been there for a few minutes when the bomb exploded ... I lost consciousness for a few seconds. When I came to I saw around me a ruin of wood and glass. I staggered to my feet, got out through one of the window frames, then sprinted around the hut to the main door. My head was buzzing, I had been deafened and I was bleeding from the head and neck. At the door a terrible scene greeted me. Severely injured officers lay around on the floor, others were reeling around and falling over.[15]

The noise of the explosion caused no alarm in the Wehrmacht adjutant's building, where Sanders commented that animals often triggered mines in the minefield that surrounded the Wolfsschanze. The car to take Haeften and Stauffenberg to the airport then arrived and, as they climbed into the car, they saw a body covered by Hitler's cloak being carried from the barracks on a stretcher and they believed, or chose to believe, that they had killed the Führer.

The guard at the entrance to the Fuhrer Restricted Area, Kurt Salterberger, states that, in his opinion, Stauffenberg was too far away from the *lagebarache* by the time that the bomb went off for him to be able to see clearly any of the casualties.[16]

Stauffenberg told the driver, Lieutenant Eric Kretz, to take him back to Rastenburg airfield. The first control post (Wache I) was less than 200 yards from the wrecked *lagebaracke*, and this was passed without difficulty. Though the barrier was down, Stauffenberg was carrying the correct identification pass and was, anyway, known to the sentry. He allowed the car through, noting in his log: '12.44. Colonel Stauffenberg passed through.' This was only about a minute after the explosion. Salterberg, being much closer to the scene, knew immediately that the explosion had occurred in the conference barracks but even he did not close the exit from the Führer Security Zone until the general alarm had sounded, by which time Stauffenberg was already approaching the last checkpoint.

But this outer control point had already been alerted by the time the car reached there and the conspirators' way to the airfield was barred by an anti-tank gun and portable barbed-wire entanglements. The guard, Sergeant Kolbe of the Führer-Begleit-Bataillon, informed Stauffenberg that the alarm had been raised and that he was not allowed to let anyone pass. There was no possibility of trying to break through the roadblock; somehow Stauffenberg would have to bluff his way through.

Stauffenberg declared that he had come straight from the Führer with urgent instructions to fly back to Berlin at once. Sergeant Kolbe was unimpressed. The entire conspiracy hung in the balance at this moment.

Stauffenberg entered the guardhouse and telephoned Captain von Möllendorff, the camp commandant's adjutant, with whom, it may be recalled, he had eaten breakfast that morning. He told Möllendorff: 'I'm in a hurry. General Fromm is waiting for me at the airfield.'

Möllendorff, at that stage of events, had no idea why the alarm had been given and, knowing that Stauffenberg had every right to enter or leave the Wolfsschanze, instructed Kolbe to let the car through. As they drove off towards the airfield, Lieutenant Kretz saw Haeften dismantle the second bomb and throw it into the woods. This was later discovered, following a search of the area.

The guards at the airfield had not yet been notified of the assassination attempt, and the car passed through unchallenged. Kretz said nothing. By 1315 hours the two conspirators were in the air and on their way to Berlin.

It did not take long for it to be realized that of the men in the room before the explosion all could be accounted for except one – Stauffenberg. His hurried departure and strange behaviour was soon remarked upon. Stauffenberg had left the briefing to make, or take, a telephone call to Berlin. Yet, according to Wachtmeister Arthur Adam, the telephone operator, Stauffenberg left without making or taking any such call. (Again, there is a slightly different version of Stauffenberg's departure from the briefing room, with one source stating that Stauffenberg asked to be connected to Erich Felgiebel and that when the connection was made the phone was handed to Stauffenberg who 'lifted the telephone receiver [and] put it down immediately'.)[17] Adam also noticed that Stauffenberg had left behind his cap and belt. Adam pointed these facts to Major Josef Wolf and then to Martin Bormann who immediately took him to Hitler. Coupled with Vogel's comments concerning the furtive actions of Haeften and Stauffenberg when the latter was supposed to be changing his shirt, it very soon became obvious that Stauffenberg was the culprit and that he was heading to the capital of the Reich. (For his sharp observations Adam was promoted to Oberwachtmeister, and given 20,000 Reichsmarks and a small house near Berlin.)

Supposedly, a call was placed to Luftwaffe headquarters in Berlin with orders to scramble a squadron of fighters to shoot down a westbound Heinkel with the identification number of Stauffenberg's aircraft. But it seems that these instructions were intercepted and suppressed by Friedrich Georgi, Olbricht's son-in-law, who was a major on the staff of the Oberkommando der Luftwaffe, and who suspected that the extraordinary order to shoot down one of their own planes might have something to do with his father-in-law's plot to overthrow Hitler.[18]

Key to the overthrow of the existing order in Berlin and elsewhere was the control of information following the death of the Führer. The conspirators needed all contact between the Nazi leaders at the Wolfsschanze and the outside world to be blocked long enough for the conspirators to take over the reins of power and arrest the leading SS, Gestapo and Nazi leaders. All communications to and from the Wolfsschanze were handled by Fellgiebel but, while there was one main communications bunker at the Wolfsschanze, it was not the only one, as Himmler, Ribbentrop and Bormann, who had their own large bunkers within the Wolfsschanze, also had their own independent communications set-ups. There were also other means by which information could be passed from the Wolfsschanze, including a radio set in Hitler's train. However, set deep within rural East Prussia, the Wolfsschanze was a long way from Berlin and there were four repeater stations at Rastenberg, Angerburg, Allenstrin and Lötzen from where signals were transmitted to the Reich capital and beyond. While Fellgiebel clearly could not shut down these four stations by himself, numbers of his officers sympathetic to the cause had been placed in the signal stations and all were ready to act as soon as the message was received that Hitler had been assassinated. That it was possible for the conspirators to be able to shut down the Reich's communications in this manner indicated just how widespread the resistance to Hitler had become by this stage of the war.

Waiting for that call to say Hitler had been killed was Fellgiebel's chief of staff in Berlin, Generalleutnant Fritz Thiele. At 1315 hours his phone rang. It was Fellgiebel: 'Something fearful has happened. The Führer is still alive.' That was all Fellgiebel said, and it left Thiele thoroughly confused and this would have a profound effect upon the events that followed. Did Fellgiebel mean that the assassination attempt had not taken place, or did it mean that the attempt had been made but that Hitler had survived?

Thiele immediately informed Olbricht who was standing by to initiate *Valkyrie*. Neither man knew what to make of Fellgiebel's cryptic message. So, rather than commit to a course of action from which there was no turning back and, as earlier attempts had been aborted at the last minute, Olbricht decided to do nothing until Stauffenberg returned with some positive information. As a result, vital hours were lost – and with that delay the coup was fatally compromised.

Fellgiebel, unaware of the reaction, or lack of it, to his phone call, assumed that the Valkyrie operation had begun and he undertook his part in the plan by contacting his accomplices at the repeater stations, instructing them to block all communications with the Wolfsschanze for as long as they could. As it happened, this was not necessary as Hitler demanded that no one outside the Wolfsschanze should know about the attempt upon his life until the extent of the conspiracy was known. The only people who were to be informed were the leading Nazi officials who were to hunt down the conspirators, with Himmler being ordered to Berlin to take countermeasures against a possible insurgency.

That insurgency in Berlin remained on hold, pending some definite information. The conspirators gathered in increasing numbers in the war ministry complex at the Bendlerblock, anxiously awaiting the news from East Prussia. Berlin police chief Helldorf was on standby at the police headquarters at Alexanderplatz ready to arrest Nazi leaders in the capital as soon as he received word of Valkyrie being launched, and Generalleutnant Karl Paul Immanuel von Hase, the Berlin City Commandant, was poised to despatch troops to seal off the government quarter.

Stauffenberg's aircraft landed at Berlin Rangsdorf at 1545 hours. From the airport Stauffenberg rang Olbricht to tell him that Hitler was dead and expecting to hear that the Valkyrie operation was in full swing. But, to Stauffenberg's dismay, he learned from Olbricht that the confused conspirators had done nothing.

Though they had no definite proof that Hitler had been killed, the die had most definitely been cast. There was no turning back and the only chance the conspirators had of avoiding disaster was to continue the coup as planned. Stauffenberg told Olbricht to issue the Valkyrie orders immediately. His driver Schweizer raced Stauffenberg to the Bendlerblock where action was finally being taken.

Olbricht stepped into Fromm's office, informing him that Hitler was dead, and that he must sign the Valkyrie orders without delay. The cautious Fromm was not prepared to take Olbricht's word before undertaking such an irrevocable step and he was able to get hold of Keitel at the Wolfsschanze. 'There was an assassination attempt, but fortunately it failed,' Keitel told Fromm. 'The Führer is alive and was only slightly injured.'[19] Keitel also asked Fromm if he had seen Stauffenberg but Fromm was able to state quite honestly that Stauffenberg had not yet reported back from his trip to the Wolfsschanze.

From that moment, Fromm knew he had to distance himself as rapidly as possible from the conspiracy. What he did not know was that the first of the Valkyrie orders had gone out, signed by Olbricht's deputy Oberst Albrecht Mertz von Quirnheim.

At this juncture Stauffenberg arrived at the Bendlerblock. He told Olbricht and Fromm that Keitel was lying and that he himself had planted the bomb and witnessed the explosion. 'This is treason,' Fromm shouted, 'punishable by death. You will all face a firing squad.' He looked at Stauffenberg and told him that he must shoot himself at once.[20]

Olbricht calmly told Fromm he had misread the situation and that it was he who was under arrest. He was confined to his office with armed guards at the door and his telephone line was cut. Generaloberst Erich Hoepner took over command of the Reserve Army.[21]

The next step was to issue orders to all headquarters throughout the Reich announcing Hitler's death. These orders, issued by Witzleben, included a preamble which stated:

> An irresponsible gang of Party leaders, far behind the front, has tried to exploit this situation to stab the hard-pressed army in the back and seize power for its own ends. In this hour of supreme danger the Reich government, to maintain law and order, has proclaimed a state of emergency and has entrusted to me both supreme command of the armed forces and executive power in the Reich.[22]

Army commanders were instructed to occupy Nazi Party offices and to arrest all SD and SS troops. There was a considerable delay in transmitting these orders while they were encrypted – and time was rapidly running out for the conspirators.

One man who played an instrumental part in the collapse of the coup attempt now takes centre stage. Major Otto Ernst Remer, in command of the Grossdeutschland Guard Battalion, was not convinced with the orders signed by Hase to cordon off the roads into Berlin and to surround important government installations and SS barracks. Deeply troubled by the signature on the instructions he had received, he sent one of his officers, Lieutenant Hans Hagen, his liaison officer with the Ministry of Propaganda, to check with Goebbels that Hitler was really dead. When Hagen returned with the news that Goebbels had just spoken to a very-much alive Führer on the telephone, Remer knew that he was being complicit in a coup and he reacted swiftly.

Along with a number of SS units, Remer led his battalion to the War Ministry at the Bendlerblock. They fought their way through the conspirators in a ten-minute gun battle, in which Stauffenberg was wounded in his upper left arm, and they released Fromm. Other conspirators that had not already slipped away were arrested. Knowing that he had been aware for some time of a plot to kill Hitler but had done nothing about it, Fromm sought to erase the evidence by executing the leading conspirators.

Stauffenberg, weak with loss of blood from his arm wound, Olbricht, Haeften and Oberst Albrecht Mertz von Quirnheim, a member of Olbricht's staff, were taken into the courtyard of the Blendlerblock, where, in the glare of a truck's headlights, they were shot by a firing party. This act marked the end of the Valkyrie plot in Berlin, but not the end of the killing which would continue for months to follow as Hitler exacted his revenge.

In a number of places, such as Vienna and Prague, the plot was going according to plan, with leading Nazi and SS officials being rounded up by the Army following the initial announcement that Hitler was dead.

In Paris the coup was running almost exactly as planned. General Stülpnagel, whom it might be recalled was Deputy Chief of the General Staff of the Army and was to negotiate a peace deal with the advancing American and British forces which had landed on the Normandy coast in June, ordered the arrest of the senior SS and Gestapo officials in the French capital. He was contacted by Beck at around 18.00 hours, calling from Berlin, to verify that the plotters in Paris were still behind the coup: 'The blow has been struck,' Beck declared,' but we still don't have any exact information on the outcome … are you still with us, no matter what happens?'

Stülpnagel replied that he was, informing the old general that he had ordered the arrest of all the SS and SD men in the capital and that he could count on the loyalty of the troops in Paris as well as their commanding officers. The most senior of all the officers in Paris was former Army Group Centre's commander General Kluge. Having recovered from his accident, he had taken over command of German forces in the West (the *Westheer*) two weeks earlier from Rundstedt, but he was still far from committed to the cause. When Stülpnagel's phone rang again, the call was from Kluge's aide, Generalleutnant Hans Speidel who asked him to join Kluge at his headquarters in the Château de la Roche-Guyon no later than 2000 hours.

Before he left for his meeting with Kluge, Stülpnagel made a phone call himself, to check with Generalleutnant Hans von Boineburg-Lengsfeld, the commandant of greater Paris, that the round-up of the SS and Gestapo was in hand. Boineburg told Stülpnagel that he had decided to wait until it was dark before implementing the measure 'in order that we won't gratify the Parisians with the spectacle of Germans arresting their fellow countrymen'.[23] The arrests, therefore, were not going to take place until 23.00 hours that night. But Boineburg assured Stülpnagel that everything was in place with the 1st Guards Regiment at the École Militaire on standby, ready to move at the appropriate time.

With this far from satisfactory answer, Stülpnagel left for Roche-Guyon, leaving his Chief of Staff and fellow conspirator Oberst Hans Otfried von Linstow to co-ordinate affairs with Beck and Stauffenberg in Berlin. Kluge was on his first familiarization tour of his new command when he was informed that Hitler had been killed and that a new body led by Wizleben and Beck had seized power in Berlin. Kluge had received the news without comment, waiting to see how the situation would develop before committing himself to any particular course of action. When, later in the evening Beck phoned to confirm Kluge's support for the coup, Kluge was interested in the answer to only one question – was Hitler dead? That answer came not from Beck, who replied that whether Hitler was alive or not was of no consequence as long as the coup was pursued with vigour, but from one of Kluge's aides who appeared with the text of Goebbels' brief broadcast announcing to the world that Hitler had been the subject of an assassination attempt but had survived unscathed. Kluge made his excuses and ended the phone call.

Kluge received two further, and contradictory, messages in the form of telegrams. The first was from Wizleben, who called himself 'Supreme Commander of the Wehrmacht', declaring that Hitler was dead, and the second was from Keitel stating that Hitler was alive and had welcomed Mussolini on his planned visit to the Wolfsschanze.

Before he could commit himself to any course of action, Kluge needed to find out exactly what had happened. Attempts at making contact with the Wolfsschanze proved unavailing, but Kluge's deputy, General der Infanterie Günther von Blumentritt, managed to reach fellow conspirator Generalmajor Hellmuth Stief at OKH Mauerwald who confirmed the disturbing news that an attempt had been made on Hitler's life but that it had failed. That was the turning point for Kluge. The coup was clearly not going to succeed. His sole concern now was how he was going to survive the investigation that was certain to follow. He had never committed himself to the conspiracy, but he had known about it and failed to act against it.

Stülpnagel and his personal aide, Oberst Caesar von Hofacker, arrived at Roche-Guyon at 2000 hours. Hofacker, who had been involved in the conspiracy since 1942, opened the conversation, talking about the overthrow of Hitler. 'But Hitler is not dead,' interrupted Kluge – and that was the crux of the matter.

Ever the well-mannered Prussian aristocrat, Kluge led his guests into the dining room. The atmosphere in the room was extraordinary, with Kluge's forced joviality a stark contrast to the gloom emanating from the other officers.

Kluge's mood soon changed when he heard that the Gestapo and SD officers were about to be arrested – Stülpnagel had not told Kluge about this until then. If that move went ahead it would indicate that Kluge was involved in the plot to assassinate Hitler, the consequences of which were only too obvious. An enraged Kluge ordered Blumentritt to immediately put a stop to the arrests. He was too late. The arrests had already begun.

A clearly terrified Kluge told Stülpnagel that he, and he alone, must take full responsibility for his actions. 'Quite impossible,' Stülpnagel retorted, 'We cannot turn back. What is done is done.' Kluge knew that the action he took next might mean the difference between life or a grizzly death at the hands of the SS. So, he told Stülpnagel to consider himself suspended from duty, but privately he told him to dress in civilian clothes and disappear 'until this has blown over'.[24]

As it transpired the round-up of the SS and SD in Paris was carried out very effectively. The troops marched into the Gestapo headquarters at 82–86 Avenue Foch and arrested those inside without resistance. By midnight, the Army was in full control of the French capital, with more than 1,200 Gestapo, SS and SD members safely under lock and key. As has been observed, if the conspirators had acted with the same degree of efficiency in Berlin, the events of 20 July might have had a very different conclusion.[25] The conspiracy collapsed, according to Hans Gisevius, not because they failed to kill Hitler, but because 'there was too much incompetence, too much carelessness, too much indecision'.

The thick oak support of the table in the briefing room unquestionably saved Hitler from serious, possibly even fatal, injury. Of the twenty-four people in the room at the time of the explosion only four subsequently died of their wounds, thanks to that wooden table support. The fatally or severely injured had all stood to the right of Hitler, on the right half of the table, while all who had suffered only moderate or minor injuries had been on the Führer's left. Those that had worn trousers suffered cuts to their lower legs, while those wearing high leather boots were largely spared such injuries.

Salterberg saw Hitler shortly after he had emerged from the wrecked building:

> Hitler was completely slumped, he did not speak and just stared absent-mindedly ahead. His black pants were completely torn up to the knee. The hands and face were smeared with blood. I couldn't see any other injuries. After the group was a few metres away from the barracks, Adolf Hitler turned around again, stood for a long moment, looked at the building.

Heinz Linge recalled that fateful day in his memoirs:

> At that time I was about 100 metres away discussing details of the forthcoming Mussolini visit with the head of protocol, von Dörnberg, and other officials. Suddenly there was an explosion. We continued to talk, assuming that Hitler's German shepherd, which had the run

> of the place, had set off one of the landmines which surrounded FHQ for its security. A few minutes later an orderly came running to our room and cried in a trembling voice: 'Hauptsturmführer Linge, go at once to the Führer!' I sensed immediately that something terrible had occurred. As I was running to Hitler's bunker, Major von Freyend, Keitel's adjutant, came up at the trot. He was greatly distressed, blood running down his face. Horrified, I asked what had happened. He gasped: 'The Führer is alive and is in the small dining room of the bunker.' When I got there Hitler looked at me questioningly with great eyes and noticed my concerned expression. With a calm smile he said: 'Linge, someone tried to kill me.'
>
> His uniform was in ribbons. His hair was singed and hung down in strands. My knees were trembling, but he acted as though nothing had happened.[26]

After Hitler had the splinters from the wrecked table removed from his leg, and his wounds dressed by Dr Hasselbach, Linge helped Hitler put on a new uniform and then went to see the scene of the crime for himself:

> There were still some soldiers outside, groaning. Berger, the stenographer who had been seated opposite Hitler, was dead. The bomb had torn off his legs. The chief of the Luftwaffe General Staff, whose legs had been crushed, was groaning close to death. He and Dr Karl Brant, who had been standing next to Hitler and had taken most of the blast, died almost immediately afterwards. Schmundt, who lost an eye and a leg, died two weeks later in the military hospital at Rastenburg.

Later that day, at around 1500 hours, Hitler asked his secretary, Christa Schroder, to come and see him. 'As I entered his bunker,' she wrote in her memoirs,

> he rose with some effect and gave me his hand. He looked surprisingly fresh and spoke about the assassination attempt: 'The heavy table leg diverted the explosion. The stenotypist sitting near me had both legs blown off. I had extraordinary luck! If the explosion had happened in the bunker and not in the wooden hut, nobody would have survived it. But haven't I always anticipated that happening?'[27]

As Hitler correctly assessed, the blast from the explosion would have been concentrated had it occurred in Hitler's windowless concrete bunker but, in the wooden hut, its windows open, much of the strength of the blast was dissipated. Damage to the hut itself was considerable: the heavy oak table had collapsed, at least one of the supports and about a fifth of the tabletop had been shattered. The walls to the east of the aisle, adjacent to the storage room, were torn down and a hole in one of the wooden floors gaped half a metre wide where the bomb had exploded. The windows and curtains, telephones, lamps, etc. had been damaged or torn to pieces. A number of floorboards had been pushed up as the blast erupted through the floor cavity.[28]

At 0100 hours on the morning of 21 July Hitler delivered a six-minute broadcast which told the German people of the assassination attempt and finally ended all hope of a coup:

> For the third time an attempt on my life has been planned and carried out. If I speak to you to-day it is, first in order that you should hear my voice and that you should know that I myself am unhurt and well; second, in order that you should know about a crime unparalleled in German history. The claim made by the usurpers that I am no longer alive is being contradicted at this very moment now that I am speaking to you.
>
> The bomb was placed by Colonel Graf von Stauffenberg. A number of colleagues very dear to me were very seriously injured. I myself sustained only some very minor scratches, bruises and burns … The bombs exploded two metres to my right. One of those with me has died. I myself am completely unhurt.
>
> It has again been granted to me that I should escape a fate which would have been terrible, not for me but for the German people. They see in this again the pointing finger of Providence, that I must and will carry on with my work.[29]

Even after Hitler's broadcast, Stülpnagel still believed the coup could succeed. When he finally had to concede that the tide had turned against him, and he was ordered to return to Berlin, he tried to commit suicide with his pistol, but only succeeded in blinding himself. He did not need his eyes covered when he was marched to the gallows.

At Zossen, some twenty miles to the south of Berlin, the notes and plans for the coup compiled by the conspirators, including a long list of names, were discovered by the Gestapo on 22 September, revealing just how many people were involved in the plot.[30] Whereas it had been thought the assassination attempt had been conducted by a small number of Army officers, it then became clear the opposition was much wider spread. Approximately 7,000 people, the vast majority of whom had nothing whatsoever to do with the Valkyrie plot, were subsequently arrested by the Gestapo of whom it is known that 4,980 were executed.

Indeed, the great irony in all of this is that rather than toppling the Nazi regime, the failed attempt actually strengthened the Party's grip on the Army, as every moderating or dissenting voice was eliminated in the arrests and executions that followed. The main beneficiary was, in fact, Himmler. He took charge of the Reserve Army from Fromm after the latter was executed for failing to act against the plot, which enabled Himmler to greatly expand the SS and consolidate even more power in his hands.

Possibly the most revealing assessment of the 20 July assassination attempt came just one day later. One of the concerns that had always troubled the conspirators was how the German people would react to the murder of their Führer. It is known that even after the war a very large percentage of Germans still approved of Hitler and his policies, and the immediate response to the news of the attempt on Hitler's life reflected this widespread sentiment.

On 21 July, chief of the Reich Main Security Office, SS-Gruppenführer Kaltenbrunner, submitted a report on 'initial effects of the attempt on the Führer's life on the mood of the nation' to Martin Bormann:

> Based on the information received so far from various parts of the Reich, the first radio broadcast [of the assassination attempt] … was heard by only a small proportion of the population. However, the news spread like wildfire, as even complete strangers told others on the streets or in the shops …
>
> All accounts agree that throughout the nation, the news of the assassination attempt triggered shock, the deepest consternation, horror, profound disgust and anger. From several cities (e.g. Königsberg and Berlin), there are reports of women breaking into

> tears in the shops and on the streets, often stunned and unable to comprehend what had happened. There was great joy over the relatively harmless outcome. Everywhere, people breathed a sigh of relief: 'Thank God, the Führer is alive!'[31]

A report compiled by the SD dated 28 July noted a similar reaction across the Reich:

> A dampening of the mood has not occurred according to the available reports. The population is breathing a sigh of relief that the leader did not become the victim of this assassination. Almost without exception the ties to the leader have been deepened and trust in the leadership which demonstrably has control of the situation strengthened. Only occasionally concerns are expressed that the events of 20 July damage our political situation abroad… . In general a heightening of morale and strengthening of the will to persevere at all costs is noticeable.'[32]

The only conclusion that can be drawn from this is that for all the good intentions of the conspirators, both in moral and military terms, had they succeeded in killing Hitler at any stage from the Anschluss onwards, they would have failed to overthrow the existing order. In 1952 Friedrich Lenz, emphasizing his earlier quoted words, wrote: 'It is clear that from the very start all actions directed against Hitler were also in effect directed against the will of the people, since after all they had chosen this man Hitler as their leader.'[33]

Theodore Hammerow understood this:

> Even if he [Hitler] had been killed it is dubious whether the final result [of the coup] would have been that much different. The fatal weakness of the anti-Hitler conspiracy was its isolation. It had no significant support – neither in Germany nor abroad, neither among liberals nor among conservatives, neither among sympathisers nor among critics of the regime, neither among the elite nor the working class. The conspiracy to topple Hitler's dictatorship … collapsed in a single day, because it had never been more than the conspiratorial attempt at a palace revolution.[34]

Those 'regicides' would have been treated as traitors and executed accordingly. Anton Gill agrees, declaring: 'Had the Resistance succeeded in toppling Hitler, it is very unlikely that any of their theoretical schemes for government would have come to fruition.'[35]

This became clear on 20 July. As Joachim Fest pointed out, not a single officer who had not been involved in the plot in advance of the coup decided to join the rebels when the news of Hitler's death was announced. Rather than blindly obeying the orders issued from the Benderblock, the commanders of the military districts in Hamburg, Dresden and Danzig immediately contacted their local Nazi Party headquarters or local Gestapo officials for 'clarification', and most officers 'instinctively dismissed the rebels as insurgents or traitors'.[36]

It was also noted in a report on the assassination attempt compiled for the OSS on 27 July 1944 that 'there was no indication that the fighting spirit of the German Army had been impaired' and it was even possible that:

> The common soldier may actually experience a certain upswing. He may even believe that the defeat in the East was due to treason rather than faulty German strategy and Russian superiority. If this is his reaction, then he will be compelled to revise his views if he is ordered to retire further.

The report concluded: 'It can now be assumed that the Nazi leadership is committed to a fight to the finish and will not hesitate to make Germany a battlefield.'[37]

For many years after the war the conspirators were not talked of by the German community, and some of the families were denied the state pensions to which they were entitled. Bearing the name of a prominent conspirator was a severe handicap in the immediate post-war years in Germany.[38] For example, Rudolf von Gersdorff, one of the few survivors of the conspiracy, tried to enlist in the Bundeswehr, the armed forces of post-war West Germany, but was denied because he was considered a 'traitor'.

This reaction was anticipated by Treckow when it had become apparent that the assassination attempt had failed, telling Stauffenberg, 'the world will vilify us.'[39] His prediction was hauntingly accurate, with the *New York Herald Times* describing the assassination attempt as being reminiscent of 'the atmosphere of a gangster's lurid underworld',[40] and the diplomat Professor John Wheeler-Bennett writing that the failure of the plot and the subsequent widespread arrests and executions have 'done us an appreciable service in removing a selection of those who would undoubtedly have posed as "good" Germans after the war'.[41]

Another view is that given in an OSS/CIA report:

> It is hard to say whether or not it is better that the plot should have failed. If Hitler had been killed German resistance would have collapsed and the war would have ended in 1944. But possibly the crimes of the Nazis were so great that nothing short of total destruction could have sufficed, despite the cost to the Allies and the loss to Germany of a group of men who are solely needed now in the task of German reconstruction. At least one thing is clear. We have the evidence that there were some Germans who were willing to make the attempt to do away with Hitler and his regime, even though they received no encouragement from Hitler's enemies, and even though it was clear that if their effort was successful it would mean the total military defeat of Germany.[42]

Chapter 29

Vienna, 'Vilmar', 1941; Obersalzberg, SOE, 1944

It might seem surprising that it was not until the summer of 1944 that Britain, in the form of SOE, undertook a serious investigation into the practicalities of assassinating Hitler. But efforts to establish a solid Resistance base in the Third Reich, as SOE had in other countries during the war, had achieved little, and the Führer's popularity was such that the consequences of killing Hitler were incalculable and, as we have seen, as likely to galvanize the Germans into even greater efforts against those who had killed their remarkable leader as to create chaos throughout Germany.

SOE had, in fact, been approached as early as 1941 by a Macedonian, referred to only by his cover name of 'Vilmar', who offered to assassinate Hitler. Recruited by SOE Middle East in Cairo, Vilmar, who had a record of violent crime, claimed to be a good shot but, according to his SOE handler, Julian Amery he was also 'fat, middle-aged and often drunk'. He claimed he was terminally ill with cancer and therefore was unconcerned with the unavoidable fact that his attempt on Hitler would see him gunned down. Consequently, he sought no financial reward for killing Hitler, other than the necessary expenses involved and the promise of a posthumous gallantry award if he did indeed lose his life during his assassination attempt.[1]

Julian Amery was concerned with the would-be assassin's reliability:

> Vilmar was very emotional and, in his cups, sometimes wept like a child. I had the gravest doubts as to whether he would make an effective killer but he was certainly a crack shot with a revolver ... As there was nothing to lose but the few hundred pounds of expenses involved, I recommended that we take the chance.[2]

Vilmar was provided with the necessary forged documents by SOE, portraying him as a Bulgarian businessman, which enabled him to be infiltrated into Portugal and from there into Switzerland. From Switzerland he was able to monitor German newspapers and radio broadcasts regarding Hitler's public appearances. Upon learning that Hitler was to visit Vienna, Vilmar travelled through Germany and into Austria. He made his way to the Bulgarian embassy two days before the date of Hitler's visit where he asked if he could be granted an audience with the Führer or be presented to him at a function. The consul was able to promise to allow Vilmar to accompany him at a diplomatic function which Hitler was due to attend.

Vilmar certainly had nothing to lose and could quite possibly have succeeded. Unfortunately, the night before the function, believing, no doubt that it was to be his last, Vilmar went out on the town. At a nightclub he began drinking heavily and showing off. To a group of girls, he rolled up his trouser leg to proudly reveal the scar of a gunshot wound from his shady past, and then let them see the pistol he was carrying – the one, no doubt with which he intended to kill Hitler. This was too much for one of the girls and she called the police. He was arrested and deported to Bulgaria a few days later. On arrival in Bulgaria he was arrested again and that was the last anyone heard of the man who just might have succeeded where all others had failed.[3]

The Vilmar episode apart, SOE had not officially contemplated an attack upon the closely guarded and highly popular German leader in the intervening years. But, by 1944, Hitler's great successes were a distant memory and whilst it was impossible to gauge the level of support for his regime across Germany, that it had waned was a certainty. Nevertheless, eliminating Hitler did not mean the end of the Nazi Party, which still held, by every known measure, an unbreakable grip on all the levers of power – and there were plenty of ambitious fanatics waiting in the wings, such as Himmler and Bormann, to take over the leadership. The extent of the opposition to Hitler in the *Heer* was unknown to SOE until the 20 July bombing at the Wolfsschanze, and then almost all internal opposition to Hitler, real or imagined, was wiped out.

Exactly why SOE decided to look into the practicalities of killing Hitler in 1944 have never been revealed, especially as by the time the feasibility study was undertaken Allied troops had gained a foothold in Normandy and a German defeat was inevitable.

It has been suggested that the spark which ignited the idea of assassinating Hitler stemmed from a telegram from Duff Cooper, the

British pepresentative on General de Gaulle's Free French Committee of National Liberation in Algiers, on 20 June 1944, concerning a 'project' to kill the German leader. Supposedly, a French colonel had discovered that Hitler was hiding in a château in Perpignan in south-west France near the Spanish border. Though this was so obviously improbable, it was taken at face value and the head of SOE, Major General Colin Gubbins, instructed his team to investigate the possibility of killing Hitler 'in the greatest detail'. He passed on the information from Algiers to the Chiefs of Staff, asking them if they would approve in principle the execution of Hitler if it should prove practicable. The Chiefs of Staff were unanimous that 'from the strictly military point of view, it was almost an advantage that Hitler should remain in control of German strategy, having regard to the blunders he has made, but that on the wider point of view, the sooner he was got out of the way the better.' The Chiefs wrote to Churchill, stating that they were in full agreement with the project and all that was required was the Prime Minister's approval.[4]

The most likely reason, however why it was thought that an assassination attempt at that point in the war was worth considering must have been the supposed, or assumed, decline in Hitler's popular support, possibly gleaned from PoW interrogations. Consequently, on 27 June, a meeting was held at SOE headquarters in Baker Street to discuss the question 'of a deliberate and continuous effort to try and liquidate Hitler'.[5] A second meeting took place the following day during which it was decided that a study should be undertaken to examine the possible means by which Adolf Hitler could be murdered.

Over the course of the next four months a vast amount of information was compiled under the codename Operation FOXLEY by an agent known as LB/X, whose identity has now been revealed as Major H.B. Court. His report was submitted to the SOE Council in November 1944. It was an impressive document, containing 131 pages of photographs, drawings, maps and highly imaginative methods by which Hitler might be killed.[6]

The objectives of FOXLEY were spelt out as 'The elimination of Hitler and any high-ranking Nazis or members of the Führer's entourage who may be present at the attempt'. The prospects of assassinating Hitler in Berlin were so slight that this was never even contemplated by Court who saw that it was only at the Berghof, or whilst en route between

Bertchesgaden and the German capital, that opportunities to kill Hitler might present themselves. The most favoured of the plans, if the quantity of information gathered is a determining factor, was where Hitler felt relaxed and secure – at his lovely Alpine retreat.

The information gathered by SOE on Hitler, his habits and his movements, was surprisingly detailed, and whilst it has been stated that most of this had been gleaned from open sources and radio intercepts, much of the information appears to have been drawn from the interrogation of a prisoner of war, eighteen-year-old Schütze Obernigg of the 3rd Company, 1st Battalion, 2nd Panzer Grenadier Regiment, who was captured on 19 July 1944. From the beginning of August 1943 until April/May 1944 he was stationed at the Berghof. His interrogation report totals twenty-six highly-relevant pages.[7] The positioning and number of all the SS pickets was known to SOE and most of the buildings inside the Berghof estate had been identified. The planners knew where their agents could stay in Berchtesgaden, and which types of person lived, worked and convalesced there, and where they could hide immediately before the operation.

Hitler had first rented a holiday home, the Haus Wachenfeld, on the Obersaltzberg on 15 October 1926. Sitting 1,200 feet above the alpine village of Berchtesgaden, it was just seventy miles from Munich and close to the Austrian border, with Salzburg being just sixteen miles away. As his popularity grew in Germany, and thanks to sales of *Mein Kampf*, (Hitler had earned around 1.2 million Reichsmarks in royalties by 1933) he was able to approach the owner, Frau Winter-Wachenfeld, with an offer to purchase the property and, on 26 June 1933, six months after becoming Chancellor, Hitler took possession of the house.[8]

Mein Kampf was made compulsory reading in many educational establishments throughout the Reich, with millions of copies being sold and distributed. This enabled Hitler to acquire surrounding land and buildings, with Martin Bormann taking charge of purchasing the properties and organizing the layout of the estate. By 1943 the estate included barracks and an SS guardroom, a theatre, a small farm, administration offices, and workers' accommodation, as well as the hotel zum Türken, the guesthouse Hoher Göll, and residences for Bormann, Göring and Speer. The estate was heavily guarded by the SS, with the RSD and *Führerbegleitkommando* acting as close bodyguards, the *Wachkompanie Obsalzberg* responsible for guarding the estate, and the *SS-Sonderkolonne* providing motor transport for Hitler and his entourage.

The security arrangements at the Berghof were extremely tight, though with the Obersaltzberg being heavily wooded and readily accessible on foot in the summer, the Berghof was not an easy place to guard. It was also overlooked by points on the Obersaltzberg from where the Berghof estate could be observed. When Hitler was in residence, a Nazi flag was flown from the estate's flagpole.

There was no such thing as a casual visitor and in 1943 all tourists and hikers were banned from the area – though it is said that on one occasion a 'mad' woman managed to get up to the Berghof undetected, climb the outer fence and walk into the guesthouse, where she was arrested.

Only persons on invited official business, or those employed on the estate, were permitted entry to the grounds of the Berghof. Visitors travelling up from Berchtesgaden had to go through a number of checkpoints, where their passes and their identities were carefully scrutinized. A different pass was required for each checkpoint, allowing access to only that specific area. This ensured that only those that had genuine reasons for being at the Berghof could get anywhere near the Führer's residence. It was said that Bormann insisted that everyone, even the most senior Nazi officials, including himself, underwent the same rigorous security checks every time they drove up to the estate.[9]

When Hitler was in residence at the Berghof nineteen armed RSD officers were on duty at their headquarters in the hotel (or Gästhaus) zum Türken (which still welcomes visitors today). One of these always patrolled in front of the Berghof on a three-hour shift rotation and another patrolled around the nearby buildings. Two others patrolled the surrounding area between 0800 and 2000, i.e. during daylight hours.[10] As so often is the case, a degree of complacency had crept in over the years. It had been noted that security was lax on the bus carrying workmen from Bertchesgaden to the Obersaltzberg, the conductor merely calling out 'Everyone got passes?' and being satisfied with a chorus of 'Jawohls' he let the workers board the bus without further ado.

Despite the frequent changes of routine which had helped frustrate his would-be assassins, when at the Berghof Hitler maintained a predictable routine. Almost every day between 1000 and 1100 he would take a morning stroll from the Berghof to the Mooslahnerkopf Teehaus for a light breakfast. The only occasions on which it was noted that he did not undertake the walk to the Teehaus was when snow on the ground was too heavy. In his report, Court gave the weather conditions from August 1943 to May 1944, indicating not only when snow fell on the Obersaltzberg but the depth of snow on the ground.

Hitler valued his morning walk immensely, and he always insisted on walking without a close bodyguard, often alone or with a friend or colleague. This was the only time that he could relax as an ordinary man, strolling through the pleasant Bavarian countryside untroubled by the war that raged across Europe, to enjoy the simple pleasure of a glass of milk and a slice of toast at the Teehaus. Though the SS guards watched him throughout most of his walk, they did so from afar, with a patrol following him discreetly at a distance, and if he spotted any of them he would turn on them angrily, shouting 'If you are frightened, go and guard yourself.' But this insistence upon privacy could potentially prove his undoing.

There were ten static pickets around the estate, plus one-man patrols, but only one of the former, that stationed at the Gutshof – a farm complex set in the woods – had the specific task of watching Hitler during his morning walk. He was observed, though, by SS pickets at the Theaterhalle and Göring's residence as he crossed a concrete path from Oberau road to the Führerstrasse. These guards, however, were more than 500 yards from the path. After his breakfast at the Teehaus, Hitler was driven back down to the Berghof, so the only time that the Führer was alone and vulnerable was during that fifteen to twenty-minute stroll through the woods.

It was only at this time that Hitler was alone and virtually unguarded. If a sniper could get within range, the chances of killing Hitler were very good. Fortunately, the trees through which Hitler walked were part of a forest which continued beyond the perimeter of the estate to the River Larosbach. The forest was dense and, as the trees were mainly non-deciduous they still held their leaves throughout the year, and would provide excellent cover both in the approach to the perimeter, and while the sniper waited for the arrival of the target. At the selected point in the woods, the sniper would only be about 100 to 200 yards from the path taken by the Führer. The wood beyond the perimeter was not patrolled or guarded.

The wire-mesh perimeter fence was 220 centimetres high, supported by steel tubes at three to five metre intervals. The tubes were bent inwards and laced with three or four strands of barbed wire. This perimeter was patrolled by an RSD dog team at 10.00 hours to make sure the area was safe before Hitler started on his walk. The sniper would not be able to take up his position until after the dog patrol had passed, which meant he only had a few minutes to get into position before Hitler left the Berghof. Timing would be everything.

The majority of the soldiers at Berchtesgaden were men of the *Gebirgsjäger*, the Alpine troops, many of whom were admitted to the military hospital, the Platterhof, and were a common sight around the village.

It was one thing dreaming up such a scheme, but it was quite another to find a man, or men, with the credentials and courage to attempt such a complex and dangerous task. In Court's report, he suggested that Austrian or Bavarian PoWs with an 'animus' against Hitler and the Nazis might be recruited, or Poles or Czechs, in view of the large number of foreign workers in the Berchtesgaden-Salzburg area. Court proposed that such individuals could be trained in the UK or in Italy or Slovenia and parachuted into the region. They could then make contact with friends or relatives in the area.

In view of the massive reprisals which had taken place in Czechoslovakia after the assassination of Reinhard Heydrich in Prague in 1942, when two villages supposedly linked to the killing were razed to the ground and their populations of more than 1,300 murdered, there was little prospect of finding any persons from the occupied countries willing to put their families at such risk.

It was not until January 1945 that an officer in the Military Research Section of the British Defence Attaché in Washington, a Captain Edmund Hilary Bennett, came to the attention of X Section as a likely, and willing, candidate. The twenty-five-year-old intelligence officer was not told the exact nature of the operation he was being considered for, only that it would require him to lie low in Germany for a considerable period while gathering the necessary intelligence to enable him to do the job. Bennett was more than willing to undertake such a task, asking only that he should not find himself out of work when he returned to the UK after completing his mission or if the war should end before he was able to finish the job.[11]

The dossier prepared by Court enabled the SOE planners to identify another area where Hitler might be vulnerable. This was as he returned, by car, from the Teehaus. If the sniper failed to kill Hitler, then an alternative plan would be undertaken. This was for a two-man team to fire a PIAT anti-tank weapon at the Führer's car from the woods near the tea-house as he returned to the Berghof.

Another option was also considered – that of aerial assault. It was suggested that if advanced notification of Hitler's arrival at the Berghof could be obtained, it would be possible to mount a combined operation which would see RAF aircraft bomb the estate, including the SS barracks, followed by the dropping of a parachute battalion or possibly the SAS into the Berchtesgaden area. A battalion of 800 men would be able to completely overwhelm the 300 or so combat troops stationed in and immediately around the Berghof estate. The German troops at the Berghof, except for those committed to anti-aircraft duties, would make their way to the large air raid shelters dug into the hillside when the bombing began. The parachutists would therefore face little opposition upon landing when they would be at their most vulnerable. Nor would it have been possible for the garrisons at Salzburg or Bad Reichenhall to reach Berchtesgaden in time to have any effect on the operation.

According to the FOXLEY file, this offered the best chance of eliminating Hitler as well as other leading Nazis who were in the Berchtesgaden area at the time. This last statement, that of eliminating other senior Nazis, was of particular importance. As the various incarnations of the Oster/Stauffenberg group had concluded, there was no point in simply killing Hitler if the Nazi Party remained in power. The war would continue as before, and possibly to the Allies' disadvantage, as Hitler's decisions had become increasingly bizarre and his insistence on refusing to allow his generals to conduct strategic withdrawals in the East had cost the Wehrmacht dear. With saner heads and wiser counsel, Germany might well recover from the reverses it had recently experienced.

The regime in Berlin had to receive such a shock that it would be driven into a realization that its leading figures could be killed off whenever the Allies decided. So, to coincide with the assassination of Hitler, further strikes would be made against other leading Nazi members. The targets, though, would not be the likes of Göring or Himmler. These were the men most likely to assume power once Hitler was dead and it was seen that these two had the most to lose if the existing regime was dismantled. Their desire to keep their wealth, power and influence would induce them, it was believed, to approach the Allies with an offer to surrender, providing the Nazi Party, or some form of it, remained in government.

The alternative to surrendering for these two would for them also to die at the hands of a British sniper, a point that would be made abundantly clear to them by the other assassinations planned by SOE under the codename FOXLEY II or LITTLE FOXLEY.

The man at the top of the list of LITTLE FOXLEY was Reich Minister of Propaganda Joseph Goebbels. Surprisingly, he was seen as an easy target. He rarely left Berlin except at weekends and much information had been gathered on his official and private addresses, his usual travel arrangements, the men he was normally in company with and, most importantly, the occasions when he was not closely guarded.

With his 'diminutive stature and clubbed foot' Goebbels was instantly recognizable, more often than not wearing civilian clothes. He usually arrived at one or other of his Berlin offices between 09.00 and 10.00 hours in the winter months. Anyone wishing to see the Reich Minister, other than well-known members of the party, had to make a written submission. This application was vetted by his personal adjutants. When in, and whilst travelling to, any of his official addresses he was closely guarded, with his personal bodyguard, SS-Untersturmführer Wilhelm Kruse always close by.

It was in his off-duty moments that Goebbels was most vulnerable. He entertained a considerable number of 'bathing belles' from the Universum Film AG at his various residences around the city when his wife Magda was out of town. Access to any of these, when Goebbels could, quite literally, be caught with his trousers down, though, would be virtually impossible.

He was known to frequent a few bars, cafés and clubs, and it was at one of these that SOE would strike. These included private clubs, where access would be difficult, and the Jockey Bar which had been taken over by the Propaganda Ministry. There was one place, however, which was open to the public. This was the Kunstlereck am Zoo (today simply the Hotel Zoo) on the Kurfürstendamm. Shooting Goebbels there would be comparatively easy, but there would be little or no chance of escape for the assassin.

Eventually, it was decided that it would be one of Goebbels' infrequent visits to his residence outside Berlin, the Sommervilla Waldof, which was on a road that joined the Prenzlaur Chausee to the Berlin-Stettin autobahn. This single-storey white house with a grey-blue roof, was set in large grounds surrounded by a two-metre-high fence topped with barbed wire. Though a strike on his car whilst travelling to or from the villa to Berlin was considered, the dates and times of such a journey could not be discovered by SOE. Other individuals on the SOE list included Generalleutnant Bruno Ritter von Hauenschild, Generalmajor Otto Ernst Remer and SS-Obersturmbannführer Otto Skorzeny.[12]

The main target, though, was still Hitler and, as attacking him at the Wolfsschanze and the Chancellery was impossible, and at the Berghof impracticable, other methods were explored.

Chapter 30

Schloss Klessheim, SOE, no fixed date

If an assassination attempt proved too difficult to mount at the Berghof, the possibility of killing Hitler as he travelled between Berlin and Berchtesgaden was given detailed consideration. His usual mode of transportation was in his special train, 'Brandenburg'.

As we have seen, attempts by the Polish resistance at derailing the *Führersonderzug* had already been made without success, but the FOXLEY papers do state that derailing a train in Germany would be far from impossible as the railways across Germany were only lightly guarded compared with those in occupied countries where troops were positioned in some places at intervals of only 100 to 200 yards. Preceding the *Führersonderzug* was an advanced train consisting of a locomotive with one or two coaches carrying *Bahnpolizei* (railway police) who were dropped off to reinforce the local railway police when deemed necessary

If any action was to be taken against the *Führersonderzug* it would be in Austria, however, where the guarding of the trains was 'slacker' than elsewhere in the Reich. The details of this were as follows:

> Signal boxes are not guarded as a rule, bridges and tunnels are guarded as a rule, bridges and tunnels are guarded by the military, and the stations by the *Bahnpolizei*. Guards at bridges and tunnels are said to consist of only two men and to be very slack in performing their duties … The *Bahnpolizei* normally carried out single patrols and were armed with rifles and hand grenades.[1]

The favoured spot for a derailment was in a tunnel. 'A sabotage party', the FOXLEY report continued, 'disguised as *Bahnpolizei* with one member in mufti (as Gestapo men), or as *Landesschützen* [second-line troops] would not arouse the suspicion of the guards, and should be able to "take over", lay their charges and destroy the train in the tunnel'. There was just one tunnel on the route between Berlin and Salzburg, where the *Führersonderzug* was kept when Hitler was at the Berghof.

There were other tunnels along the routes normally travelled by Hitler's train, such as the one at Stuttgart. This was a long tunnel and it was suggested that it might be possible to lay charges on the track entering it through a ventilation shaft.

In either scenario, it would be necessary for an operative with a wireless transmitter to be posted further up the line to warn the demolition party of the approach of the *Führersonderzug*.

Another suggestion was to derail the train by switching the points so that the *Führersonderzug*, rushing along at 120 km/h, would be diverted into a siding where it would crash off the rails. Alternatively, as it was passing through a station where an individual would throw a suitcase full of explosives under the oncoming train: for this to be practical, the *Führersonderzug* would have to be on the track adjacent to the platform where the agent was standing. It was thought that a suitable individual for this task could be recruited from disaffected German PoWs.

The *Führersonderzug* must have presented an awe-inspiring sight steaming across the countryside. By 1944 the dark green of the other special trains, the *Sonderzüge*, used by other prominent Nazis, had been changed to what was described as a 'dirty' violet or dark blue and comprised of sometimes two locomotives and up to twenty coaches, many of which had been specially constructed entirely from steel and weighed more than 60 tons. It acted as a fully functioning mobile headquarters which was in constant communication with the rest of the Reich. If the train stopped, the Führer's personal Pullman carriage, the dining car and sleeping cars could be connected quickly with the postal telephone network. When on the move, communications were conducted by encrypted radio. Telephone lines ran the full length of the train. The total strength of the train's personnel, including the flak troops, the Begleit-Kommando, waiters and railway employees was around 100–120.[2]

The first and last carriages were flak wagons, both of which had an armoured cupola mounting an anti-tank gun or quadruple 20 mm anti-aircraft guns. These were manned by officers and men from 9 Fallschirm-Panzer-Artillerie-Regiment 'Hermann Göring'. The second carriage was for the twenty-two men of the SS-Begleit-Kommando and the RSD detachment which followed Hitler everywhere. Two of these men were always on duty at both entrances to Hitler's coach. At any station where the train was to stop, *Bahnpolizei* armed with pistols and sometimes rifles or machine guns and detachments of Gestapo, some in plain clothes, guarded the platform, though the station was not cleared of civilians. At longer stops where Hitler left the train, the Begleit-Kommando also got off the train to form a bodyguard around the Führer, never leaving his side.

As mentioned earlier, such was the security around the movements of Hitler's train, there was little chance of discovering such information and this was the main reason not much attention was given by SOE to this form of action against Hitler.[3] It was also highly unspecific in that there could be no guarantee that Hitler would be amongst those who might be killed in the crash.

Attention, therefore, turned to conducting some form of sabotage when the train was in sidings. When Hitler was in Berlin, the *Führersonderzug* was usually stationed at Tempelhof maintenance depot and was shunted to the chosen departure station, usually taking two hours.

From what was known about the guarding of Ribbentrop's *Sonderzug* 'Westfalen', four of the flak gunners were on duty during the daytime, and by two *Bahnpolizei* armed with pistols at night. When Hitler was at one of his *Führerhauptquartiere* away from Berlin or the Berghof, the *Führersonderzug* was guarded by the Begleit-Kommando.

The *Führersonderzug* was normally serviced, washed and provisioned at sidings by the magnificent Schloss Klessheim, the work generally being carried out by Begleit-Kommando personnel. This Baroque palace is around two-and-a-half miles to the west of Saltzburg, and it was used by Hitler after the Anschluss for conferences and to host important guests. Today it is the home of Casino Salzburg.

With the *Führersonderzug* being so heavily guarded, and its movements difficult to discover in advance, it was suggested that it might be more practical to attack Hitler as he was being driven to the train when it was at the Schloss Klessheim sidings. If an agent was based in Salzburg, he would be able to watch for the arrival of the train at Schloss Klessheim. With Hitler's presence being so badly needed in Berlin or the Wolfsshanze, the agent could be absolutely certain that the Führer would only be at the Berghof for a few days. The agent would not have long to wait in his chosen spot with his high-powered sniper rifle before Hitler returned to the schloss.

Hitler's cavalcade always followed the same route between the Berghof and the schloss which, almost as far as the autobahn beyond Grödig, is heavily wooded, the tree line being very close to the road, providing excellent cover for a sniper. This route was known to be guarded by the SS and the RSD, but this is a distance of almost fifteen miles and it would have been impossible for these men to provide anything other than a token presence, with large gaps between them.

Occasionally, Hitler's train was moved down to the station at Berchtesgaden for Hitler to board. The road down to the station was similarly heavily wooded, but the distance was far shorter and could therefore be more easily secured.

The *Kolonne* usually consisted of three or more Mercedes-Nurberg six-seater limousines preceded by an RSD motorcyclist armed with a sub-machine gun. Hitler's car was always the first or second in the *Kolonne* and was distinguishable from the others in that it carried a large swastika symbol on its right mudguard. Hitler, helpfully, always rode in the front passenger seat, unless he was travelling with a fellow dignitary and then he rode in the back with his guest.

Attacking Hitler's car while travelling at speed could not be regarded as a certain method of killing Hitler. So consideration was given to shooting him as he stepped out of the vehicle – when he would be fully exposed and at his most vulnerable. Yet, while the route to the schloss was predictable, SOE did not know which direction Hitler's cavalcade took after leaving the schloss to reach the railway sidings. If it took the right-hand fork or carried on along the autobahn without actually going to the schloss itself, then Hitler would possibly have disembarked from his car to walk to the train at the south-east end of the sidings. This, though, would be 300 yards away from the nearest cover, a wood that extended to the north of the schloss, where a sniper could conceal himself. This was regarded as beyond a sniper's range, bearing in mind that Hitler would be a moving target. The alternative to a rifle would be for the assassin to use a PIAT to blast Hitler as his car drew to a stop.

If the column took the left-hand fork, the road ran alongside the wood to reach the sidings and a sniper hidden at the edge of the wood would have a comparatively easy shot (under 100 yards) as Hitler stepped out of his car. The concern here, though, was that the wood was 'uncomfortably' close both to the sidings and the schloss and any activity there might be detected by the Begleit-Kommando. This might be a particular concern during winter, as the forest included many deciduous trees which would have shed their leaves.

Such was the detail in the planning of FOXLEY, two safe places for the would-be assassin to stay were identified in the Saltzburg area. These, the Gasthof Meyer at Hof, a small township eight miles east of Salzburg, and at Ainringweg 13, Salzburg. These were places one could stay where 'no questions would be asked'.

There were occasions, it was noted, when the *Führersonderzug* was left in the sidings at Salzburg which offered another possibility contemplated by SOE – that of poisoning the train's water supply. Hitler had a persistent fear of being poisoned (possibly stemming from the incident at the Kaiserhof in 1932) and all vegetables and fruits prepared for the Führer were grown on the Berghof estate under close supervision, with bread and similar products coming from Himmler's SS bakeries. A team of female food-tasters was also employed. So there was little chance of tampering with Hitler's food.

It was the same with the Führer's medicines. The supply of medicines to Hitler were controlled by the SS and the Police Medical Ordnance Officer, Dr Carl Blumenreuther, with all medicines given to Hitler being administered solely by his personal physician, Doctor Theo Morell. Each month Morell would submit Hitler's requirements to Blumenreuther who would order them in, the items being randomly analyzed by the SS. This may sound like a secure procedure, but Morell owned two pharmaceutical companies in Olmütz and Pilsen from where some of the medicines were obtained. In his factories Morell employed mostly Czechs and forced Russian workers, as well as a Jewish doctor, Wolfgang Laves. The potential for contamination in the factories by such possibly disaffected types was obvious and it was believed that there was at least one unspecified plan to sabotage the consignments. It is known that one batch of medicines was rejected by the SS, so it may well have been the case that one poisoning attempt was made.[4]

With Hitler's food and medicines being so carefully controlled, it was considered that the only possible medium through which he might be poisoned was through his drinking water. When the *Führersonderzug* was at the Saltzburg sidings, the outside of the train was washed not by the Begleit-Kommando, but by a team of six French female workers. According to the FOXLEY report these women are 'apparently approachable'. It was known that they were often to be found in the evenings, after 17.00 hours, at local cafés, particularly the Café Funfhaus and the Café Pitter (the latter was subsequently developed and extended and is today the 4-star Hotel Pitter). Though the girls had to be back at their work camp by 22.00 or 23.00 hours, they were known to be 'dateable'. They could be identified by their black, buttoned, knee-length overalls.

The idea of contacting these women was in the hope that one of them would be able to 'doctor' the water in the tank above the kitchen of the *Führersonderzug*'s dining car. The capacity of the tank was 120 gallons, which would necessitate dropping into it approximately 768 grams of the poison in the form of a strong solution. The movement of the train as it chugged along the track would distribute the poison evenly throughout the water. This would have to be done when the train received its final washdown on the day before leaving the sidings.

The poison in question, only identified as 'I' in the FOXLEY file, was tasteless and odourless. Its other great advantage was that it took six or seven days for any symptoms to appear, by which time it was too late for any antidote to work.

How practical all this was is open to question, and was thought so at the time, particularly as the French women only cleaned the outside of the train, the inside being serviced by Reichbahn employees. Another method of introducing poison into the water tank as it was being filled up was also investigated. But at Salzburg, the train was moved from the main sidings to a goods siding, where water was taken onboard from a hydrant which stood between the rails. Water for drinking and cooking purposes was also taken on at station stops en route, once again by means of a rail hydrant. With no practicable means of contaminating this mains water, the idea was not progressed.

Why then was Operation FOXLEY not carried out? The subject of assassinating Hitler had first been considered as early as 1941, though such ideas were shelved until the FOXLEY plans were drawn up. Opinions were divided amongst SOE staff about the desirability of killing Hitler, and doubts about the morality of assassinating a head of state caused them considerable agony. Even in the midst of the most devastating war in history, there was something unseemly about an assassination of that nature. Equally, there was a chance that with an enemy government assassinating Hitler he would be turned in the eyes of many from being a monster into a martyr, thus, as was observed after the Valkyrie debacle, encouraging the patriotic Germans to fight on with even greater tenacity. Also, all the senior Nazis who might take over from Hitler were well aware that they were likely to face prosecution for war crimes if they lost the war; there was, therefore, little likelihood of a German surrender. In his Foreword to the published FOXLEY files, the renowned historian Ian Kershaw pointed out that in a survey of public opinion in West Germany in 1952 a third of those interviewed still condemned Stauffenberg's actions.[5] This attempt was conducted by fellow Germans, so it is easy to imagine how strong the response to an assassination of the Führer by Britain might be. That same survey, incidentally, also revealed that a quarter of those questioned still 'thought well' of Hitler.

It must not be forgotten that, at the end of the First World War, it was the German claim that they had been 'stabbed in the back' by their politicians who had surrendered, refusing to acknowledge that their armed forces had been defeated on the battlefield. A similar outcome in the Second World War might produce the same conviction, with untold potential consequences. Germany's belief in its military strength had to be utterly demolished. Allied leaders fully understood this which is why they announced that the only terms they would accept was unconditional surrender.

On the other hand, it was argued that the entire Nazi structure had been built around Hitler and that his death would see the whole of that flimsy edifice crumble almost overnight. If this would have happened and the war shortened, even if only by a few months, hundreds of thousands of lives would have been saved, for it was in the latter stages of the war that the casualty count reached appalling numbers.

FOXLEY continued to have its advocates even into early 1945, but the strongest argument against the assassination of Hitler is revealed in the FOXLEY papers in a minute written on 9 October that year by Lieutenant Colonel Ronald Thornley, the Deputy Head of the German Directorate:

> As a strategist, Hitler has been of the greatest possible assistance to the British war effort … his value to us has been the equivalent to

an almost unlimited number of first-class SOE agents strategically placed inside Germany. Although the military situation has been temporarily stabilised on the western front and the German army appears to have regained cohesion, Hitler is still in a position to override completely the soundest of military appreciations and thereby help the Allied cause enormously … .

To remove Hitler from the wheel at a time when he and his fanatics have pledged themselves to defend every street and every house on German soil, would almost inevitably canonise him and give birth to the myth that Germany would have been saved if he had lived. If, as is almost inevitable in my view, the assassination was traced to Allied sources, the repercussions would probably be grave. It would be disastrous if the world came to think that the Allies had to resort to these low methods as they were otherwise unable to defeat the German military machine. From every point of view, the ideal end to Hitler would be one of steadily declining power and increasing ridicule.

Chapter 31

Schloss Klessheim, Erwin Giesing, 1 October 1944

Hitler was more seriously injured by Stauffenberg's bomb than is often appreciated. Though he had more than one hundred oak splinters removed from his legs, mainly his right one, at first it appeared that Hitler had survived the blast surprisingly well. When Morell rushed into Hitler's quarters after hearing the explosion, the Führer remarked, 'It's nothing really.' Then with an actual smile on his face he declared, 'I'm invulnerable. I'm immortal!'

Hitler was also well enough to receive Mussolini on his planned visit, at 15.30 hours. Hitler went to the Wolfsschanze barnhof to greet Mussolini, the pair driving back to the Sperrkries I accompanied on the short journey by armoured vehicles. Hitler took his old friend to the situation barracks to show him the damage done by Stauffenberg's bomb and to revel once again in his remarkable survival.

The two leaders had tea together and when walking down to the tearoom Hitler was determined to show everyone that he was alive and seemingly untroubled by the event, with the Führer making a point of talking to the Todt workers as he passed by them to assure them that they were not under any suspicion. At the meal were Göring, Himmler and Ribbentrop, as well as an interpreter who recorded the following:

> At the beginning of the talk the Duce congratulated the Führer with heartfelt words on his survival of the bomb attempt. The Duce was deeply moved upon hearing the details related to him by the Führer concerning the train of events surrounding the assassination attempt. He interpreted the Führer's escape as a clear indication of the intervention of the Almighty. It was certain that anybody who always miraculously survived the assassination attempts of his enemies must also be led to a victorious finale in the current conflict.[1]

One of the most remarkable immediate effects of the explosion was that the trembling in his left leg which had manifested itself in recent times disappeared. But he had second-degree burns on his calf and two fingers of his left arm. His hair was singed and he had severe bruising and open flesh wounds.

Other symptoms also developed and, as the weeks passed by, Hitler's health deteriorated rapidly. His right arm, which had been damaged in the explosion, trembled constantly and his skin and eyes became noticeably jaundiced.

He increasingly secluded himself in his quarters, becoming more and more withdrawn. He shuffled around his bunker and, occasionally, the Führer Restricted Area, like an old man, due to a wound to his head which caused damage to his inner ear. This affected his balance. He believed that he was falling to the right and when he was walking outside his bunker at night he would stumble to the right off the path into the darkness. Gradually, the damage to his ear became less pronounced, but then the trembling to his left leg returned.

He was also racked with stomach cramps which were so severe that one morning he could not get out of bed, would not eat and showed no interest in the war situation. His stomach pains continued remorselessly. Often, he would struggle to stand upright, suffering severe and painful flatulence.

Morell believed that the conditions at the Wolfsschanze were adding to Hitler's problems: 'I again proposed most urgently a change of air (to Berlin) either for two or three days and then to the mountain for twelve to fourteen days, or just Berlin for eight to ten days,' the doctor wrote in his diary.

> He rejects the Berghof out of hand and says Berlin is unsuitable as he (the patient) would have to keep going down into the bunker, and he cannot walk much at present, he is too weak. I referred to the unsuitability of the new bunker for him, the living and sleeping quarters are tiny and despite the ventilation system there is far too little oxygen.[2]

Martin Bormann was equally concerned about the state of Hitler's health, writing the following to Frau Gerda on 1 October 1944:

> The Führer lives downstairs in his bunker room, has only electric light, and where the air pressure is constantly too high because fresh air has to be pumped in – and it is exactly as if he was living in a basement… . He also nags about our huts with the brick walls that, he says, are destroyed in the first heavy air raid… . I have made myself unwell worrying about the Führer's illness. Finally everything depends on his health! … the briefing had to be cancelled for the third day in a row today.[3]

It had also become noticeable to those close to Hitler that the booming voice which had thrilled the thousands at the great rallies of the past was reduced to a weak whisper. In fact, there was a medical reason for the weakened condition of his voice. Otorhinolaryngologist Dr Carl Otto von Eicken examined Hitler on 16 November and conducted an X-ray on the Führer two days later, which showed a shadowing of the left maxillary sinus and s small polyp (about 20mm) on his vocal chord.

Some of those around him believed that the pressures of the failing war against the Soviets, coupled with the shock of almost being killed by Stauffenberg's bomb, had finally broken his spirit and they thought Hitler would never recover. The daily situation reports had to be taken to his bunker, being read to him by Admiral Puttkamer who was also still suffering from the effects of the explosion of 20 July and had to limp across on crutches from the conference room.

Inevitably, added security measures were put into place immediately after the assassination attempt. This included, predictably, searching the briefcases of any person who was likely to be in the presence of the Führer. This led to an alarm when a hand grenade and a bottle of petrol were found in the briefcase of Captain Ötting, Ribbentrop's adjutant. Ötting was in fact carrying out a rarely followed rule which dictated that personnel carrying top secret papers should have with them the means of destroying those papers to ensure that they did not fall into the hands of the enemy.

While the workers at the Wolfsschanze were not in any way involved in the assassination attempt, they were also subjected to heavily increased security measures. They were subjected to almost daily searches and their every move in the compound was monitored by the SS and RSD officers and, when being driven to and from the Wolfsschanze, the lorries they were transported in were escorted by armoured vehicles and motorcycle combinations with mounted machine guns.

During his periods of illness at the Wolfsschanze, Hitler was once again the subject of a failed assassination attempt, though he was completely unaware of it. Doctor Erwin Giesing, chief medical officer of the Luftwaffe and an ear, nose and throat specialist, was called to treat Hitler's ear injuries. This treatment included doses of highly pure cocaine. This he administered in the form of nose and throat dabs, a highly effective surface application. The cocaine was delivered by courier train from Berlin. According to Giesing, he administered the cocaine to Hitler more than fifty times between July and November 1944. Hitler had become profoundly bothered by the noise from the construction work being carried on at the Wolfsschanze and the cocaine mitigated the effects of the banging and crashing of the workers.

The procedure was carefully monitored. In the morning, assistant surgeon Karl Brandt took Giesing to a tent behind the guest bunker where they went through the strict security measures in place since 20 July. Giesing's bags were emptied, every instrument was examined – even the lightbulbs of the otoscope were taken out and screwed back in again. Giesing had to hand over his uniform cap and his dagger, empty out the contents of his trouser and jacket pockets on to the table, and turn out his pockets. He got only his handkerchief and keys back, and his fountain pen and pencil were returned afterward. He was frisked from top to bottom. The cocaine was left out of these rigid controls; it was already inside kept under lock and key by Hitler's valet Linge. It was then that the valet performed his part of the ritual, taking the bottle of cocaine out of the drugs cabinet in the orderly room and inviting Giesing to make his examination.[4]

On one of these occasions, on 1 October, after receiving his dose of cocaine, Hitler's eyes fluttered, he turned a deathly white and passed out. At first, Giesing was terrifyingly alarmed that he had given the Führer a fatal overdose. Then, he realized that Linge had left the room and that he was alone with Hitler, and he saw his chance to get rid of the tyrant: 'At that moment', Giesing wrote in his diary, 'I did not want such a man to exist and exercise the power of life and death in his purely subjective manner.' He plunged the swab he had been using back into the cocaine bottle, knowing that a second dose could be lethal. He began swabbing

Hitler's nose when he was startled by Linge who had walked back into the room and demanded to know how much longer the treatment was going to take.

Giesing said he was just about finished. He left the bunker not knowing whether or not he had killed the Führer. Giesing then excused himself, saying that he had to return to Berlin, ostensibly claiming that he had to check on his office which had been bombed. He telephoned the Wolfsschanze the following day from Berlin and was relieved to learn that Hitler was still very much alive.[5]

Chapter 32

Berghof, USAAF, June 1944; Berlin, Rupprecht Gehring, January 1945

If SOE had rejected the idea of killing Hitler, others had not. The USA was late both to join the war and to contemplate assassinating the German leader. US General Carl Andrew Spaatz, the commander of Strategic Air Forces in Europe in 1944, looked at the possibility of killing Hitler when he was in residence at the Berghof. It will be recalled that Hitler's presence at the Berghof was always announced by the flying of the Nazi flag, so it would be possible to know exactly when to strike.

Spaatz, therefore, requested aerial reconnaissance of the Berghof and Berchtesgaden district in June 1944. His proposed method of attacking the Berghof was to use Lockheed P-38 Lightning fighter-bombers of the US Fifteenth Air Force based in Italy. But, as with the conclusions drawn by SOE, Henry 'Hap' Arnold, commanding general of the US Army Air Forces, believed the 'general impression among the higher officers in the Allied Air Forces is that … "Our secret weapon is Hitler, hence do not bomb his castle. Do not let him get hurt, we want him to continue making mistakes".'[1] It was also considered that, due to the strength of the defences of the Obersalzberg and the underground shelters of the Berghof, Hitler was likely to survive such an attack causing the German people to once again rally round their Führer. The scheme was dropped.

As it happened, a raid very similar to that proposed took place just a few months later on 4 November. Four Republic P-47 Thunderbolts from the US 27th Fighter Group of the Mediterranean Allied Tactical Air Force bombed a hotel in Milan where it was thought Hitler was staying. Hitler was in fact at the Wolfsschanze, spending his last few days at his East Prussian headquarters before his final trip to Berlin.

Berchtesgaden was in fact attacked on 20 February the following year, much as had earlier been envisaged, when eight P-47s from the Fifteenth Air Force bombed the area and attacked a train, after being unable to complete a mission in Italy. Initially, the commander of the squadron did not realize the significance of the place he was attacking, and he was driven off by heavy anti-aircraft fire without attacking the Berghof.

When this was revealed to the general public there was widespread disappointment. In a letter to the *Washington Post* one reader wrote: 'within the many months that our and British planes have been flying from Italy to bomb certain localities in Austria, there must have been some occasions when it would have been convenient to leave a calling card at Hitler's place.'[2]

There was, therefore, a public mood for bombing the Berghof but it was not until 25 April 1945 that the Berghof was targeted, under the operational name of HELLBOUND. But on this occasion it was the RAF's Bomber Command which struck with a massive force of 359 Avro Lancasters drawn from twenty-two squadrons. Many reasons have been suggested as the motive, or motives, for the raid, but one thing can be certain: killing Hitler was not one of them, regardless of such speculation in the press. The Führer was known to be in Berlin where, even in the last months of the war, plans were afoot to assassinate him.

One of these was a hastily- and ill-conceived idea dreamt up a Leutnant Rupprecht Gehring who claimed to be present at the Führer's headquarters from time to time which would give him the opportunity to strike. As with so many of those who sought Hitler's downfall, he had once been a staunch National Socialist. But he lost a leg in fighting in 1939 and, as early as the winter of 1942, he had contemplated assassinating Hitler with a bomb hidden in his false leg during one of his visits to the Chancellery. At the time he also commanded a tank company in Wünsdorf near Berlin and wanted to lead it against the government.

It was in January 1945, however, when Gehring seems to have developed a more specific plan. On 15 January Hitler left the Berghof for the last time and arrived at Berlin-Grunewald aboard 'Brandenburg' the following morning. It was during one of the *Führersonderzug*'s 'customary' stops en route, it has been suggested, that Gehring aimed to attack the train with explosives. Nothing came of this and, on the 18th or 19th, he came to the attention of the Gestapo and was arrested. Gehring made other fanciful claims, including one that he had been given 'the mission' to fly to England to arrange for Allied paratroopers to land at Potsdam and Berlin to support the overthrow of the collapsing Third Reich. [3] Predictably, Gehring was executed.

Implausible as this sounds, it is claimed that contact had been made once again with Dulles in Geneva by a Berlin resistance group which would guide American paratroopers to key targets in the city or, possibly, to simply capture Hitler before the Soviet armies overran the German capital. The Americans, however, were not going to renege on their promise that the Soviets would take Berlin and the scheme was never taken up by Dulles.[4]

Nevertheless, there was one supposed final effort by the Americans to assassinate Hitler. The person who had handled Alexander Foote when he contemplated blowing Hitler up at the Osteria Bavaria was the most unlikely Oxfordshire housewife, Mrs Burton. She had been born Ursula Kuczynski and served the Soviet Union as a colonel in the Red Army and was a highly trained spy. As such, she recruited two German nationals living in England, Paul Lindner and Anton 'Tony' Rush. These two were to be parachuted into Germany to send local information to US intelligence. It is said one of the last messages that was sent to Lindner and Rush in April 1945 was from the OSS asking for the exact 'whereabouts of Hitler', with a view to killing him with a 'surgical bombing strike'.[5]

Chapter 33

Führerbunker, Berlin, Albert Speer, February 1945

It was on 19 October 1945 that a certain Dietrich Stahl was interviewed by Major E. Tilley of the Enemy Personnel Exploitation Section concerning Albert Speer's alleged assassination plans. Speer, it was claimed, planned not only to kill Hitler but also what was described as 'the Big Three' – Himmler, Goebbels and Bormann.[1]

Stahl was involved in the plot, which, in its essentials, was a scheme to inject solid poison gas into the air-raid shelter at the Reich Chancellery in February 1945. Stahl was a munitions expert, becoming honorary Head of the Main Committee for Munitions (*Hauptausschuss Munition*) and Chairman and Liaison Officer of all Chiefs of Main Committees in Speer's ministry.

According to Stahl, it was sometime in the middle of February that he and Speer were sheltering from an Allied air raid in the bunker by Speer's ministry at Pariser Platz in Berlin, that Speer first mentioned his plan. They talked for an hour and a half. After dealing with some official business, Speer revealed his thoughts, in particular the instructions that Hitler had given regarding 'the insane measures for destruction, against the defence of towns and villages which were worthless from a strategical viewpoint, against the Volkssturm, etc., and he expressed his great sorrow that nothing sensible or serious was done to terminate this lost war.'

Stahl agreed with his boss which encouraged Speer to reveal more.

> I simply cannot stand it any longer and be witness to a government by lunatics. The nation will perish completely if nothing decisive is done about these insane plans for destruction. I have finally come to the decision to end this state of affairs, if necessary by force. However, there is no use in removing only one, the most dangerous and closest of his entourage must be removed… Himmler, Goering and Bormann.

Speer then told Stahl exactly how he intended to dispose of all these four. 'He intended to throw into the ventilators of the ARP bunker in the Reich Chancellery some poison gas shells or canisters, on the assumption that these canisters would burst open during the descent and the escaping gas would penetrate the bunkers.' Speer apparently added that the bunker doors would have to be locked to make sure that no one inside could escape. The reason that Speer had confided in Stahl was because he needed advice on what type of shell and gas to use, and Stahl was an expert in that field. Stahl told Speer that he did not know much about poison gas, but he knew someone who did – his Army liaison officer.

The man Stahl turned to was Oberstleutnant Diplom-Ingenieur Soika. What Stahl learned was that solid poison only turns to a gas when the container or shell explodes, thus splitting the poison into minute particles. This was a serious setback because an explosion would have shattered the thin walls of the air ducts. The scheme had to be dropped.

Speer, having taken the mental leap from loyal servant to assassin, was not about to give up. Certainly, it is a fact that Hitler had told Speer to make sure that Germany's industrial infrastructure was destroyed rather than allowing any part of it to fall into Allied hands. This was Hitler's *Zerstörungsbefehl*, or destruction command. Hitler believed that the German nation would never be allowed to rise again. So, if Germany was finished, then, in his eyes, everything should be destroyed. Speer, as Reich Minister of Armaments and War Production, was the man who had guided German industry since 1942. He could not bring himself to destroy what he had created and he secretly ignored Hitler's order.[2]

Still determined to find a way of killing Hitler, Speer considered the use of a more traditional type of gas which he could introduce into the bunker's ventilation system. Filters protected the system from drawing in any poisonous air so these would have to be removed beforehand. Speer was acquainted with the Chancellery's chief engineer, Johannes Henschel. He advised Henschel that the system's filters had been in use for a long time and should be renewed, Hitler having genuinely complained of bad air in the bunker.

Henschel duly removed the filters, leaving the ventilation system unprotected. But when Speer next invented a reason to inspect the ventilation shaft, he found armed SS guards posted on the roofs of the entire complex where searchlights had also been installed. He also saw that where the ventilation shaft had previously been at ground level, there was now a chimney rising at least ten feet high (poison gas being heavier than air) putting the air intake completely beyond his reach.[3]

In March Speer again spoke to Stahl and told him of his latest plan:

> Himmler, Goebbels and Bormann gathered almost every evening in the Reich Chancellery for the purpose of hatching their fiendish plans and imposing the most terrible death sentences etc. During night air raids all three drove in their cars from the Reich Chancellery to the suburbs of Berlin and such a moment was to be used for an ambush. He [Speer] said that he had found a few brave men experienced in the use of arms and that he himself would take on one of the three cars.

Speer asked Stahl to provide him with a dozen machine carbines and pistols, along with enough ammunition for the job. He also asked Stahl to get him Very flares. These would be set off in the road as the cars approached to imitate incendiary bombs. This would cause the cars to stop, triggering the ambush.

It was at this point where Stahl later changed his story slightly, by stating that Speer intended to shoot Himmler, Goebbels and Bormann as they exited the Chancellery at the start of an air raid to make for the bunker. Speer, nevertheless, asked Stahl for a further delivery of guns and ammunition in April, which was the last time that the two men had the opportunity to speak together in private.

Nevertheless, Stahl's testimony was very similar to Speer's own version of his plot to kill Hitler with poison gas, leading to the conclusion that Speer had certainly considered killing Hitler and 'the Big Three'.

Many have doubted the veracity of Speer's claims to have tried to assassinate Hitler, suggesting that the story was concocted by Speer to save himself from the gallows after the war. There is, however, evidence of Speer's opposition to Hitler at an even earlier date. Axel Bussche wrote of this after Kurt Plettenberg had told him of a surprise visit he had received from Speer in the autumn of 1944: 'Speer implored him, Plettenberg, to activate any existing contacts to the English, for now the Führer had to be removed.' Suspicious that Speer might be trying to induce him to betray himself and his fellow conspirators, Plettenberg said nothing, but he later blamed himself 'for having missed the last opportunity to put a stop to further crimes and destruction'.[4]

With the war in Europe reaching its final weeks, Himmler stepped up his attempts at persuading the Allies to accept him as the German leader who would take over from Hitler, even though the German forces were on the verge of complete collapse and the world had begun to learn with horror of the death camps which had been under Himmler's control. He engaged in a series of four secret peace meetings to end the war with the vice president of the Swedish Red Cross, Folke Bernadotte, Count of Wisborg, beginning on 12 February 1945. Count Bernadotte's terms were that Hitler must give all powers to Himmler, who must in turn remove all Nazi Party officials and release all Danish and Norwegian prisoners to Sweden via the Swedish Red Cross – but it was made clear to Himmler that he would not have any part to play in post-war Germany.

Himmler then tried to persuade Eisenhower to join with Germany in an alliance against the Soviet Union and, surprisingly, the new US president, Harry S. Truman discussed this proposal with Churchill by transatlantic telephone on 25 April, but it was, of course, rejected.[5]

However, Reuters news agency learned of Himmler's offers to the Allies and this was broadcast on 29 April. The Reichsfuhrer's double dealings had at last been exposed. Hitler immediately stripped Himmler of all his offices and ordered him to be shot. Himmler quickly made his escape from the Führer's clutches but committed suicide after his capture by British forces on 23 May.

All the plots and plans, schemes and dreams of the multitude that had opposed Hitler over the course of some fifteen years had, ultimately, come to nothing. Equally, the huge security apparatus which surrounded Hitler and the extreme measures undertaken to safeguard the Führer had been in vain, for everything he had achieved had crumbled into dust among the ruins of Berlin.

In one of history's most ironic twists of fate, the man who had been possibly the subject of more assassination plots than any individual before him was compelled to take his own life to avoid capture by his enemies.

At around 14.45 hours on the afternoon of 30 April 1945 Adolf Hitler and the woman he had married the previous day, Eva Braun, said their final farewells to their closest staff. Hitler moved only slowly, stooping more than ever, a man broken in both body and spirit. The Hitlers shook hands with everyone before they retired into Adolph's study.

Hitler's adjutant, Otto Günshe, stood guard outside the room. Others, not knowing what to do, just hung around nearby. A little after 15.30 hours there was the sound of a gunshot. Rochus Misch, at his post on the switchboard, heard someone calling for Hitler's valet, Heinz Linge, and he went with Linge and Günshe, into the study: 'I looked only for a few seconds,' Misch later wrote,

> but I have never forgotten what I saw. My glance first fell on Eva. She was seated on the sofa with her legs drawn up, her head inclined towards Hitler. Her shoes were under the sofa. Near her – I cannot remember whether on the sofa or the armchair near it – the dead Hitler. His eyes were open and staring, his head had fallen forward slightly. I saw no blood. I shrank back. All I wanted to do now was get away. Eva did not want her head to be blown away by a gunshot. She did not want to be a disfigured corpse and chose cyanide instead but, in case the poison did not work, Hitler had taken two pistols into the room. Though Eva did not want to spoil her looks, the cyanide had distorted her face.[6]

Linge spread out two blankets and placed the two bodies separately on them. Eva was carried out first by Martin Bormann, assisted by Hitler's chauffeur, Erich Kempka, and then, with the help of officers from Hitler's SS bodyguard detachment, Hitler's body was taken up the stairs of the bunker, his shoes protruding from under the simple covering. 'Immediately in front of the bunker door, in the Reich Chancellery garden, his body was laid out next to Eva's in a small depression,' recalled Linge, 'where gasoline was poured over the cadavers.'

It took two attempts before Hitler's petrol-soaked body, and then that of his wife, caught fire. Standing in the bunker entrance shielded from the Soviet artillery shells which fell around the grounds of the Chancellery, Hitler's closest associates, his valets, chauffeur, Bormann and Goebbels raised their hands in one final Hitler salute.

Notes & References

Introduction

1. Nigel Jones, *Countdown to Valkyrie, The July Plot to Assassinate Hitler*, p.192.
2. Eberhard Zeller, *The Flame of Freedom, The German Struggle Against Hitler*), p.100.
3. Friedrich Lenz, *Worm in the Apple, German Traitors and Other Influences That Pushed the World Into War: The little-known story of the men who destroyed Adolf Hitler's Germany*, Preface, wintersonnenwende.com/scriptorium/english/archives/worminapple
4. Hans Rothfels, *The German Opposition to Hitler*, pp.14–15; Anton Gill, *An Honourable Defeat, A History of German Resistance to Hitler, 1933–1945*, p.20; Herbert Molloy Mason, *To Kill Hitler, The Attempts on the Life of Adolf Hitler*, p.156.
5. white-rose-studies.org/The_Leaflets.
6. Annedore Leber, *Conscience in Revolt, Sixty-four Stories of Resistance in Germany, 1933–1945*, pp.16–17.
7. The German Resistance Memorial Centre, biographies.
8. Hermann Graml, Hans Mommsen, Hans-Joachim Reichhardt and Ernst Wolf, *The German Resistance to Hitler*, pp.5–6.
9. Michael Balfour and Julian Frisby, *Helmuth von Moltke*, p.219.
10. David Clay Large, *Contending With Hitler: Varieties of German Resistance in the Third Reich*, p.9.
11. Joachim Fest, *Plotting Hitler's Death, The German Resistance to Hitler 1933–1945*, pp.7–35.
12. Hans Mommsen, *Germans Against Hitler, Resistance Under The Third Reich*, p.24.
13. ibid, p.251.
14. Rothfels, p.15, states by 1944 the Gestapo numbered 40,000.
15. Helmut Ortner, *Hitler's Executioner, Roland Freisler President of the Nazi People's Court* pp.102–15.
16. ibid, pp.7–10.
17. Peter Hoffmann, *Behind Valkyrie, German Resistance to Hitler [Documents]*, pp.269–70.
18. ibid, 341–2.
19. Gill, p.169. Many would consider that Germany has now achieved this goal with its unchallenged leadership of the European Union.

20. Roger Manvell & Heinrich Fraenkel, *The Men Who Tried to Kill Hitler*, p.15.
21. Mommsen, p.6.
22. Zeller, p.205.
23. Böhm-Tettelbach, who re-joined the Army with the rank of Oberstleutnant, made a second visit to London in the summer of 1939 but again to no avail.
24. Michael Thomsett, *The German Opposition to Hitler, The Resistance, The Underground, and Assassination Plots, 1938–1945*), pp.46–7.
25. Anton Gill, p.2.
26. Mason, pp.94–5.

Chapter 1

1. Extracted from *Mein Kampf (My Struggle)*, Fairborne Publishing, The Colchester Collection, online PDF.
2. '*Freiheit*'.
3. Ian Kershaw, *Hitler 1889–1936: Hubris*, p.114.
4. Richard Dargie, *The Plots to Kill Hitler, The Men and Women who tried to Change History*, pp.12–13.

Chapter 2

1. John Toland, Adolf Hitler, pp.137–8.
2. ibid, p.158.
3. Kershaw, p.209. The troops were each given two of these notes.
4. Toland, pp.169–70.

Chapter 3

1. *Rente* is a technical term for mortgage in German, thus the Rentenmark was mortgaged against the land.
2. Sebastian Haffner, *Defying Hitler*, p.54.
3. Martyn Whittock, *The Third Reich, the Rise and Fall of the Nazis*, p.24.
4. Will Berthold, *Die 42 Attentate auf Adolf Hitler*, p.14.
5. Dargie, p.30.

Chapter 4

1. Quoted in Toland, pp.260–1.
2. James P. Duffy and Vincent L. Ricci, *Target Hitler, The Plots to Kill Adolph Hitler*, p.16.
3. Dargie, p.39.
4. Roger Moorhouse, *Killing Hitler, The Third Reich and the Plots to Kill The Führer*, p.16
5. Will Berthold, *Die 42 Attentate auf Adolf Hitler*, p.7.
6. Rothfels, p.52.
7. Peter Hoffmann, *Hitler's Personal Security, Protecting the Führer, 1921–1945*, pp.24–5.

Chapter 5

1. Details of Kimball's communications can be found in Office of Strategic Services, CIA-RDP13X00001R000100460002-2 etc.
2. aish.com, The-Jewish-Plot-to-Kill-Hitler.
3. Dargie, pp.42–3.
4. Duffy and Ricci, p.16
5. Peter Hoffmann, *Hitler's Personal Security*, p.24.
6. Peter Hoffmann, *The History of the German Resistance 1933–1945*, p.253.
7. There were a further two members of the FSK detailed to protect Himmler, ibid, p.31.
8. Stan Cook and R. James Bender, *Leibstandarte SS Adolf Hitler: Uniforms, Organization, & History*, pp.8–9
9. Rochus Misch, *Hitler's Last Witness, The Memoirs of Hitler's Bodyguard*, pp.36–7.

Chapter 6

1. Fest, p.100.
2. kuenstlerkolonie-berlin.de/bewohner/beppo_roemer.
3. Peter Hoffmann, German Resistance to Hitler, p.54.
4. Hoffman, *Security*, p.178.
5. Kershaw, p.514.
6. Duffy and Ricci, p.17.

Chapter 7

1. These were Generals von Schleicher and von Bredow, see John Wheeler-Bennett, *The Nemesis of Power: The German Army in Politics 1918–1945*, p.336.
2. Otto Strasser and Michael Stern, *Flight from Terror* (National Travel Club, New York, 1943), pp.215–6.
3. Strasser and Stern, pp.217–18.
4. historycollection.com/18-of-the-many-attempts-to-assassinate-adolf-hitler-by-the-german-resistance
5. Peter Fotis Kapnidstos, *Hitler's Doubles*, pp.4–5.
6. 'Guarding the Dictators', *Chicago Times*, 1 Oct. 1939.
7. Michael Unger [ed.], *The Memoirs of Bridget Hitler*, p.140.

Chapter 8

1. Strasser, pp.221–3.
2. Duffy and Vincent, p.18; Berthold, pp.62–3.
3. Moorhouse, p.18.
4. David Frankfurter, *I Kill a Nazi Gauleiter: Memoir of a Jewish Assassin*, commentarymagazine.com.
5. This is stated in Duffy and Ricci, p.18, but this author has not been able to substantiate this claim.

6. Michael Newton *Famous Assassinations in World History, An Encyclopedia*, p.227.
7. Duffy and Ricci, p.43, incorrectly state that it was Hans Wiedemann.
8. 'Intelligence papers reveal Hitler's close ally sought help from British to conspire against him', News – The College of Arts and Social Sciences, University of Aberdeen
9. Newton, op. cit.
10. Adolf Hitler – Collection of Speeches – 1922–1945.

Chapter 9

1. Moorhouse, p.28.
2. Duffy and Ricci, p.20.
3. Rolf Hochhuth, *Tell '38*, p.114.
4. Moorhouse, pp.29–30
5. Duffy and Ricci, p.23–4.
6. Klaus Urner, 'Ten Prussian police officers and the "Abegg archive"', in *The Swiss Hitler Assassin. Three studies on resistance and its border areas*, pp. 131–43. The fake archive was sold for 8,000 francs in 1959.

Chapter 10

1. Mason, p.66.
2. *William L. Shirer, Twentieth Century Journey, Volume 2, The Nightmare Years: 1930–1940, p. 308.*
3. Michael Mueller, *Canaris, The Life and Death of Hitler's Spymaster*, p.135.
4. Hoffmann, *Behind Valkyrie*, p.328.
5. Duffy and Ricci, pp.66–7.
6. Terry Parssinen, *The Oster Conspiracy of 1938: The Unknown Story of the Military Plot to Kill Hitler and Avert World War II*, p.70.
7. Mueller, p.136
8. Parssinen, p.135.
9. ibid.
10. ibid, p.133.
11. Ian Colvin, *Admiral Canaris, Chief of Intelligence*, pp.64–5.
12. Zeller, p.31.
13. Mueller, p.174.
14. Telford Taylor, *Munich, The Price of Peace*, pp.64–5.
15. Hans Gisevius, p.326.
16. Zeller, p.34.

Chapter 11

1. Ewan Butler, *Mason-Mac, The Life of Lieutenant-General Sir Noel Mason-Macfarlane*, p.74.
2. Ewan Butler, 'I talked of plan to kill Hitler', *The Times*, 6 August 1969, p.1.
3. Hoffmann, *Hitler's Personal Security*, p.99.

Chapter 12

1. Adolf Hitler, *Mein Kampf*, Translated by James Murphy, p.119.
2. ibid, p.116.
3. ibid, p.118.
4. ibid, p.226.
5. *The Nuremberg Trials*, Vol. 14, p. 279.
6. Ben Mackintyre, *Agent Sonya, Lover, Soldier, Spy*, p.157.
7. Alexander Foote, *Handbook For Spies*, p.31.
8. 'Hitler's British Girl', Part Two. Channel 4 Documentary 2007.
9. Foote, pp.31–2.

Chapter 13

1. Harold C. Deutsch, *The Conspiracy Against Hitler in the Twilight War*, p.116.
2. Mark Riebling, *Church of Spies, The Pope's Secret War Against Hitler*, pp.67–8.
3. On occasion Müller met Leiber at the Universita Gregoriana, John V.H. Dippel, *Two Against Hitler: Stealing the Nazis' Best Kept Secrets*, p.105.
4. Gill, p.12.
5. Reinhard Spitzy, *How We Squandered the Reich*, p.305.
6. Mason, p.131.
7. Riebling, p.82.
8. British Legation to the Holy See, January 12th, 1940, TNA FO 800 /113.
9. ibid, February 7th, 1940, TNA FO 800/113.
10. Peter Hoffmann, *The History of the German Resistance*, p.167.
11. Otto John, *Twice Through the Lines*, p.63.
12. Gregor Schollgen, *A Conservative Against Hitler: Ulrich Von Hassell Diplomat in Imperial Germany, the Weimar Republic and the Third Reich, 1881–1944*, p.80.
13. Robin Bryans, *The Dust Has Never Settled*, p.312.
14. John Wheeler-Bennett, *Friends, Enemies and Sovereigns – The Final Volume of his Auto-biography*, p.487.

Chapter 14

1. polityka.pl/tygodnikpolityka/historia.
2. Dargie, p.129. Others, state that Hammerstein-Equord only intended to arrest Hitler, see Moorhouse, p.181 and Hoffmann, *History of the German Resistance*, p.114.
3. Mason, p.103.
4. Wheeler-Bennett, *The Nemesis of Power*, p.441.

Chapter 15

1. Moorhouse, p.43.
2. Hellmut G. Haasis, *Bombing Hitler: The Story of the Man Who Almost Assassinated the Führer*, p.3.
3. ibid, pp.24–5.

4. ibid, pp.15–16.
5. *Rogue Male* was the title of a fictionalised story by Geoffrey Household about the attempted assassination of an unnamed European dictator which was published in 1939.
6. ibid, Chapter XI.
7. *Liverpool Daily Post*, Thursday, 23 November 1939.
8. Rothfel, p.52.
9. Haasis, p.211.

Chapter 16

1. See Nigel Jones' Introduction to Captain S. Payne Best, *The Venlo Incident, A True Story of Double-Dealing, Captivity, and a Murderous Nazi Plot.*
2. Eelco Nicolaas van Fleffens, *Juggernaut over Holland, The Dutch Foreign Minister's Personal Story of the Invasion of the Netherlands*, pp.64–5.
3. Best, pp.11–12.

Chapter 17

1. TNA AIR20/208.
2. Danny Orbach, *The Plots Against Hitler*, p.112.
3. Manvell & Fraenkel, p.229.
4. ibid., p.53.
5. Ulrich von Hassell, *The Ulrich von Hassell Diaries, The Story of the Forces Against Hitler Inside Germany*, p. X.
6. Rigden, p.161.
7. Hans Bernd Gisevius, *To the Bitter End, The Insider's Account of the Plot to Kill Hitler*, p.47; Fest, p.148.
8. Balfour and Frisby, p.157.
9. James Douglas-Hamilton, *The Truth About Rudolf Hess*, p.98.
10. Hassell, p.127.
11. Clifford Fidler, *Selsey at War 1939–1945: A Village Faces the Nazis.*
12. TNA HS 6/623, p.33.
13. Balfour and Frisby, p.158.
14. Charles Messenger, *The Last Prussian: A Biography of Field Marshal Gerd von Rundstedt 1875–1953*, p.201.
15. Erich Kempka, *I was Hitler's Chauffeur, The Memoirs of Erich Kempka*, pp.23–4.

Chapter 18

1. TNA, AIR 16/619. 'Adolf Hitler: Proposed abduction to England by his personal pilot.'

Chapter 19

1. Quoted in Orbach, p.122.
2. *Daily Telegraph* 5 December 2008.

3. Anthony Beevor, *The Mystery of Olga Chekhova, The true story of a family torn apart by revolution and war*, pp.176–7.
4. Moorhouse, p.140.
5. Ian Baxter, *Wolf's Lair, Inside Hitler's East Prussian HQ*, p.27.
6. TNA HW 1/206, British Military Mission, Moscow.
7. Ray Wagner, *The Soviet Air Forces in World War II*, p.66.
8. Peter Hoffmann, *Hitler's Personal Security*, p.xxvi.
9. TNA FO 800/868. PWE Misc. Correspondence.

Chapter 20

1. M.R.D. Foot, *The Special Operations Executive 1940–1946*, p.191; Nigel West, Secret War, pp.311–12.
2. Moorhouse, p.99.
3. Operation *Foxley* file, p.120
4. Moorhouse, p.111.
5. Mark Felton, *Guarding Hitler, The Secret World of the Führer*, pp.28–9.
6. Bernard Drzyzga, *Zagra-Lin: oddział sabotażowo-dywersyjny Organizacji Specjalnych Akcji ('Osa', 'Kosa') utworzony do realizacji zamachów na terenie Niemiec*, pp.204–6.
7. Hitler travelled from the Wolfsschanze to the Berghof on 21 May 1943, Hoffmann *Hitler's Personal Security*, p.xxx.

Chapter 21

1. Quoted in Eberhard Schmitt, *The Hitler Conspirator, The Story of Kurt Freiherr von Plettenberg and Stauffenberg's Valkyrie Plot to Kill the Führer*, p.95.
2. Eberhard Schmidt, *The Hitler Conspirator: The Story of Kurt Baron Von Plettenberg and Stauffenberg's Valkyrie Plot to Kill the Fuhrer*, p.115.
3. Fabian von Schlabrendorff, *The Secret War against Hitler*, p.231.
4. This unit was actually a force established to move into action to protect the conspirators should there be an immediate counter-coup.
5. Anton Gill, *An Honourable Defeat, A History of German Resistance to Hitler, 1933–1945*, p.207.
6. Schlabrendorff, pp.232–3.
7. Duffy and Ricci, p.127.
8. Fest, p.193.
9. Helena Schrader, *Codename Valkyrie, General Friedrich Olbricht and the Plot Against Hitler*, pp.223–4.
10. ibid, p.225.
11. Schlabrendorff, p.236.
12. Fest, p.195.
13. Schalbrendorff, pp.236–8.

Chapter 22

1. Rudolf-Christolph Freiherr von Gersdorff, *Soldat in Untergang*, pp.128–9, quoted in Orbach, p.141.
2. Schrader, pp.189–90.

Chapter 23

1. Manvell and Frankel, p.49.
2. ibid, pp.36–7.
   Gisevius, p.448.
3. John Colville, *The Fringes of Power*, p. 56.
4. Martin Allen, *Himmler's Secret War, The Covert Peace Negotiations of Heinrich Himmler*, pp. 131–2.
5. Denis Rigden, *Kill The Führer, Section X and Operation Foxley*, pp.106–8 & 112.
6. TNA FO 800/868, Political Warfare Executive (PWE): miscellaneous correspondence.
7. Hassell, pp.199 & 214.
8. Rigden, pp.157–8.
9. Neal H. Petersen [ed.] *From Hitler's Doorstep: The Wartime Intelligence Reports of Allen Dulles, 1942–1945*, p.565. Gill, p.179.
10. Central Intelligence Agency, John H. Waller, *Reichsführer Himmler Pitches Washington: Dispatch from Wartime Sweden.*
11. Manvell and Fraenkel, pp.67–9, state that Himmler was aware of Hitler's failing mental and physical health and that he was expecting to take over from Hitler and thus had to consider all the options available in preparation for when that moment might come.
13. Schmidt, p.127.
14. All the details of Egon Hanfstaengl's scheme to assassinate Hitler are taken from Peter Conrad, *Hitler's Piano Player, The Rise and Fall of Ernst Hanfstaengl Confidant of Hitler, Ally of FDR*, pp.290–2.

Chapter 24

1. Hans-Heinrich Herwarth Von Bittenfeld, *Against Two Evils: Memoirs of a Diplomat-Soldier During the Third Reich*, p.254
2. Peter Hoffmann, *The History of the German Resistance*, pp.279–80.
3. Baxter, *Hitler's Military Headquarters*, p.73. See also John Grehan, *Hitler's Wolfsschanze, The Wolf's Lair Headquarters on the Eastern Front.*
4. Moorhouse, p.132.

Chapter 25

1. Schmidt, pp.121–2.
2. ibid, p.123.
3. Manvell & Fraenkel, pp.86 & 91.
4. Joachim Fest, *Plotting Hitler's Death, The German Resistance to Hitler 1933–1945*, p.202.

5. Fest, p.213.
6. All written information was typed up by Tresckow's wife, Erika, and his secretary, Countess Margarete von Oven, both women wearing gloves so as not to leave fingerprints. Fest, p.220.
7. Manvell and Fraenkel, pp.65–6.
8. Hoffmann, 327
9. Martin Middlebrook and Chris Everitt, *Bomber Command War Diaries: An Operational Reference Book* , 2014).
10. Regarding the different versions of the air raid see, for example, Dargie, pp.150–1 and Mason, pp.180–1.

Chapter 26

1. In his memoirs, Fabian von Schlabrendorff states (p.275) that Breitenbuch did gain entry to the conference room but he could not even put his hand in his pocket to pull out his gun because of the SS guards present who watched everyone in the room for the slightest suspicious movement. This is contradicted by von Breitenbuch's own testimony, recorded in Frank Werner's contribution 'Eberhard von Breitenbuch' to Schaumburger Landschaft (ed), *Gegen den Strom*, p.48, quoted in Moorhouse, p.197.
2. forum.axishistory.com//viewtopic.php?f=5&t=111316&p=980237; Fest, pp.224–5.
3. Duffy and Ricci, p.138. Further indication that this incident has been mistaken for the Kuhn and Hagen attempt at burying explosives is provided by the fact that the authors state that the investigation into the explosion was undertaken by Werner Schrader, who 'dragged his inquiry on so long that he never issued a report'. The similarities are too striking to be separate events.
4. Allen Welsh Dulles, *Germany's Underground*, p.135.
5. See the excellent websites, Third Reich in Ruins and Adolf Hitler – Collection of Speeches – 1922–1945.
6. Florian M. Beierl, *Inside Hitler's Mountain*, pp.98–9.

Chapter 27

1. Theodore Harrow, *On the Road to the Wolf's Lair, German Resistance To Hitler*, p.343.
2. Fabian von Schlabrendorff, *The Secret War Against Hitler*, p.277.
3. Schmidt, p.128.
4. Fest, p.3.
5. Schrader, p.204.
6. All ten points are listed in full in Wolfgang Venohr, *Stauffenberg, Symbol of Resistance, The Man Who Almost Killed Hitler*, p.230.
7. Zeller, p.295.

Chapter 28

1. Venohr, p.263, gives a departure time of 0800 hours.
2. Fest, p.255.

3. Hoffmann, *Zu Dem Attentat Im Führerhauptquartier 'Wolfsschanze' am 20. Juli 1944*; Jones, p.187.
4. Felton, *Guarding Hitler*, p.119.
5. Grehan, op. cit.
6. Zeller, p.203.
7. Quoted in Moorhouse, p.203
8. Fest, p.258.
9. Rigden, p.175.
10. Venohr, p.265.
11. Jones, p.189; Duffy and Ricci, p.166; Thomsett, 248 etc.
12. Zeller, p.303.
13. Walter Warlimont, *Inside Hitler's Headquarters*, p.440.
14. Quoted in Irving, p.145.
15. Below, p.209.
16. Kurt Salterberg, *Als Wachsoldat in der Wolfsschanze: Aus der Sicht eines einfachen jungen Soldaten berichtet der Zeit- und Augenzeuge über die Abläufe* (Kindle version, Helios, 2018).
17. Rigden, p.176.
18. Duffy and Ricci, p.170.
19. Orbach, p.219.
20. ibid, p.222.
21. Duffy and Ricci, p.172.
22. Peter Hoffmann, *The History of the German Resistance*, pp.755–6.
23. Jones, p.218.
24. ibid, p.222.
25. ibid, p.223.
26. Linge, pp.156–7.
27. Schroeder, p.122.
28. Hoffmann, Zu Dem Attentat Im Führerhauptquartier 'Wolfsschanze' am 20. Juli.
29. *Guardian*, Friday 21 Jul 1944.
30. Zeller, p.375.
31. Ortner, pp.134–5.
32. Venohr, p.288.
33. Friedrich Lenz, op. cit. Overview.
34. See the Preface and Chapter 10 of the above Venohr book for a more extended analysis of this.
35. Gill, p.109.
36. Fest, pp.288–9.
37. 'The Attempt on Hitler's Life and its Consequences' OSS Research and Analysis Report No. 2387, 27 July 1944.
38. Gill, p.1.
39. Mommsen, p.7.
40. *New York Times*, 9 August 1944.

41. ibid, p.261.
42. CIA-RDP80M01009A000700970065-6.

Chapter 29

1. Julian Amery, *Approach March*, pp.240–1; Rigden, pp.88–90.
2. Amery, ibid.
3. ibid.
4. TNA HS 6/623, p.62; Rigden, pp.49–50.
5. Rigden, p.50.
6. The full *Foxley* report is reproduced in Mark Seaman's *Operation Foxley, The British Plan to Kill Hitler*; Moorhouse, p.167, states that Court was assisted by the historian James Joll.
7. TNA FO 1020/3471.
8. James Wilson, *Hitler's Alpine Headquarters*, pp.11–12.
9. These security arrangements are covered in detail in Felton, pp.80–2.
10. Felton, p.77.
11. Rigden, pp.87–8.
12. Himmler, Kaltenbrunner, Bormann and Göring were all considered as other *Little Foxleys*, but no detailed planning was ever carried out.

Chapter 30

1. Foxley, p.94.
2. markfelton.co.uk/publishedbooks/planes-trains-automobiles-transporting-hitler; TNA HS 6/623.
3. Felton, *Guarding Hitler*, p.29.
4. Hoffman, *Hitler's Security*, ix-x.
5. Seaman, ix-x.

Chapter 31

1. Seidler & Zeigert, p.174.
2. Irving, pp.167–8.
3. Jerzy Szynkowski, *Wolfsschanze. Das Führerhauptquartier: Umfassende Darstellung. Umfangreiches Bildmaterial. Erinnerungen von Zeitzeugen*, pp.44–5.
4. Norman Ohler, 'Hitler's Doctor Said the Dictator Almost Died from a Cocaine Overdose', *Vice* magazine, 27 March 2017.
5. Toland, pp.827–8.

Chapter 32

1. John Huston, *American Airpower Comes of Age: Henry H. "Hap" Arnold's World War II Diaries*, p.166.
2. Despina Stratigakos, *Hitler at Home*, pp.259–60.
3. Schmidt, pp.144–9.
4. ibid, p.145.
5. Macintyre, p.275.

Chapter 33

1. TNA FO 1078/236, Interrogation of Stahl on Speer's plot to kill Hitler.
2. Alan Bullock, *Hitler: A Study in Tyranny*, pp.774–5.
3. Albert Speer, *Inside the Third Reich, The Classic Account of Nazi Germany's Armaments Minister*, pp.574–7.
4. Schmidt, p.136
5. warfarehistorynetwork.com/heinrich-himmler-the-rise-and-fall-of-hitlers-third-reichsfuhrer-ss.
6. Rochus Misch, *Hitler's Last Witness, The Memoirs of Hitler's Bodyguard*, pp.171–2.

Source Information

Unpublished documents

The National Archives, Kew:

AIR 16/619. 'Adolf Hitler: Proposed abduction to England by his personal pilot.'

AIR 20/2081, German victory parades in Paris: proposed attacks.

FO 1020/3471, SS Schütze Obernigg.

FO 1078/236, Interrogation of Stahl on Speer's plot to kill Hitler.

FO 800 /113 British Legation to the Holy See.

FO 800/868, Political Warfare Executive, miscellaneous correspondence.

HS 6/623, Politics: operation FOXLEY: plan to liquidate Hitler and/or his satellites.

HW 1/206, British Military Mission, Moscow, alerted to German high level conference at Orsha, 8 Nov.

Office of Strategic Studies, 'The Attempt on Hitler's Life and its Consequences,' Research and Analysis Report No. 2387, July 27, 1944.

Published Books

Amery, Julian, *Approach March* (Hutchinson, London, 1973) Balfour, Michael and Frisby, Julian, *Helmuth von Moltke* (Macmillan, London, 1972)

Baur, Hans, *I Was Hitler's Pilot* (Frontline, Barnsley, 2013)

Baxter, Ian, *Wolf's Lair, Inside Hitler's East Prussian HQ* (History Press, Stroud, 2009)

Beevor, Anthony, *The Mystery of Olga Chekhova* (Viking, London, 2004)

Beierl, Florian M., *Inside Hitler's Mountain* (Florian Beieri Verlag, Berchtesgaden, 2015)

Below, Nicolaus von, *At Hitler's Side, The Memoirs of Hitler's Luftwaffe Adjutant 1937–1945* (Frontline, Barnsley, 2019), p.209

Berthold, Will, *Die 42 Attentate auf Adolf Hitler* (Ueberreuter, Wein, 1997)

Bittenfeld, Hans-Heinrich Herwarth Von, *Against Two Evils: Memoirs of a Diplomat-Soldier During the Third Reich* (Encore Editions, London, 1981)

Bryans, Robin, *The Dust Has Never Settled* (Honeyford Press, London, 1992)

Bullock, Alan, *Hitler: A Study in Tyranny* (Penguin, London, 1962)

Colvin, Ian, *Admiral Canaris, Chief of Intelligence* (Colvin Press, 2008)

Cook, Stan and Bender, R. James, *Leibstandarte SS Adolf Hitler: Uniforms, Organization, & History* (R. James Bender Publishing, San Jose, 1994)

Dargie, Richard, *The Plots to Kill Hitler, The Men and Women who tried to Change History* (Arcturus, London, 2019)

Douglas-Hamilton, James, *The Truth About Rudolf Hess* (Frontline, Barnsley, 2016)

Döhring, Herbert, Karl, Wilhelm Krause & Plain, Anna, *Living With Hitler, Accounts of Hitler's Household Staff* (Greenhill, Barnsley, 2018)

Duffy, James P., & Ricci, Vincent L., *Target Hitler, The Plots to Kill Adolf Hitler* (Praeger, London, 1992)

Dulles, Allen Welsh, *Germany's Underground* (Macmillan, New York, 1947)

Dulles, Allen, [ed.], *Great True Spy Stories* (Harper & Row, New York, 1968)

Eberle, Henrik & Uhl, Matthais, *The Hitler Book, The Secret Report by his Two Closest Aides* (John Murray, London, 2006),

Felton, Mark, *Guarding Hitler, The Secret World of the Führer* (Pen & Sword, Barnsley, 2014)

Fest, Joachim, *Plotting Hitler's Death: The German Resistance To Hitler, 1933–1945* (Pheonix, London, 1997)

Fidler, Clifford, *Selsey at War 1939–1945: A Village Faces the Nazis* (Fidelity Processes, 2000).

Foote, Alexander, *Handbook For Spies* (Museum Press, London, 1949)

Gisevius, Hans B., *To the Bitter End, The Insider's Account of the Plot to Kill Hitler* ((Houghton Mifflin, Boston, 1947)

Gill, Anton, *An Honourable Defeat, A History of German Resistance to Hitler, 1933–1945* (Henry Holt, New York, 1994),

Graml, Hermann, Mommsen, Hans, Reichhardt, Hans-Joachim, and Wolf, Ernst, *The German Resistance to Hitler* (Batsford, London, 1970)

Grehan, John, *Hitler's Wolfsschanze: The Wolf's Lair Headquarters on the Eastern Front – An Illustrated Guide* (Frontline, Barnsley, 2021).

Haasis, Hellmut G., *Bombing Hitler: The Story of the Man Who Almost Assassinated the Führer* (Simon and Schuster, London, 2013)

Haffner, Sebastian, *Defying Hitler* (Phoenix, London, 2002),

Harrow, Theodore, *On the Road to the Wolf's Lair, German Resistance To Hitler* (Harvard University Press, 1999)

Kempka, Erich, *I was Hitler's Chauffeur, The Memoirs of Erich Kempka* (Frontline, Barnsley, 2010)

Ulrich von Hassell, *The Ulrich von Hassell Diaries, The Story of the Forces Against Hitler Inside Germany* (Frontline, Barnsley, 2011)

Hochhuth, Rolf, *Tell '38* (Little, Brown, Toronto, 1984)

Hoffmann, Heinrich, *Hitler Was My Friend, The Memoirs of Hitler's Photographer* (Frontline, Barnsley, 2011)

Hoffmann, Peter, *The History of the German Resistance 1933–1945* (MIT Press, Cambridge, 1977)

Hoffmann, Peter, *German Resistance to Hitler* (Harvard University Press, Massachusetts, 1988)

Hoffmann, Peter, *Die Sicherheit des Diktators* (Piper Verlag, Munchen, 1992)

Hoffmann, Peter, *Hitler's Personal Security, Protecting the Führer, 1921–1945* (Da Capo, 2000)
Hoffmann, Peter, *Behind Valkyrie, German Resistance to Hitler [Documents]* (McGill-Queen's University Press, London, 2011)
Huston, John, *American Airpower Comes of Age: Henry H. "Hap" Arnold's World War II Diaries* (Air University Press, Maxwell Air Force Base, 2002), p.166.
Irving, David, *The Secret Diaries of Hitler's Doctor* (Focal Pont, London, 2005)
John, Otto, *Twice Through the Lines* (Harper & Row, New York, 1972)
Junge, Traudl, with Muller, Melissa, *Until the Final Hour: Hitler's Last Secretary* (Pheonix, London, 2004)
Large, David Clay, *Contending With Hitler: Varieties of German Resistance in the Third Reich* (Cambridge University Press, 1995)
Leber, Annedore, *Conscience in Revolt, Sixty-four Stories of Resistance in Germany, 1933–1945* (Vaentine, Mitchell and Co., London, 1957),
Linge, Heinz, *With Hitler to the End, The Memoirs of Adolf Hitler's Valet* (Frontline Books, Barnsley, 2009)
Jones, Nigel, *Countdown to Valkyrie, The July Plot to Assassinate Hitler* (Frontline, Barnsley, 2008)
Kapnidstos, Peter Fotis, *Hitler's Doubles* (CreateSpace, 2015)
Korpalski, Edward, Szynkowski, Jerzy, Wagner, Heinz, *Wolfsschanze, und das Attentat vom 20. Juli 1944* (Algraf, Biskupiec, Bischofsburg, 2016)
Macjintyre, Ben, *Agent Sonya, Lover, Soldier, Spy* (Viking, 2020)
Mason, Herbert Molloy, *To Kill Hitler, The Attempts on the Life of Adolf Hitler* (Michael Joseph, London, 1979),
Middlebrook, Martin and Everitt, Chris, *Bomber Command War Diaries: An Operational Reference Book* (Pen & Sword, Barnsley, 2014)
Misch, Rochus, *Hitler's Last Witness: The Memoirs of Hitler's Bodyguard* (Frontline, Barnsley, 2014)
Mommsen, Hans, *Germans Against Hitler, Resistance Under The Third Reich* (I.B. Tauris, London, 2009)
Moorhouse, Roger, *Killing Hitler, The Third Reich and the Plots to Kill The Führer* (Vintage, London, 2006)
Mueller, Michael, *Canaris, The Life and Death of Hitler's Spymaster* (Frontline, Barnsley, 2017)
Newton, Michael, *Famous Assassinations in World History, An Encyclopedia* (ABC-Clio, Santa Barbara, 2011)
Orbach, Danny, *The Plots Against Hitler* (Mariner Books, New York, 2016)
Ortner, Helmut, *Hitler's Executioner, Roland Freisler President of the Nazi People's Court* (Frontline, Barnsley, 2018)
Parssinen, Terry, *The Oster Conspiracy of 1938: The Unknown Story of the Military Plot to Kill Hitler and Avert World War II* (HarperCollins, New York, 2003)
Rigden Denis, *Kill The Führer, Section X and Operation Foxley* (History Press, Stroud, 2009)
Rothfels, Hans, *The German Opposition to Hitler* (Oswald Wolff, London, 1978)

Salterberg, Kurt, *Als Wachsoldat in der Wolfsschanze: Aus der Sicht eines einfachen jungen Soldaten berichtet der Zeit- und Augenzeuge über die Abläufe* (Kindle version, Helios, 2018).

Schollgen, Gregor, *A Conservative Against Hitler: Ulrich Von Hassell Diplomat in Imperial Germany, the Weimar Republic and the Third Reich, 1881–1944* (Springer, Berlin, 1991)

Schrader, Helena, *Codename Valkyrie, General Friedrich Olbricht and the Plot Against Hitler* (Haynes Publishing, Yeovil, 2009)

Schroeder, Christa, *He was My Chief, The Memoirs of Adolf Hitler's Secretary* (Frontline, Barnsley, 2012)

Schulz, Alfons *Drei Jahre in der nachrichtenzentrale des Führerhauptquartiers* (Christiana, Berlin, 1997)

Seaman, Mark, *Operation Foxley, The British Plan to Kill Hitler* (PRO Publications, Richmond, 1998)

Seidler, Franz W., & Zeigert, Dieter, *Hitler's Secret Headquarters, The Führer's Wartime Bases from the Invasion of France to the Berlin Bunker* (Greenhill, London, 2004)

Shirer, William L., Twentieth Century Journey, Volume 2, The Nightmare Years: 1930–1940 (Little Brown, Boston, 1984)

Schmidt, Eberhard, *The Hitler Conspirator: The Story of Kurt Baron Von Plettenberg and Stauffenberg's Valkyrie Plot to Kill the Fuhrer* (Frontline, Barnsley, 2017)

Speer, Albert, *Inside the Third Reich. The Classic Account of Nazi Germany's Armaments Minister* (Weidenfeld & Nicholson, London, 1970)

Spitzy, Reinhard, *How We Squandered the Reich* (Michael Russell, Norwich, 1999)

Stahlberg, Alexander, *Bounden Duty, The Memoirs of a German Officer 1932–45* (Brassey's London, 1990)

Stratigakos, Despina, *Hitler at Home* (Yale University Press, New Haven, 2015)

Szynkowski, Jerzy, *Wolfsschanze. Das Führerhauptquartier: Umfassende Darstellung. Umfangreiches Bildmaterial. Erinnerungen von Zeitzeugen* (Algraf, Bischofsburg, 2000)

Taylor, Telford, *Munich, The Price of Peace* (Hodder & Stoughton, London, 1979)

Thomsett, Michael, *The German Opposition to Hitler: The Resistance, the Underground, and Assassination Plots, 1938–1945* (Crux, 2016)

Toland, John, *Adolf Hitler* (Wordsworth Editions, Ware, 1997)

Trevor-Roper, Hugh, *Hitler's Table Talk 1941–1944* (Weidenfeld & Nicolson Ltd, London, 1953)

Unger, Michael [ed.], *The Memoirs of Bridget Hitler* (Duckworth, Dallas, 1979)

Urner, Klaus, 'Ten Prussian police officers and the "Abegg archive"', in *The Swiss Hitler Assassin. Three studies on resistance and its border areas* (Frauenfeld, Stuttgart, 1980)

Wagner, Ray, *The Soviet Air Forces in World War II* (David & Charles, London, 1974)

Warlimont, Walter, *Inside Hitler's Headquarters 1939–45* (Weidenfeld and Nicholson, London, 1962)

Wheeler-Bennett, John, *The Nemesis of Power: The German Army in Politics 1918–1945 (Macmillan, London, 1967)*
Wheeler-Bennett, John, *Friends, Enemies and Sovereigns—The Final Volume of his Auto-biography* (MacMillan, London, 1976),
Wilson, James, *Hitler's Alpine Headquarters* (Pen & Sword, Barnsley, 2013)
Whittock, Martyn, *The Third Reich, the Rise and Fall of the Nazis* (Robinson, London, 2011)
Venohr, Wolfgang, *Stauffenberg, Symbol of Resistance, The Man Who Almost Killed Hitler* (Frontline, Barnsley, 2019)
Zeller, Eberhard, *The Flame of Freedom, The German Struggle Against Hitler* (Westview Press, Colorado, 1994)

Internet

Adolf Hitler, *Mein Kampf (My Struggle)*, Fairborne Publishing, The Colchester Collection, online PDF
Adolf Hitler – Collection of Speeches – 1922–1945.
aish.com, The-Jewish-Plot-to-Kill-Hitler
cia.gov/library/readingroom/docs/HITLER
Felton, Mark, *Planes, Trains & Automobiles – Transporting the Führer*,
forum.axishistory.com
historycollection.com/18-of-the-many-attempts-to-assassinate-adolf-hitler-by-the-german-resistance
hitler-attentat.de
Intelligence papers reveal Hitler's close ally sought help from British to conspire against him', News – The College of Arts and Social Sciences, The University of Aberdeen
David Frankfurter, 'I Kill a Nazi Gauleiter: Memoir of a Jewish Assassin', commentarymagazine.com
Hoffmann, Peter, *Zu Dem Attentat Im Führerhauptquartier 'Wolfsschanze' am 20. Juli 1944* (Vertelijahrshrshefte für Zeitgeschichte, 1964).
kuenstlerkolonie-berlin.de/bewohner/beppo_roemer.
The German Resistance Memorial Centre, biographies
white-rose-studies.org/The_Leaflets.
warfarehistorynetwork.com
wintersonnenwende.com/scriptorium/english/archives/worminapple

Newspapers and Periodicals

Butler, Ewan, 'I talked of plan to kill Hitler', *The Times*, 6 August 1969
'Guarding the Dictators', *Chicago Times*, Oct. 1 1939
Kelly, John 'Adolf Hitler's food taster tells how she cried with relief at surviving after every meal' The *Mirror*, 19 September 2014
New York Times
Ohler, Norman, 'Hitler's Doctor Said the Dictator Almost Died from a Cocaine Overdose', *Vice* magazine, 27 March 2017

Index of People and Places